MAKING SENSE OF NORMANDY

A Young Man's Journey of War and Faith

E. Carver McGriff

INKWATER
PRESS

PORTLAND • OREGON
INKWATERPRESS.COM

THIS BOOK IS DEDICATED TO ALL WHO SERVED, BUT ESPECIALLY TO the boys who never had time to grow up, and whose valor defined for all time the meaning of the word "nobility."

TABLE OF CONTENTS

ACKNOWLEDGEMENTS

FIRST OF ALL, THANKS TO MY WIFE MARIANNE, WHOM I LOVE VERY much, and who patiently endured my extended absences while in the next room as I journeyed back in time.

Thanks to Bob Zehr for his gift of encouraging others, and to Kent Millard for his loving spirit, and especially to Lori Crantford whose good-humored and patient intolerance of clumsy sentences and bad punctuation made this whole thing a lot more readable. These three made this book possible.

Thanks to Jim Enzor, Doug Horth, Lefty Huntzinger, Tom Jones, and Bob James. They were there, on a battlefield, and they helped to keep me honest.

Thanks to the members of The Service Club of Indianapolis who continually remind me that incredibly old guys were once America's only hope for continued freedom, and that when they were kids they stepped up and fought for their country so now I can say and write anything I want.

Thanks to the people of St. Luke's United Methodist Church simply because I love them and they have continued to make me feel loved.

FOREWORD

As a teenager I was drafted into the United States Army in time to serve as an infantryman in Normandy. I was there for two months during what General Dwight Eisenhower considered the worst fighting of the war, a campaign he feared was about to fail. He wrote, "It was doughboy fighting at its worst." German General Erwin Rommel called it "one terrible blood letting." In a few weeks 29,000 American boys died on that small peninsula. More than 106,000 were wounded. I was one. Finally, it all ended and I returned to a normal life: school, marriage, vocation, family. Like so many of my comrades I pushed all those memories of war into a hidden corner of my mind and happily accepted the privelege of serving God as a pastor. Those memories were merely part of a long-ago past.

In retirement I began to remember. I thought of men I'd barely thought about since Normandy, saw their faces again. I've begun to wonder what happened to Huey and Duey, to John and "Meejy," to Jimmy, and George, and Bruce and all the others. People have asked me how I'm able to remember so much after all these years and I can only answer that it's all burned deeply into our very souls. I have begun to wonder why such a thing could have happened in the first place, what meaning it had, what sense I could make of all that happened, what part God may have played. Here is what I've decided.

The America we know and most of us treasure today is largely the result of the minds and hearts and muscles of that World War II generation. Through the years which followed the war it was these men and women who ran for office, started businesses, studied for the professions, led the religious and educational institutions, and produced a "Baby Boom" generation who run things today. The values which have shaped America are profoundly a result of the influence of the men and women of that era. I confess a bit of fear that those values are being eroded today by negative cultural forces, and if we allow ourselves to lose the train of honor which reaches back to Granddad and Grandma it may be hard to recover.

We've been called The Greatest Generation by Tom Brokaw. That reminds me of an old preacher joke, about the conservative Christian who asked his pastor "Can a Christian dance?" His answer was "Some can, some can't." Were we the greatest generation? Some were, some weren't. I've depicted my generation of men who served in the armed forces as we were, warts and all. The great and the not-so-great. But this is what it was really like from the view of the young men who fought among the hedgerows.

My generation is nearly gone. The men who served are either very aged or have died. Many of those who have passed did so without saying much about the experience of fighting for their country. We had our reasons. I've spoken to several school groups recently and heard many young people say they wish they'd learned more about "Granddad's experiences in the war." I presume to speak for some of those men, to reveal many of the stories they never told, and to remind their descendants of the price they paid, without complaint, so we could enjoy the freedom we so prize today.

Most of the current generation base their vision of that war on the entertainment media. It's taught in the schools but many kids tell me they find that boring. Those war movies are long on entertainment, short on history. It makes better theater to depict elite organizations, paratroopers and Rangers, men who trained for years together, true professionals, as they heroically fought gallantly to victory. They were the real thing of course, but they were a very small percentage of the men who fought in and finally won the war. Most who served were kids, barely trained, and all too often poorly trained; boys like my two best friends who left high school in their junior year to serve in the Navy in the Pacific. One recent book, *The Boy's Crusade*, points out that the war on the ground was won by teenagers. I've spent a lot of time with people like myself, back then and since, which lets me feel I have the right to speak for them.

As for a clergyman writing this, we clergy have influenced many people through the years since. Not everyone has been Christian or Jewish, but the values of the Old and New Testaments determine what most of us today consider to be right and good. Those who think clergy are far removed from any understanding of war might be surprised to learn that just among my clergy friends in Indiana are a First Sergeant of Infantry in the Pacific, a gunnery officer in the Navy, a decorated former prisoner of war in Germany, a combat platoon leader of Infantry who served in France, and a former chaplain who came home from Europe with a Purple Heart. And those are just men with whom I have often eaten lunch. This also allows me to share some of our reflections on the war which grow out of our Christian faith.

Getting out of Normandy was the most important single undertaking of World War II. It was the military archimedian point, that at which everything which went before would have been too little, and nothing could follow which would have been sufficient for complete victory. Allied troops were dying in Norman fields by thousands. General Dwight Eisenhower, Allied Supreme Commander, feared at one point that we would never get out. The fact that we did is one of the greatest stories of American courage under the most extreme circumstances in our nation's modern history. Worse than the Battle of The Bulge, worse than Iwo Jima, worse than Gettysburg, the battle for Normandy would determine the future of humanity in modern times. This also helps put some of our current wars in perspective. So here's the story as seen by the men who fought; our fears, our hopes, our sins - and our triumph.

"That night we moved into a field and I walked past a dead man. No one seemed to pay any attention to the body and I assumed someone would later gather the poor guy in. In retrospect, it's disturbing to recall how quickly we found ourselves able to look at dead bodies and, provided we didn't know the man, feel very little emotion. That was a terrible realization, and yet to have reacted otherwise would have quickly drained us of the will to go on. Today I think back to that moment, the placid face of death, a kid, someone who had loved ones waiting at home, who had friends, not long out of high school, a kid with hopes and dreams, a person who that very day had smiled, had laughed at some childish joke, maybe written a reassuring letter to his mom. Now he was dead, lying uncared for along a nameless country road as one by one we walked by and turned quickly away. Now, shrouded in darkness, unknown, he lay there. No one should die that way. These are the photographs of the mind which dispel any idea of the romance of war."

–Carver McGriff, Making Sense of Normandy

INTRODUCTION

"The enduring memory of Normandy is that of the dramatic and heroic invasion of 6 June and the great breakout and pursuit emanating from COBRA at the end of July. Yet most of the campaign was a grim struggle and those who fought there are more likely to remember that dreadful bocage; the heat, mud, and dust; the terror of unseen mortar and sniper fire; the loss of many comrades to an enemy that was rarely seen. Certainly few who fought there in the hot summer of 1944 would dispute Rommel, who gave the campaign its epitaph: 'It was one terrible blood-letting.'"

Carlo D'Este in Decision In Normandy"[1]

THE BATTLE FOR NORMANDY, FRANCE, WHICH BEGAN ON JUNE 6, 1944, was the single most crucial battle of World War II. The leaders of the Allied nations knew that without a foothold on the continent of Europe there was little hope of defeating Nazi Germany. The Germans were already developing long-range missiles which could destroy distant cities, planes which could fly at twice the speed of those flown by Allied pilots, and most frightening of all, Nazi scientists were surging forward in the race for the unleashing of nuclear power. Meanwhile, Joseph Stalin, president of our Russian allies, was considering a separate peace with Germany which would have released the full might of the Nazi war machine to repel any attack. We had to invade, and we had to do so quickly. The result was the invasion code named Operation Overlord, and it almost failed.

In a sense, the Normandy campaign was World War II in microcosm. It was the largest sea-borne invasion in history. It involved nearly 3,000,000 men. It required two-and-a-half of the eleven months xvi | E. CARVER MCGRIFF

required for the Allies to conquer all of Europe, yet it was confined to a small peninsula on the northern coast of France. American casualties, 29,000 dead and 106,000 wounded or missing, equaled the total of the five costliest battles in the Pacific Theater of war. The Allied Air forces suffered an additional 12,000 casualties and lost 2,000 planes in the period of April and May preparing for the invasion. Failure would have postponed the end of the war indefinitely, probably would have cost us the victory. Adolf Hitler, when informed of the landings in Normandy, said "If the enemy here succeeds...consequences of staggering proportions will follow within a short time." General Rommel, commander of German forces in France, wrote toward the end of the campaign "Sometimes I was near collapse. I have never seen such losses." Of the many battles of World War II Normandy, more than any other, had to be won if the Allies were to win the war.

Because of the hedgerows which tangled the Norman landscape - one aerial photograph showed 3,900 hedgerowed fields in an eight-square mile area - and the absence of all but a few main roads, plus the record-breaking constant heavy rains which turned secondary roads into muddy quagmires, American tanks were almost useless. Historian Robin Neillands wrote that "The hedgerow country was dense and claustrophobic, where visibility was rarely more than a few yards. Fighting forward called on first-class infantry skills." The Germans, having had years to prepare for this defensive battle, had zeroed in their artillery and were able to fire with pinpoint accuracy on advancing American troop formations. Allied GIs, most just kids a year or two out of high school, had no experience by which to understand close-quarter combat while fighting experienced German forces which had been carefully trained for close combat for years.

It appeared for some time that we would not be able to get out of Normandy and into open country where tanks and air support could be effective. There were only two ways out. One, the city of Caen, was surrounded with German Panzer divisions, Adolf Hitler having realized that preserving that city was essential to German victory and having therefore massed his strongest formations to prevent its capture. The only other way out was through the little town of Saint Lo where all the useful roads converged, and beyond which lay the open plains of Brittany to the south and open country east to Paris.

The approaches to Saint Lo led through hilly terrain with high peaks from which the Germans could observe Allied preparations and from which German artillery could rain down murderous fire from distances up to several miles. Much of the surrounding countryside was a swamp, deep in water released by the Germans from the rivers and fed by the persistent rain. American tanks and other motorized equipment had no choice but to to approach Saint Lo by roads exposed to that fire. First, the hills had to be captured. One key strong point was a hill, listed on maps as Hill 122, located in the Mont Castre Forest. More than 300 feet high, it had been an important military strong point since the Gallic Wars, the remains of a stone fort from that era still visible at its peak. The German 5th airborne division had been assigned the hill's defense. As General Charles Corlett, commander of our 35th Infantry Division, told Army commander General Bradley: "Saint Lo cannot be taken without possession of Hill 122."

Here, then, is part of that story from inside the campaign that even Supreme Commander Dwight D. Eisenhower feared would not succeed. It's the story of men, most of them teenagers or kids just into their twenties, overcoming egregious mistakes at every level of preparation and execution, battling a far more experienced enemy under seemingly impossible conditions, suffering unthinkable casualties, yet going on to victory, following which they all came home asking little more in return than a chance to build a peaceful life and to enjoy the freedom for which they paid an exorbitant price. This is, rather than just a history, a look into the hearts, minds, and spirit of the men who were there. This is the story of what it was like for young men drafted away from home and ordered to do battle with one of the most formidable war machines in history. More than 400,000 of those boys, along with several hundred American young women, would never return from the war.

CHAPTER ONE

DARKNESS FALLS

ALMOST EVERYONE IN AMERICA LISTENED IN SHOCKED DISBELIEF to the radio on Sunday afternoon, December 7, 1941, while the announcer talked in excited, disbelieving tones, reporting the first scattered reports of the bombing of Pearl Harbor in Hawaii. It was believed, he said, that the waves of planes which had left America's battleships burning as half-sunken hulks in the water off Ford Island were Japanese. Survivors told of dive bombers bearing the rising sun insignia on their wings screaming down to release their bombs; fighter escort planes strafing the port installations, some flying on over nearby neighborhoods where young Navy and Army men lived with their families, and where some of their wives were cut down by machine gun fire. Hundreds of people were dead, maybe thousands, the announcer reported, his own voice uncharacteristically shrill from shock.

In the days that followed, America reeled in horrified fury. As more details were revealed, it became clear that some 2,400 people, mostly sailors on the sunken ships, had been killed. We soon learned how the planes from six Japanese aircraft carriers which had been at sea for several days approaching Pearl flew down from the east between the Pearl Harbor Navy yard and the Navy's submarine base, and at 7:55 a.m. Hawaii time began the destruction of the neatly lined-up planes of the Army and Navy air forces on Ford Island as following torpedo planes delivered their weapons into the battleships Nevada, Utah, and Maryland off the western side of Ford Island, while other flights hit the California, the Oklahoma, the West Virginia, and the Arizona on the east side, then returned to bomb the USS Pennsylvania in dry dock. The battleship forces of the Pacific Fleet were effectively destroyed.

2 | E. CARVER MCGRIFF

In a radio address the following day President Franklin Roosevelt announced to the American people that "Yesterday, December 7, 1941 - a date which will live in infamy - the United States of America was suddenly attacked by the naval forces of the empire of Japan." He said that a state of war exists between America and Japan. Four days later, Chancellor Adolf Hitler of Germany, following a declaration of war against America by Benito Mussolini of Italy, announced to the Reichstag in Berlin that Germany hereby declares war on the United States. And so World War II had begun.

In the months that followed, America underwent a dramatic transition. Thousands of young men lined up at recruiting stations all over America, seeking to enlist in one of the armed services. The Selective Service draft was quickly expanded and those who delayed volunteering were soon being called to service in the thousands, then in the millions. Rationing was ordered, and supplies of such common products as sugar, shoes, tobacco, rubber products, especially car tires were drastically limited. Gas for cars was in such short supply that the average driver was only able to drive a few miles each week, and the national speed limit was cut to thirty-five miles per hour. Patriotic groups began collecting metal, paper, records, books, whatever a family was willing to give for the war effort. Bond drives flourished as Americans invested much of their wealth in War Bonds. Boy Scout troops began training older boys to be civil defense workers. Women soon left home and swarmed by hundreds of thousands into defense factories making airplanes, submarines and artillery shells, as Rosie the Riveter became a feminine icon in America.

In one way or another, everyone was mobilized to fight the enemy. I, at the age of seventeen, along with several classmates at Shortridge High School in Indianapolis, began attending classes to learn how to be an Air Raid Warden in preparation for what we then considered to be the imminent possibility that enemy airplanes would one day raid our city. We were issued white helmets and arm bands and, truth to tell, were having a great time as adventure loomed on our teenaged horizon.

The Japanese had accomplished in one blazing day something politicians had never been able to accomplish: an outburst of patriotism in America. Small red, white and blue flags, each bearing a blue star, began to appear in the windows of American homes as proud families announced that a young man from that home had gone to war. Headlines proclaimed defeats and victories as everyone's first concern was the progress of the war. Soon, virtually every family either had a member or a friend in the service. The daily papers began to feature announcements of casualties as every city began to count the cost in young lives, and a growing number of those blue stars were changed to gold. Like never before the people of America were proudly joined together.

In Europe things did not go well for awhile. American troops, poorly armed and inadequately trained, went into action in Africa against Germany's famed Afrika Korps which was led by the renowned General Erwin Rommel, the "Desert Fox." It was a disaster. We had landed in North Africa on August 8, 1942. Blasé and overconfident, lacking the know-how and the determination to fight the Germans successfully, the American forces were soon badly defeated in the Dorsal mountains of Tunisia, in the battle of Kasserine Pass. Our Grant tanks were no match for the German Panthers and Tigers with their 75 mm and 88 mm weapons. Our tactics were outmoded World War I tactics, one tank against another, while the Germans ganged up, used massed fire power. A thousand GIs died and hundreds were marched off into captivity. The Germans, examining our equipment, smiled, sent back word that our tanks would be easy to defeat, and this enabled them to design their equipment accordingly. Only the British succeeded, under Field Marshall Bernard Montgomery, in finally driving the Germans back across the sands of North Africa, capturing large numbers of German troops. But even then the major factor in Rommel's defeat was not superior tactics but the shortage of oil supplies for his tanks.

We were, however, learning. Our Sherman tank was developed which, still lacking the power of the German tanks, was far more maneuverable than our older tanks, with a more powerful main gun. New tactics were developed. Infantry leaders began to learn how to lead. Slowly, the American army, disdained by the Nazis, began to learn how to fight. Before long we'd capture Tunisia. Then, under a soon-to-be-famous general, George Patton, we'd capture Sicily. General Mark Clark would be leading the American Fifth Army into the mountains of Italy. And so, for the many months to follow, America and Britain were engaged in costly battle with the enemy. President Roosevelt, deciding that America lacked the resources to engage in full-scale war on opposite sides of the world, ordered that most of our resources be directed to the war in Europe, thus consigning many embattled American forces in the Philippines to defeat and capture by the fast-advancing Japanese.

For awhile the Japanese continued to rampage through the Far East. Their goal was to gain control of the oil and rubber, and the rice fields of the countries controlled by the Chinese. The Japanese sense of destiny, what they called their Greater East Asia Co-Prosperity Sphere, required the conquering of that part of the world, and their leaders believed that by depriving the United States of the maritime facilities of Pearl Harbor they would make it impossible for us to ship the necessary military materiel to the endangered nations in time to help them. They were determined to attack Australia and made bombing raids on Darwin and Port Moresby. They assaulted Guam, Borneo, Hong Kong and Bangkok, and were preparing for an assault on Singapore. They bombed the port of Ceylon to prevent delivery of supplies, and won a naval battle against allied forces in the Java Sea. For five months following the attack on Pearl Harbor the Japanese forces appeared to be invincible.

But the Japanese had underestimated the United States Navy and Marine Corps. American pilots were winning victories, shooting down hundreds of Japanese planes. The Japanese had made some fatal mistakes. Our aircraft carriers were safely at sea during the attack on Pearl. Our destroyers and cruisers had generally survived and the Japanese had failed to hit our fleet oil supplies. It would not be long until the U.S. fleet would strike back. On May 7 and 8, 1942, the U.S. fleet engaged the Japanese fleet in the vicinity of the Solomon Islands and though both suffered losses -- coupled with the mere fact that the

American fleet demonstrated such offensive power in what became known as the Battle of Coral Sea -- the Japanese drew back in surprise. The two again met in a decisive battle a month later near the island of Midway. In this battle three Japanese aircraft carriers were sunk and another was damaged and sent running at the cost of one American carrier. The victory was complete as the Japanese navy never again launched any offensive action.

On April 14, 1942 Air Corps Colonel Jimmy Dolittle led a raid on Tokyo of sixteen B-25 bombers manned by eighty heroic volunteer airmen knowing they had little chance of returning safely. They made the first bombing raid on the city, then flew on, either to crash or crash land in Chinese territory. The damage to the city was minor, but the psychological effect on the Japanese was profound. Now they knew we could reach them where they lived. Eventually, seventy-one of the fliers were returned safely, thanks to the help of the Chinese who rescued the downed men.

On a faraway island named Guadalcanal, on August 7, 1942, American marines landed and began the first major Pacific land battle against the Japanese following the capitulation on Bataan. The island was chosen as an outpost strategically located to defend any possible Japanese attempt to invade Australia. A long, hard-fought campaign followed in which 7,100 American men died, both from battle wounds and from disease, especially malaria. But several thousand Japanese soldiers died and American forces had won their first land victory.

There would follow a succession of bloody engagements on islands like Tarawa on November 20, 1943, where 1,000 Americans died, and Saipan on June 15, 1944 with the loss of almost 3,000. On February 19, 1945, one of the bloodiest Pacific battles of the war would take place on Iwo Jima. Lasting thirty-six days and costing more than 7,700 American lives, it was a battle which would become famous for the flag raising memorialized in the honored photograph, an event recently depicted in the movie *Flags of Our Fathers*.

Then, on April 1, 1945, the costliest battle of the war in the Pacific took place on the island of Okinawa. So many American marines and soldiers died there, 12,000 men. It's believed it was this battle which finally convinced President Truman to agree to the use of the atomic bomb on Hiroshima. It was followed by the fighting in the Philippines as General MacArthur made good on his promise that "I shall return." All of those battles ended in victory for American forces.

In Europe, the situation looked bleak for some time. British Prime Minister Winston Churchill believed a victory must be won in the Mediterranean. The Russians, long engaged in ruthless give-no-quarter battle with the Germans, insisted that the Americans and the British open a Second Front, an invasion of the European continent as the only solution to the seemingly endless fighting. Russian president Joseph Stalin hinted that he might seek a separate peace with Germany thus releasing millions of Nazi troops, currently suffering defeat after defeat on the frigid plains of Russia, to regroup and turn their attention to the British and Americans, making the possibility of a successful invasion of Europe very remote. Roosevelt believed we must invade through the shores of France. Bottom line: Churchill, Stalin, and Roosevelt knew it was of crucial importance to find a way to land armies in France, and to do so as soon as possible. American forces were fighting in Italy, but the mountainous terrain proved a nightmare for any offensive action and progress was slow and plodding. Defeat of the Nazis was not going to be possible without a landing directly on the continent with access to Germany.

The decision was made to land on the beaches of Normandy, France. It would all come down to this. It would prove to be the make or break action of the entire war. The proposed campaign was given the code name Overlord, and an obscure peacetime Lieutenant Colonel, Dwight D. Eisenhower, promoted to full general, would become Allied Supreme commander, an office coveted by the successful British General Bernard Montgomery who was not at all popular with the Americans. It was Eisenhower's splendid skills at diplomacy, a skill at which Monty was deficient, which won him the command. The day for invasion was chosen: June 5, 1944. Nearly 3,000,000 people would be involved in the cross-Channel action.

By June 4 thousands of men of the attacking units were already boarded on the invasion flotilla, many of them already having been there for several days. Others would soon board. Weather forecasters had predicted a bad storm almost certain to lash the Channel the next day. The logistics of unloading the troops only to load again in time for the crossing would have been too complex and time-consuming to be practical. The men had to remain on the ships while the seas pounded and churned violently. Eisenhower knew that to cancel the June 5 invasion could mean a lengthy postponement, one which would surely mean its failure as elaborate deceptions designed to make the Germans expect the attack in the Pas de Calais area, and which the Germans so far believed, would be exposed. The only alternative was the possibility that the following day the weather would subside sufficiently for the ships to cross, but the decision had to be made quickly. Men of the airborne divisions were already putting on their equipment in preparation to board the C-47s which would carry them to France. General Eisenhower spent a miserable day through the 4th of June struggling with the decision. British General Montgomery as well as several others of the planners urged Eisenhower to stay with the decision to go on the 5th. Finally, Eisenhower, disregarding the urging of others, in an act of moral courage which history will forever applaud, made and announced his decision at 4:15 on the morning of the 5th: the invasion would be postponed one day, thus risking the strong possibility that the whole thing would have to be canceled. He then wrote a statement taking full responsibility for the decision, to be published in the event the invasion proved to be a disaster. They waited. In his memoirs he wrote "at 3:30 the next morning our little camp was shaking and shuddering under a wind of almost hurricane proportions and the accompanying rain seemed to be traveling in horizontal streaks."[1] Had they gone on June 5 the invasion would certainly have met with disaster.

The Germans had had four years to prepare and reinforce their elaborate defenses. Sinking thousands of metal barriers in the shallow water where landing craft would be pierced and sunk, they sowed the Channel waters with hundreds of mines, and built mammoth steel-reinforced concrete fortifications concealing hundreds of artillery pieces and machine guns along the high ground overlooking the beaches. By every measure the defenses were impregnable. Unaware of all of this, several thousand young men, British and American, were asked to throw their unarmored bodies against this waiting defense. In the cool light of day it's unimaginable to believe what those men were asked to do that day.

In the early hours of June 6 hundreds of ships loaded with troops, arms and equipment set forth across the still-heaving English Channel and anchored off the beaches of Normandy, France, Americans on the two westernmost beaches designated as Utah and Omaha, the British and Canadians on those designated as Sword, Gold, and Juno. They were preceded by 16,000 men of the American 101st and 82nd American Airborne Divisions and 8,000 men of the British 6th Airborne Division who landed by parachutes and gliders in the pre-dawn darkness. And so the long-awaited Second Front, the one hope to end the war, had begun - in utter chaos as would soon become apparent.

The 101st Airborne troopers were scattered over an area of fifteen by twenty-five miles, most of them far from their drop zones. Sixty percent of their equipment was lost or destroyed, and within hours they'd suffered 1,500 casualties; only at such cost did they succeed in their objective of securing the four causeways leading in from Utah beach. The 82nd Airborne Division was scattered over thirty-five square miles, and many men wearing heavy equipment drowned in the marshes which the Germans had flooded with water from the Merderet River. Most of the paratroopers were dropped miles from their planned drop sites, some of them directly on the town square of Saint Mere Eglise, where surprised German troops shot them as they landed. Officers usually had no idea where the men under their command had landed. Majors and colonels fought for awhile as squad leaders, leading small groups of men from various units.

Pathfinders who had been flown in ahead of the troop carriers to land and light the way were flown off course. Only thirty-eight of those men landed on their objective; many were shot, others drowned. One team landed on the front lawn of the general commanding the

German 711th Infantry Division and were immediately captured. The weather had contributed, but many troopers later spoke bitterly of the failure of their transport pilots to maintain course and altitude as required for the drop. Ironically, some historians would later view this as providential as many advantages were gained by the Germans' inability to ascertain just where the troopers were. As one Nazi General, Gerhard Trilpel, was later quoted in a bit of understatement, "Parachutists appeared everywhere to our discomfort."

As for the gliders which came in in two waves, one early, one later in the day, the first glider to land in the darkness proceeded to crash through the landing lights provided by their pathfinders who'd flown in ahead of the oncoming waves, leaving the following glider pilots to guess where to land in the darkness. Many landing gliders were torn apart by large poles installed in fields along the coast by the Germans for just that purpose. One glider carried a general, and a jeep for the general's convenience had been strapped in behind him. The glider smashed into a hedgerow, the jeep crashed forward killing the general, and the whole operation lost its commanding officer. Of the second wave of gliders arriving in the afternoon, fifty in all, thirty-seven were hit by enemy fire, fortunately only two of them shot down, with, of course, the loss of all the men on board. Many gliders crash landed with dozens of men killed or injured.

C-47s which carried the paratroopers and pulled the gliders, unlike the bombers which had self-sealing fuel tanks, were vulnerable to incendiary bullets which could explode the plane's fuel. Below the planes were suspended parapacks, many of which contained explosives which could also be ignited by incendiary fire, so the pilot's maneuvers, if not admirable, were certainly understandable. In fact, many C-47s were shot down carrying their paratroopers to fiery deaths. The pilots, while heroic in the sense that they were there at all, were in too many cases derelict in their duty in failing to fly the course as instructed. Once a few pilots changed course while flying in darkness, most of the rest had to veer away to avoid midair collisions.

Chaos also beset the ground troops. Since troops had boarded ship on or before June 5, seasickness was rampant as the men rode out the violent storm. The landings began at 6:30 a.m. The Navy men in charge of the landing craft were often carried off course by the tides, and many infantrymen complained that they were forced to disembark long before they were close enough to shore, sometimes because of underwater obstacles, but too often because the pilots of the craft wanted to get the hell out of there. Many GIs, burdened with heavy equipment, drowned. Lieutenant Elliott Johnson, an officer in the 4th Infantry Division artillery, trying to land a 155 mm self-propelled artillery piece, reported that the Navy man steering his small craft toward the beach pulled up some distance out, in deep water, and said he couldn't go any closer. Johnson argued with the man, telling him the gun would founder and be lost but the seaman refused. Johnson then drew his pistol and literally pushed it into the man's mouth saying he'd shoot and drive the damn boat himself. The man then relented and drove as close as he could.

Men assigned to land on Utah Beach were landed 2,000 yards south of their assigned location, again providentially, as the defenses where they landed were much lighter than those at the assigned objective. They were opposed by one battalion of the German 709th Infantry Division plus elements of the 91st Luftlande Division whose commander, General Falley, was killed by 82nd Airborne paratroopers while trying to get back to his unit from a planning meeting in Rennes. This caused consternation among the men of the division and resulted, fortunately, in a sluggish response to the Americans.

The Rangers assigned to capture Pointe-du-Hoc boarded their transports and were fed spoiled hot dogs. Many men became so sick they thought they wouldn't be able to fulfill their mission, which was to destroy five artillery pieces thought to be concealed at the top of the pointe and aimed at Omaha Beach. The 225 Rangers assigned to attack the cliffs were loaded into landing craft and lowered into surging four-foot seas. Immediately one boat sank, killing four men and sending twenty-one to the hospital in England. Then another sank drowning most of the men on board. The 2nd Rangers had lost forty-five men just getting ready to start their trip inland some ten miles off shore.

As the Rangers approached what they believed to be their objective, their commander, Colonel Darby, realized that thanks to the mistake of the British Coxswain driving their boat they were three miles from their correct destination. Darby hurriedly turned them along the shore toward Pointe du Hoc, but precious time was lost. Darby later said that had they arrived on time they could have taken their objective without losing a man.

The heights were to be climbed on ropes tied to grappling hooks and shot from cannons. However, heavy rains had drenched the ropes adding significantly to their weight and preventing many of the ropes from reaching the heights. The Rangers heroically began to climb the 180-foot cliff, under the most extreme difficulty, only to discover, after suffering heavy casualties, that the guns they sought to destroy had already been moved.

Meanwhile, the Air Corps, fearful of hitting our own troops on Omaha Beach, had dropped their bombs so far inland they not only missed American troops, they also missed the waiting German troops. Ranger First Sergeant Lommel, seriously wounded, still managed to climb the cliff, only to discover the absence of the guns they were there to destroy. He started inland with another man, Sergeant Kuhn, finding that the guns had been moved 500 yards from the top of the cliff, aimed at Utah Beach. While enemy gun crews conferred a hundred yards away, the two sergeants quietly crept over and placed thermite grenades in the five artillery pieces, destroying them and no doubt saving hundreds of lives on Utah Beach. Lommel received a Distinguished Service Cross, Sergeant Kuhn received a Silver Star.

Offshore, Colonel Benjamin Talley was cruising a few hundred yards out in a small boat responsible to report to the generals waiting anxiously on the naval ships. He sent word to General Gerow that LCTs (Landing Craft-Tanks) were churning around in the water "like a stampeding herd of cattle," and General Bradley, listening to the reports, later wrote that he had "gained the impression that our forces had suffered an irreversible catastrophe." Closer in, the ocean waves were threatening all armored vehicles, as one by one they foundered, all too often taking their crew members to their deaths. Of thirty-two amphibious tanks launched to support the infantry, twenty-seven sank and were lost. All supporting artillery was lost. Into the hedgerows of Normandy, the soon-to-be-hated *bocage* country, streamed thousands of British and American infantry troops, going up against crack German troops instead of the old men and young boys they'd been told to expect, almost all their armor and artillery at the bottom of the Channel.

On Omaha Beach the landing was a slaughter. As the ramps dropped on the landing boats, machine-gun fire often killed the occupants before they could even exit the vessel. Many of the boats were impaled on underwater obstacles, occupants often drowning as they jumped out in deep water. Other men drowned as, loaded down with weapons, ammunition, radios, equipment of all kinds, they were disgorged from the landing boats in deep water too far from shore. Still other men, wading chest deep, then waist deep, were easy targets for the Nazi snipers on the hill before them, the water red with blood, bodies floating everywhere. Mines exploded, blowing men apart. Those who made it to the beach were ripped by artillery and machine gun fire. Soon the beach was littered with wounded men, medics who went to aid them soon themselves among the dead. Once a man stepped out of a landing boat there was nowhere to hide, though a few men tried to conceal themselves behind beach obstacles made of metal poles, or tree limbs. Along the seawall inland hundreds of men crouched, many without the weapons they'd lost in the water, most of them with no idea at all what they must do next. Officers ran among them trying to rally their men, many to be shot down before the men's eyes.

A few men who realized their only hope was to get inland from the beach tried to move forward, only to be shot down. Men of the 29th Infantry Division were virtually paralyzed, hundreds crowded together under the protection of a seawall, having no idea what to do next. None had experienced battle. Most were in some state of shock. Fortunately, some men of the 1st Division had been in battle and had some realization that there was no alternative to facing the fire and heading inland. Brigadier General Norman Cota of the 29th Division finally began to move among his men, trying to encourage them to get up and try to advance inland. Staff Sergeant William Courtney started up the steep hill as one man shoved a Bangalore torpedo under some barbed wire, opening a lane. Another man dashed upward and was shot dead. Still another ran on past him, Courtney leading the way. Lieutenant John Spalding led twenty-three men safely up the hill and after a lengthy battle managed to capture a German officer and twenty of his men.

A Ranger Sergeant, Mike Rehm, had hunkered down against the seawall for two hours with several other men when General Cota came by and asked who they were. When Rehm said they were Rangers, Cota shouted at him "then dammit, if you're Rangers get up and lead the way." They did just that, blasting their way through some wires with Bangalores, then finally making their way to the top of the hill, and in moving along the crest of the hill they found themselves in behind some of the most dangerous German fortifications. As more GIs followed they began killing Germans, while others surrendered. Finally, the slaughter on the beach began to abate.

Other units were also making headway, finally getting in behind German fortifications. General Cota found men paralyzed with fear, but under his urging they came to life and began to take part in the battle behind the German emplacements. Thanks to the constant supporting fire of American destroyers standing offshore, some of the German emplacements had already been demolished. Now others were neutralized. At last the German casualties began to number in the hundreds as dozens surrendered and the bulk of the German division began to withdraw. This is how the Americans finally got past Omaha Beach, dozens of small battles by unbelievably brave young men, many of those battles lost but an increasing number won. Americans were still dying, the fighting continuing, but by the end of the day the Americans, along with the British units to the east, were securely established in Normandy. Now the gathering of thousands of dead and wounded would begin, as hospital ships waited offshore. Many officers served with splendid courage and audacity. The battle was finally won, by those officers and non-coms who served above and beyond the call of duty, and by those young GIs who, having no previous experience which could have prepared them for the most costly day of fighting in the war, went forward, stepped over the dead and dying and pressed on until the battle was finally won because of them.

There would be many other battles in Normandy, and the casualties of that day would soon merge with those which lay just ahead. Thousands of men would yet die before any Allied soldier reached Paris. But on that day, in one small area of sandy beach, more than 3,000 courageous American men were killed or wounded in just a few hours in one of history's most incredible examples of collective heroism. General Bradley wrote later that "Even now it brings pain to recall what happened there on June 6, 1944. I have returned many times to honor the valiant men who died on that beach. They should never be forgotten. Nor should those who lived to carry the day by the slimmest of margins. Every man who set foot on Omaha Beach that day was a hero."

Terrible as those casualties were they could have been far worse save for the bizarre fact that Hitler and his Chief of Staff, General Jodl, were sound asleep and everyone was afraid to waken them. However, that may not have made a difference as Hitler had actually bought into some clever deception leading him to believe the real attack would come in the Pas de Calais area. He'd been deceived into believing that General George Patton was in command of an entire Allied Army, one which in fact did not exist. Instead, rubber replicas of tanks and other vehicles had been arranged in the fields of England to appear seen from an airplane to be large armored units, leading Hitler's Intelligence people to believe in the fake 5th Army. He therefore kept his Panzer units in reserve until it was too late to help repel the Allies on the beaches.

History has paid less attention to the men of the 4th Infantry Division who landed on Utah Beach. Officially, the roll of their casualties was listed as 197. General Bradley called it "a piece of cake." Certainly, by comparison it was. But not many days later the the 4th Division would lose thousands of men in other battles. Later accounting would in fact raise that number to around 300. I suppose as military histories are concerned those losses are small. Three hundred families across America grieved when the word reached home.

East of the American portion of the peninsula the British were fighting just as tenaciously, though their landings were far less costly than the Omaha Beach landing. While our purpose here is to record the American part of the invasion, it can't be overlooked that our Allies were also heroically fighting and dying. Their primary objective was the capture of the city of Caen which would afford road and rail facilities necessary for the quick run to Paris. North of Caen was the Orne River across which the Pegasus Bridge enabled the British access to their forces east of the Orne. The Germans knew how important the bridge was to the British, that if it could be destroyed their forces to the east would be trapped. The saving of the Pegasus Bridge is one of the most heralded British actions of the Normandy campaign. They succeeded, and in so doing caused the Germans to need reinforcements, which came from the reserves of their 352nd Division causing so much trouble at Omaha Beach. The loss of those reserves by the Germans probably saved many American lives.

Due to faulty intelligence, two crucial planning mistakes had been made by the planners in preparation for the invasion. One, they failed to learn that one of Germany's first-line infantry divisions, the 352nd, first-class troops specially trained by General Rommel for defense, was newly encamped near Omaha Beach. Only second-rate troops composed of old men and new recruits had been expected, but the powerful new division had been moved in for rest and refitting and was loaded and ready when the Americans arrived. Second, no one knew of the hedgerows which would impede our troops for many weeks in the effort to drive toward Germany. The consequences of these errors in intelligence would prove disastrous, very nearly fatal. It seems unbelievable that planners, many of whom must surely have visited France in earlier years, could not have known of the existence of the barely penetrable hedgerows. But they did not. No doubt from the air the hedgerows looked like the shrubs that bordered my grandmother's front yard.

CHAPTER TWO
MARCHING OFF TO WAR

BACK IN INDIANA I WAS THE KID IN THE BACK ROW OF THE MATH class, staring out the window. The teacher's words were lost on me as was true for most of us boys in that Shortridge High School senior class of 1942. Our country had been attacked by the Japanese at Pearl Harbor and as America mobilized for war we dreamed of high adventure in faraway places. My two best friends had already left in their junior year to join the Navy. I had copies of *National Geographic* magazine on the table by my bed, the pages turned to photos of artillery men, shirts off, suntanned, shoving shells into their cannons as they bombarded the jungles of Guadalcanal. My copy of *Life* magazine featured photos of B-17 bombers ducking ack-ack in the skies over Germany, and the radio music program "Your Hit Parade" was playing the newly popular song "Coming in on a Wing and a Prayer." We would soon feast on movies like *Bataan* and *Wake Island*, American marines battling the now hated "Japs." It was obvious we'd all be in uniform and all those childhood dreams of heroism on some far battlefield would, for many of us, become reality. Of course we had no real idea what that would mean to us. We were seventeen- and eighteen-year-old kids. But our country was calling and, with millions like us, the boys I knew were ready and willing to serve. Most of us only dimly appreciated the seriousness of the threat to our nation. For most of us teenagers it was a summons to adventure, and we could hardly wait. We took small note of the increasing number of reports of the deaths of kids who'd graduated a year or two ahead of us.

My turn came on September 17, 1943 twelve days after my nineteenth birthday, with a notice from my draft board calling me to the service. I'd been called six months earlier but had been deferred for a minor health problem. In the next few days a physical exam was followed by assignment to the United States Army, a brief time at home, a week at Fort Benjamin Harrison to receive a uniform, then a train ride to Camp Blanding, Florida for seventeen weeks of basic training where I was made an acting sergeant.

Basic training, required of every man destined for the Infantry, was a time of extremely strenuous training in military customs, drills, use of firearms, tactics in battle, and most of all, training in doing without the amenities of everyday life to which we'd been accustomed. We learned to get by on little sleep with small quantities of basically tasteless food while running, jumping, marching, racing over obstacle courses, until we were rid of fat, honed down to bone and gristle, and ready to exist under the most primitive conditions of extreme privation. It was all designed to create in us an unquestioning obedience to the orders of anyone holding higher rank than we did, and an uncomplaining acceptance of harsh discomfort in everyday life. However much we may have grumbled then, those who survived would look back on "basic" as one of the best things that ever happened to us.

After a brief visit with my family I was shipped, along with several friends from Camp Blanding, to Fort Meade, Maryland, then to Camp Shanks, New York, and finally aboard a transport vessel, the Bienville Victory, and off to the high seas of the North Atlantic. For thirteen days I was a member of a Navy gun crew standing a twelve-to-four watch twice a day. As I stood in the open gun pit as it was swept by sometimes violent winds, clinging to the metal edge of the canopy for four hours at a time as the ship plunged and rose in the heavy seas, I was afforded plenty of time to contemplate the demanding life which lay ahead. Harley Masters, a friend from Bloomington, Indiana, and I - Harley was on the port side gun - would sing a duet of "Oh What a Beautiful Morning" over the ship's intercom as the sun began to break through the early morning gloom. For a kid who'd only been out of Indiana once, it was an exhilarating beginning to my great adventure.

The Allied forces had begun to win the war in the Atlantic as hundreds of German U Boats (submarines) had been destroyed. But some were still out there roaming the Atlantic searching for convoys like ours. My job was to scan the water for any sign of a periscope or surfacing submarine. Toward the end of our voyage a nearby naval ship launched a search plane, and I was able to overhear radio traffic on the intercom and learned that there had been some kind of suspicious sighting a mile or so to our port stern. Whatever was sighted was either nothing or a sub that moved on. It did, though, give me something to think about for the rest of the trip.

We landed at the pier of the little town of Greenock, Scotland, and were soon moved by train, then by trucks, to a remote hillside camp in southwest England where we would remain for six weeks undergoing advanced combat training, mostly in what seemed to us like perpetually cold drizzle, living in six-man tents, spending most days climbing hills, doing calisthenics, and learning tactics we'd never use in battle.

One night we saw in the far distance a series of flashing lights reflecting off low-lying scattered clouds followed seconds later by the sounds of *crump, crump* and later we learned that we had seen the town of Cardiff, Wales many miles away as it was hit by enemy bombers. On another occasion, a British Spitfire fighter plane screamed out of nowhere, then over us at treetop level as we stood at attention in our company street. I could see the smiling pilot as he greeted us new arrivals with his deafening prop wash. I envied him as he rocketed off into space while I stood there in muddy shoes and wondered why I had passed up the Air Corps. For a moment, watching that sleek craft quickly disappearing into the sky, I wished I hadn't. I'd chosen, instead, to walk and crawl in the mud. Still, I was having a great time.

We should have begun to face the sobering probability that we were heading for the hell of battle, but we were kids. We'd heard of war in far-off places, places like Italy and Africa, and the far away Pacific, but we were in England. We thought life would go on like this with excitement, new places to see, friends we'd never otherwise have met, a sense of manhood new to most of us. On our rare days off we'd wander in groups to a pub some two miles down the road from our camp, and it was there I had my first drink, a pint of "half and half" English beer. I'd been a somewhat lonely kid growing up and I luxuriated now in merely being one of the guys in the camaraderie with friends who shared the hardships of combat training. My dreams of adventure were coming true. We'd sit around and tell tall stories and jokes, then stroll back to camp yelling and roughhousing all the way. Of course we complained about everything - the food, the weather, the early sound of a whistle in the morning. But beneath it all it was our great adventure. Complaining was a necessary part of Army life. There was an old saying that you only need to worry about morale when the troops stop bitching. What we were doing wasn't fun, after all, and complaining was a necessary part of our daily therapy.

How little we knew. Barely more than children, soon to suffer the death of innocence. So very sure of ourselves, so confident, off on our journey into darkness. Joseph Conrad said it for us: "I remember my youth and the feeling that will never come back anymore... the feeling that I could last forever, outlast the sea, the earth, and all men, the deceitful feeling that lures us to joys, to perils, to love, to vain effort - to death."

After six weeks of this, we were ordered to gather our equipment and prepare to move. A line of trucks arrived, and the 150 or so of us in our provisional company climbed aboard. The trucks rumbled off through scenic Somerset, passing through small villages where the people lined up to greet us, and we watched as a flight of large transport planes pulling gliders thundered overhead. It was June 6, 1944.

We arrived at the portside area of a town we believed to be Southampton, and there we joined with hundreds of other GIs as sergeants and lieutenants shouted orders with an authority we'd not experienced thus far. There was tension in the air, a sense of impending violence. We all felt it, felt that our lives were about to change profoundly. We'd paused for a day and a half at a barbed-wire enclosed camp patrolled by guards carrying Tommy Guns. There we were issued ammunition for our rifles, a hand grenade apiece, plus some colorful play money which we learned was invasion currency. We also were issued uniforms which had been treated with some foul-smelling chemical making the cloth slightly unpleasant to the touch with a slight swishing sound as we walked. Only after a few days of rain were our clothes fairly normal. We were told the chemicals would protect us if the enemy used gas as a weapon.

My closest friends, Duey and Huey McMillion, Tony "Meejy" Mejia, Harley Masters, Floyd Lainhart, Dallas McKinney, and Harold Brown and I searched each other out as we clambered aboard an overloaded ship. Once on board we were told to find a place, we wouldn't need a bed as we'd only be on board a few hours. The normally wild English Channel was churning from the effects of a violent storm only just having passed, and soon we were in its midst, the ship plunging deep into thundering waves, then rising skyward as men jammed together clung to rails and lifeboats as we tried to find a place to wait out the voyage which none of us cared for at all. Nothing had been said to us as to a destination, but it was obviously somewhere in France. We watched a constant flow of airplane traffic as two or three times sleek fighter planes, P-38s and P-51s, passed over us at a few hundred feet, all pointed toward the French shore.

The water had calmed as, after several hours, we started toward shore where we saw literally hundreds of ships and small vessels, several only barely visible above the threshing surf, obviously having been sunk. After an hour of negotiations among some officers who had come aboard our ship, we were ordered to climb over the side on heavy webbed nets, then drop into LCIs (Landing Craft: Infantry) each holding what appeared to be about twenty-five of us, and once loaded, we began puttering toward shore.

Fifty yards from shore our craft stopped. With a resounding crash the ramp on the front splashed down and we were ordered to get off. I was near the front and had little choice as men farther back surged forward. I found myself in four feet of surf and, burdened with a large loaded barracks bag, a pack, M1 rifle, and belt loaded with canteen, ammunition, first aid packet, and bayonet, struggled ashore where we dropped the bags, never to see our personal possessions again. Dripping sea water, we started inland. We crossed a sandy beach teeming with stacks of boxes, yelling men, the grinding roar of tractors and bulldozers, trash strewn everywhere, and down the beach a hundred yards a hospital tent surrounded by men on stretchers and what appeared to be medical people kneeling beside them.

Soon it all became real. We passed a dead sergeant wearing the insignia of the 101st Airborne, his hand covering his face as though he was ashamed to have been killed. It was severely traumatic for nearly all of us. He was our first dead man. Dressed as he was, we saw him as one of us, a GI, a kid who'd shared our dreams, been excited at the prospect of adventure. For two years he'd trained to serve his country, then died the first day. For the first time I reflected that a mother and father were sitting home somewhere, just as my parents were, hoping, praying for their son. Now he was dead, his body already bloating as the 101st Airborne had jumped four days earlier and he'd been left there in the sun and the rain, the ultimate obscenity of war. No one spoke. We silently proceeded forward, each alone with his thoughts.

A large flight of American bombers passed overhead and we watched as little black puffs of smoke began to pop around the planes. Ack-ack, it was called, the words a contraction of the sound of anti-aircraft fire. Soon we heard the deep rumble of bombs exploding among the enemy forces. The sound was comforting to us. We did not yet, however, realize how fortunate we were that the German Air Force, the Luftwaffe, was virtually non-existent, thanks to our fighter pilots, so we wouldn't have to put up with German bombers or strafing fighters. Captured German troops told how horrible it was to be bombed, many of those men mentally disabled by the experience.

Paratroopers had managed to capture the causeways leading inland from Utah beach sparing the land invaders many more casualties. Lieutenant Richard Winters, celebrated on the HBO Channel series "Band of Brothers," led a dozen men of the 506th Regiment of the 101st Airborne in knocking out four artillery pieces being used to pummel Utah Beach at Brecourt and won the Distinguished Service Cross.

We passed a broken road sign bearing the words Ste-Marie-du-Mont, so we knew we were in France. The invading units had moved inland and our replacement company began walking toward the sounds of battle. We still had no idea what was happening. No one told us anything. All the men we saw who were already there were grim-faced, stoic. Our imaginations ran wild but we had yet to hear the word "Normandy." The day would come when we would learn that hundreds of thousands of young men about our ages would have similar experiences as they arrived to replace a like number of casualties.

We passed a farmhouse and a stern-faced French woman of some thirty years standing along the road staring impassively at the passing lines of men. Beside her was a small child, her little face a mystery. I wonder now what they must have thought. After five years of life under Nazi rule, suddenly to see the arrival of supposedly friendly troops, yet to be surrounded by the maelstrom of war with explosions and death suddenly filling the neighborhood had apparently left them stunned. I assumed they'd been looking forward to an end to the occupation, but to have it all taking place where they had lived their lives in relative peace must have produced a kind of psychic shock: a confused wonder at the threat to their way of life, yet a hope for a new way of life with freedom from the tyranny of the Germans. I wondered, though, just how welcome we must be. People adjust.

Perhaps the family had learned to live with things as they were and didn't welcome this disruption of their world as being too exorbitant a price for what difference our presence could make. I certainly saw no sign of pleasure on the woman's face, only that grim, shocked acceptance. Some of the men waved a friendly greeting at the pair and I hoped that would reassure them that at least these bedraggled young men came in peace. It dawned on me that the cost of freedom could prove to be stratospheric for the people of France. One GI stepped across the road and handed the little girl a piece of candy. Solemnly, she accepted the gift, but her face revealed no emotion.

We passed a field littered with the remains of several badly broken gliders. Later we'd learn about the airborne invasion, but for the present we stared and just accepted everything we saw as being the way it was supposed to be. The whole experience had, for me, a kind of dream-like quality. The young lieutenant leading us seemed uncertain, pausing often to consult a map. He led us for more than an hour through a progression of small fields until we finally found ourselves on a winding country road where we stopped to take a break alongside another glider-littered field. I stood with Harley Masters and Duey McMillion as we shared our observations thus far. Then Duey pointed to the gliders and said, "I think those are the same gliders we saw an hour ago." He was right. We'd been walking aimlessly, in a circle. Our lieutenant leader, probably a 21-year-old but to us an older man, was obviously lost. Eventually he apparently got his bearings, and we set out once more and proceeded toward enemy lines.

It was nearly midnight when we stopped in a field and, exhausted, most of us just flopped down on the ground and were soon asleep. On waking at dawn one man let out a yell as he stripped off a field jacket he'd found there and worn through the night. It was stained with still tacky dried blood. We'd stopped where another unit had been decimated by enemy mortar fire earlier. An officer pointed out to us that the previous occupants who'd camped where we were now had failed to dig slit trenches and were caught in the open, suffering heavy casualties. Lesson learned: don't fail to dig in ever again. The Germans had, as we would learn, chosen areas where they thought it likely we would gather and they zeroed in their artillery, then waited. When some GIs arrived, the artillery opened up with perfect accuracy.

Another man was sent to fill our canteens in a nearby well, only to return white-faced, carrying our still empty canteens to announce that he'd found the body of a dead German floating in the well. By this point we kids were vividly aware that we were approaching the real war. We were issued K rations to be eaten on the march and we started at dawn, once more in the direction of the sounds of artillery and mortar fire.

We alternately walked and waited through the day as our guide tried to find his way. Shortly before midnight we stopped in a field where several men were standing, veterans of three days of heavy fighting, men who'd come in with the unit to which we were now to be assigned. Three days earlier, those men would have been just like us, young men with no real idea what lay ahead. Now they were separated from us by 1,000 miles of experience, glancing at us like we were children.

Finally, after standing around in the darkness, completely confused, we were ordered to form a line in the corner of the hedgerowed field and, one by one, we walked over to a makeshift table and there, in almost total darkness illuminated only by a carefully shaded flashlight, an officer informed us in whispered tones that we were assigned to the 90th Infantry Division, a National Guard division from Texas and Oklahoma, and we were in an area called Normandy. It felt weird, standing in line as though waiting to buy a movie ticket, then to be assigned the role that would determine our fates for life. I was to become a member of M Company, 357th Infantry, and would be a member of a machine gun squad. Just like that, the man I replaced was dead and I had his job. I'd later learn that our new company had already lost twenty-four of the 160 who had landed on Utah Beach. Where a replacement went was just luck of the draw. Max Hastings described it this way: "countless thousands of infantry replacements shipped to Normandy in June 1944 in anonymous packages of 250 men to be directed wherever casualties dictated."[1]

It was pitch dark, a starless sky, as we crossed into another field where other men were digging silently. Huey, Duey, Meejy, Floyd and I were in the same squad. Harold Brown was separated from us and only years later would I learn that he was killed in action shortly after our arrival. The "older" men glanced over briefly, then ignored us. Technical Sergeant Clayton Story whispered "dig in" and that was it. We would soon learn that there was a profound difference between us and the men who'd been there from the beginning. The title Combat Infantryman was to be earned in combat. For the present, we were just a bunch of kids who might or might not qualify. The brotherhood of men in combat was a closed corporation. You had to earn your membership. New men were socially ignored. We knew not to laugh at their jokes, or try to be friendly. Later, if we measured up, passed the test of enemy fire, then one of the "old" men might smile at us or ask us where we came from, or perhaps might help us at some task, then we'd know we were in, we were members. Until then our job was to dig a hole in the hard Norman ground and try to sleep for the three or four hours until dawn, and to keep our mouths shut. Men who had not been tested under fire were mere non-entities to those men.

The Army had made a grievous mistake, one finally corrected for future wars, in sending replacements in piecemeal. We were utterly bewildered, had no idea who was to be trusted, didn't even know who were our leaders. We would be in combat long before we knew the other men in our units, and they certainly knew nothing about us. Tragically, many young kids were killed before they even knew what they were doing. Only those of us fortunate enough to survive long enough to learn all we'd need to know, and long enough to prove ourselves to the men already there, would we in due time become accepted members of the unit to which we were assigned. Statistically, the greatest probability of becoming a casualty was in the first few days in combat.

The young lieutenant who'd led us to our division assignment and gotten us lost was only a couple years older than the rest of us. It worried me to think someone would follow him into combat, and I wondered if he was ready to go up against the German infantry company officers who'd been fighting successfully for a long time. I was soon to learn that nearly all of our infantry officers in Normandy were men with no experience in actual combat, and because the invasion planners hadn't known about the hedgerow country which redefined infantry combat, even the training those young officers had received was impractical for the close-in combat they were about to lead.

My disquiet was not exclusive with me. General Eisenhower's aide, Navy Captain Harry C. Butcher, on a tour with the general, had written in his diary that "I am concerned over the absence of toughness and alertness of young American officers whom I saw on this trip. They are as green as growing corn. How will they act in battle and how will they look in three months' time?"[2] His concern was not misplaced as later events would reveal. Casualties among the younger officers in the early going were horrendous despite their heroism. Eleven Second Lieutenants landed in our group, and a week or so later I ran into one of them who told us that he and one other were the only ones still in combat. Unlike the German junior officers who had been in combat for a long time, American junior officers, those who would lead platoons and companies, the basic fighting units of Normandy, had mostly been drawn from college ROTC units or were "ninety-day wonders," many having been officers for a matter of weeks or a few months. They faced the added disadvantage that because Army Intelligence had completely failed to anticipate the terrain of the *bocage* country, new officers had no idea what to expect when they arrived, nor had they any training to prepare them for the hedgerows.

Senior officers were little better off. Most had risen in the ranks as peacetime officers, been hurriedly jumped more than one grade in rank following the attack on Pearl Harbor, were accustomed to the mundane life of the barracks and were suddenly plunged into the quagmire of Normandy. Too many infantry commanders were peacetime administrators, men woefully ill-equipped for battle. My division would have three commanders in the first weeks. My regimental commander was also sacked before long. So was my battalion commander. They simply were in over their heads. Thousands of men died unnecessarily because of the mistakes of such men. One historian, Max Hastings, observed that "by 1944 it was evident to America's commanders that serious errors in judgment had been made in mobilization of the nation. The most critical, which would markedly influence the campaign in northwest Europe, was that too little emphasis had been placed on manning the infantry regiments at the very tip of the American spear."[3] Mercifully, there were a few experienced leaders who made the difference. Still, as the most heroic and thus most out-in-front officers were killed or wounded, many units began to flounder for lack of strong leadership. It took time for the others to learn the art of small-unit warfare, an art long since mastered by the Germans. It is indeed a wonder that we won in Normandy given the disparity in combat capability between German and American officers in the beginning. It wasn't our fault. There was just one way to learn, and that was on the job.

We, of course, were blithely unaware of all of this, assuming that anyone with rank must know what he's doing and - we didn't question this for a long time – must be courageous enough to go out ahead of us whenever we were ordered to go where we could get shot.

These were all issues which troubled Dwight Eisenhower as we new recruits tried to drift off to sleep in mud-filled slit trenches, still finding it hard to believe that we were actually here, in an Infantry division, in a war, in France, where they actually shot people. But then there was that dead paratroop sergeant.

It was only breaking dawn as we were rousted out of our troubled sleep and ordered to gather our equipment and get ready to move. We would soon learn that we'd not stay in one place very long. Sergeant Earl Brewer introduced himself to us and told us he'd be our squad leader. We met a few other men, Leo Buchanan, Don Cerulli our medic, and a couple others. A case of K rations was opened and the old timers hurriedly grabbed off their preferences. Almost all the food we would eat in the days to follow would be in the form of K Rations. The army provided three of these a day, Breakfast, Lunch, and Dinner, each of which came in a small rectangular box. Ironically, the box was about the size of the case which came with a Purple Heart. Men who suffered slight wounds used them to mail their medals home.

There was also a backup ration for dire emergencies called a D Bar. It was a chocolate bar said to contain 600 calories and was so hard as to require about an hour to consume. I think, though, someone realized we'd eat them along with our regular rations unless they tasted terrible.

Most of this day was spent walking, digging slit trenches, walking, digging, walking, digging. It was axiomatic that we begin preparing some form of protection the moment we were stationary because mortar rounds or the soon to be hated and feared 88 millimeter artillery rounds slammed in without warning. I had soon torn the fingertips out of my gloves digging. Some men were supplied with what the army called entrenching tools, what ordinary people call shovels. These, though, were ingenious items with a ratchet at the joint of the blade to the handle. The blade could be fastened in line with the handle forming a shovel, or turned at right angle to the handle, locked into position, and used as a pickax. Thank the good Lord for that because Norman ground was as hard as asphalt. Hopefully, one of every two men had one of these. You'd chip away some ground and scrape it out with gloved hands (until the gloves were worn away and the hands toughened). You were lucky to get deep enough to flatten yourself to ground level.

Civilians heard a lot about foxholes in World War II. These were, ideally, deep enough for a man to stand in straight with the ground about chest level. I saw few of them myself. They must have dated from the war in Africa where the digging was easier. It would take a strong man two days to dig one with the tools we had. Instead, we scraped a depression in the ground long enough and wide enough to lie in, hopefully deep enough that flying shell fragments could not hit, and called them slit trenches. One of those could be dug in fifteen to twenty minutes. Most of the ones I dug were probably six to eight inches deep, and rarely were we in one place long enough to complete the job. If we were lucky, we might commandeer one someone else had dug before moving on. It was sometimes like musical chairs: you'd see some slit trenches in the direction you were moving and hoped if you were ordered to stop, you'd be the man closest to one already dug. Only if you stopped for some length of time, overnight say, or for a couple days, did you dig anything better.

We could also use our metal helmets to scrape loose dirt from a trench. The helmet came in two parts, a plastic helmet liner, plus the metal shell that fit on top. Parade ground activities usually meant wearing the liner without the outer metal shell. There was a chin strap but no one ever used it. We were told that concussion from a near-miss artillery shell could rip that helmet off your head or it could rip that helmet off *with* your head if it were buckled. Instead, it was buckled over the back of the helmet. I'm not sure I believed that stuff about the concussion, and I found that running with the unbuckled helmet often sent it flying off my head, but we soon learned to cope with all of that. The metal shell also had other uses, like as a place to wash your socks, and as a toilet during an artillery barrage, and as a water trough during a rainstorm, though one needed to be very thirsty to use it for that after it had been in general use for awhile.

If Adolf Hitler had ordered the use of gas as a weapon, we would have lost the battle for Normandy. Each of us was supplied with a gas mask, and most of us threw the darn thing away within hours of arriving there. You could track the trail of newly arrived replacements by the discarded equipment we left along the way. Gas masks were cumbersome and no one seriously thought the enemy would be crazy enough to use gas. Chlorine, phosgene, mustard, whatever else would do the trick would have caught us totally unprepared, and when we considered the other means to inflict death and suffering used by Hitler, gas must surely have seemed a logical weapon. Why it was never used even though the Geneva Convention prohibits its use I have never heard. It may well be that the Germans realized two could play at that game and the result would be mutual catastrophe. Still, they used it in the first World War. Anyway, none of us ever gave it much thought. The few men who hung onto their masks said they used them when encountering groups of dead soldiers who had lain untended for days.

CHAPTER THREE

ON TO THE FIELD

ALL INFANTRY COMPANIES HAD A LETTER DESIGNATION TO WHICH was assigned a word; so companies A, B, C, and D, in the First Battalion, for example, were Able, Baker, Charlie, Dog. My Company was "M" Company, called Man Company (sometimes Mike Company). The Company to which we were usually attached was "L" Company, known with a bit of unintended irony as Love Company. M Company was a Heavy Weapons Company. Whereas the Weapons platoon in a rifle company was armed with air-cooled, 30-caliber machine guns which could only fire about six-round bursts without overheating, and with small, short-range sixty millimeter mortars, the Weapons Company was supposed to be armed with water-cooled guns which could fire a much more sustained rate of fire, and with larger 81 mm mortars with longer firing range. For our first week, however, we only had light air-cooled guns. This made us more mobile as the guns were lighter, allowing us to run with the rifle companies.

An Infantry Division in World War II was composed of roughly 16,000 men and was commanded by a two-star Major General, assisted by a Brigadier one-star. Called a triangular division, there were three regiments in a division, in our case 357, 358 and 359, each commanded by a full colonel, and each was divided into three infantry battalions plus an artillery battalion. These were commanded by Lieutenant Colonels, (or sometimes a Major). Each infantry battalion was divided into three rifle companies and a Heavy Weapons Company commanded by captains (or sometimes a First Lieutenant); each rifle company had three rifle platoons, plus a weapons platoon, each commanded by a lieutenant, each with three twelve-man squads commanded by a staff or buck sergeant. Ideally, a company might have had about 160 men but the reality was many less. The actual number fluctuated wildly in battle where the basic combat unit was the platoon.

There were, of course, numerous other units in a division including communications, ordnance, quartermaster, intelligence, cannon companies, graves registration, on and on. Tank companies were normally of great importance, but because of the hedgerows and the marshy ground they were of limited importance in Normandy. There would also be an artillery battalion. Many men served in infantry divisions without ever hearing a shot fired from closer than a mile or so. Historian Lee Kennett wrote "Fifty percent of division personnel were primarily involved in non-combat logistics. The other fifty percent, at the most about eight to nine thousand men per division fought, bled, and died and along the way determined the outcome of the war."[1] For example, only about half the members of the 82nd and 101st Airborne Divisions actually jumped into Normandy.

There would be much jealousy and resentment among the various units. Historian Paul Fussell has written, "It is true of every war that much as he may fear and perhaps hate the enemy opposing him, the combat infantryman broods with deep and bitter resentment over the enormous number of people in his rear who sleep safely at night."[2] Men would later return from brief visits to the rear areas and report that everyone was wearing the new field jackets not yet issued to those of us at the front. I don't suppose any one man thought he was hurting a comrade. He just saw huge stacks of new clothing, thought no one would miss one jacket and so helped himself. But when several hundred men did the same it could mean a whole regiment of men would suffer. In the winter, combat men have been known to suffer frozen feet while rear echelon troops headed off supplies of the new winter shoes for themselves though they lived in commandeered homes and offices.

One survey revealed that sixty-five percent of Infantry noncommissioned officers reported "A significant degree of resentment among themselves or their men. Only six percent felt that there was no resentment at all."[3] To be fair, while rear echelon men were safe as compared to combat men, their lives could be very uncomfortable, and it was not unheard of that rear units were overrun and suffered casualties. The great majority of those men did their jobs, else the front-line units would have been unable to function. Still, while I don't remember feeling "bitter resentment" I certainly envied those men who slept safely at night.

Since seventy percent of all casualties were inflicted by enemy artillery and mortars - some estimates place that percentage of Normandy casualties as more nearly eighty-five percent - the odds were pretty similar for all of us. In combat there was some of this feeling that "my job is worse than your job" among most men at the front. Riflemen who were literally face to face with the enemy believed men on machine guns were safer, while we knew the machine guns were the first things the enemy went after. We, of course, viewed the light-mortar men as rear echelon while the few of them still around after the first few days scoffed at that and wished they could be back with the artillery units. The tankers were lucky, we thought, since they were surrounded by thick walls of steel, while people who saw the casualty reports referred to the Sherman tanks as Ronsons, a reference to a then popular cigarette lighter, because one round from a German Tiger tank would light up a Sherman and burn the occupants to death. A Sherman tank was no match for a German Tiger tank one on one, the German having better armor and a far more powerful gun.

The basic American tank was the M-4 Sherman which weighed about 34 tons and had two-and-a-half inches of armor and a 75 mm gun, not high velocity. The Germans had two tanks which were far superior: the PzKw "Panther" at 53 tons and three-and-a-half inches of armor with a 75 mm high velocity gun, and the horrifying PzKw VI "King Tiger" weighing 64 tons, twice that of our Sherman, with its 88 mm high-velocity gun which could destroy a Sherman at 2,000 yards, its velocity such that on at least one occasion the shell penetrated through one Sherman and set another beyond it on fire. With its six-inch armor face "glacis" plate, it was virtually immune to the Sherman gun's shell, even with its maximum effective range of 600 yards and which often failed to penetrate the Tiger's hide. To make matters worse the Tiger was more maneuverable, and the only way Shermans could destroy one was for several Shermans to maneuver so one could get a side shot, while, too often, one or two of the other Shermans were being destroyed. Shermans also had a higher profile making them easier to see at a distance. Tank battles were only won by swarming enemy tanks with superior numbers.

A former lieutenant in an armored division named Belton Cooper recently wrote a book with the suggestive title *Death Trap*, telling of his experiences during the war of trying to keep the Shermans of the 3rd Armored Division working. He reported that once the division was in combat and had faced the Germans "the myth that our armor was in any way comparable to the German armor was completely shattered. We realized that we were fighting against German tanks that were far superior to anything that we had to offer. As a result, many young Americans would die on the battlefield."[4] He also reported a little-known fact that American designers had developed the prototype of a new, far more formidable and more maneuverable tank, the M26. Several generals of the armored force had immediately asked for these tanks, but the idea was finally nixed by no less a man than General George Patton who believed the Sherman was better because it could move around a lot. So, as Cooper points out, many young men needlessly died. The truth is that men who manned those Shermans were all heroes.

So it went with men in combat. Everyone thought his job was the most dangerous. Statistics would finally show that in World War II, fourteen percent of the men sent overseas would serve as infantry, and would suffer seventy percent of the casualties. Author Stephen Ambrose put it this way: "Normandy was a soldier's battle. It belonged to the riflemen, machine gunners, mortar men, tankers, and artillery men who were on the front lines. There was no room for maneuver. There was no opportunity for subtlety. There was a simplicity to the fighting, for the Germans, to hold; for the Americans, to attack." He quoted one veteran of the fighting to some new arrivals: "Now if you guys are around this time tomorrow you can call yourselves veterans."[5]

This was how most of us sized up our situation at the time. We had very little regard for anyone not immediately exposed to battle with the enemy. The day would come, however, when we'd see things quite differently. There'd been a lot we didn't know that would have changed our attitude toward those rear echelon people. Historian Robin Neillands wrote that the work of supplying arms, ammunition, food, equipment and other needed supplies to front-line units may be "dry stuff" to discuss, but without an efficient system for supply, battles would quickly be lost. By June 18, 106,000 tons of supplies and 41,000 vehicles had been landed in the American sector along with 314,000 troops. The British had landed about the same number of troops with a 102,000 tons of supplies and another 54,000 vehicles. Each day thousands of additional tons of supplies and thousands more men were arriving, all of this in a small peninsula, much of which was submerged in marshy water and with roads which today we'd consider country lanes. By June 19 a brutal storm had begun which was destined to last four days, destroy one and badly damage the other of the two artificial piers that had been prepared in England and floated across the Channel, bringing the unloading of supplies almost to a standstill. Thousands of men were being killed, wounded or captured every day while thousands of replacement troops, most of them teenagers, were arriving daily. All of this created a nightmare logistical situation as wounded were being evacuated, dead were gathered, replacements troops were shuttled forward, essential supplies were distributed. The problems facing men in the rear seemed at times almost impossible to solve.

Take gasoline. Delivering the gas, or any material, was a major problem. Many bridges had been destroyed and truck drivers didn't always know which road was passable. Most of those roads were winding and narrow, bordered tightly by hedgerows, with barely room for an Army truck. Heavy rains which would persist through June and July turned vast areas into quagmires, farm roads into muddy swamps. Drivers searching for passable roads had to be very careful not to take a wrong turn and run into a German patrol.

Food? We lived on K rations packed in rectangular boxes. Figure fifteen divisions with as many as 9,000 front-line troops in each - I assume those lucky fellows in the rear were eating hot meals - that would be a 130,000 men, plus tankers, medics, all the other front-line men, times three meals a day - it was close to half a million meals that must be delivered to the front lines every day with the number increasing daily. It wouldn't help to deliver too many meals to one company and too few to another. Distribution had to be near perfect.

Ammunition. I have never heard how much ammo we expended in Normandy. I know a shell for a big 240 mm artillery piece weighed 95 pounds and one gun could fire off 30 or 40 of those in a day, often more. There were thousands of artillery pieces of various sizes spread all over Normandy, each needing a constant supply of heavy shells.

The most gruesome work of all -- caring for the dead -- required many men. Our own dead had to be carefully returned to gathering points and temporarily buried. Same for enemy dead we recovered. Many of those dead were badly mutilated and in too many cases had lain where they died for several days. I could never imagine what that cleanup job must have been like for the men who did it, or what kind of nightmares they must have had.

Also, in the matter of gruesome work: damaged tanks, which eventually numbered in the thousands, had to be returned for repair, and often they contained the remains of dead gunners and loaders, the tank interiors blood-soaked. Someone, someone whom God will surely bless, had to climb inside those tanks and clean them up so they could be used again. Mechanics must have numbered in the hundreds to make sure we had as many workable tanks in the field as possible.

Wounded men had to be evacuated to aid stations for emergency care, then on to station hospitals and, if their wounds were at all serious, back to England to general hospitals. There was a constant flow of thousands of wounded men, each requiring the attention of doctors, nurses, ward workers and ambulance drivers, which meant that medicine and other medical supplies must be constantly delivered to hundreds of locations immediately adjacent to battlefields. Captured German wounded were added to this, and the number of personnel required to move wounded men from the field and process them through to places of recovery must also have numbered in the thousands.

None of this would have been possible without good communication facilities. Today's cell phone user would be amazed to discover how rudimentary telephone and "walkie-talkie" communication was back then by comparison. Then there were all those other jobs, record-keeping, mail handling and distribution, meal preparation for the hundreds of thousands of men and many women doing all these other jobs, overseeing the daily arrival of thousands of replacement troops, receiving millions of other items as they streamed onto the beaches and into the ports, military police keeping order, guards overseeing captured prisoners, people in the various Intelligence sections trying to make sense out of information derived from captured prisoners, and from photos taken by pilots flying flimsy Piper Cubs over enemy territory. It seems almost endless. And all of this crammed into an area so relatively tiny that one British division had to sit offshore on their ship for two days because there wasn't enough room on the beaches for them to unload. There were people in transportation, public relations with the French, people looking after arrangements for housing of rear echelon troops, people in charge of supply and distribution of clothing, on and on went the requirements to maintain the elaborate machine which enabled men in combat units to do battle with the enemy.

Had any of us had the slightest comprehension of all of this, understood that when a case of rations or a case of M1 bandoliers arrived it was made possible by all those people working tirelessly, doing their jobs, we would have thought quite differently than we did. Had we understood the colossal work of supply and troop maintenance going on back in England, men and women assembling all these essential materials, getting them loaded and dispersed where they were needed, we again would have felt quite differently, far more grateful for all those "blue star rangers" getting the essential jobs done so we could do ours. We just didn't know any of this back then. We had it all wrong. But we were scared kids wanting to survive, perhaps prove ourselves worthy, needing the sense of importance to the cause that could sustain us in battle. Wisdom would come much later. Today former combat men are far more respectful of all those other men who made it all work than we once were.

A few men survived in front-line units a long time without becoming casualties, some individuals surviving for months, but they were rare. The 90th Division, in just over two months' fighting in Normandy, lost the equivalent of 100 percent of its enlisted men and one 150 percent of its officers, those on the front line.[6] That was about 9,000 casualties out of 16,000 men of whom probably 8,000 were non-combat personnel in a period of eight-and-a-half weeks. Obviously there weren't very many individuals around by the end of the campaign who were there when it started.

Men who survived for longer periods in combat often had very mixed feelings about men who, though having served honorably and well in combat, were wounded sufficiently early to escape further service. Veterans could be very competitive about this. Those who saw the television series "Band of Brothers" which depicted in almost documentary style the adventures of the men of the 506th Regiment of the 101st Airborne Division, may recall the scene in which Private Webster who jumped in Normandy, then in Holland, had been wounded and hospitalized, thus missing the combat at Bastogne. When he returns to his unit expecting to be warmly welcomed by old friends he is instead greeted coldly and told by former friends to go to a different squad. All his past service notwithstanding, he hadn't been *there*. Even some new men who hadn't seen as much combat as Webster took up the disdainful attitude. They *had* been at Bastogne. Webster had to prove himself all over again. Combat men tend to be conscious of who has seen how much combat and which battles were the most dangerous. It was a subtle "but you weren't in Normandy," or "yeah, but you weren't in the Huertgen," or "maybe you guys had it bad but at least you missed the Bulge."

In other words, each unit was something of an entity unto itself with its own culture, values and prejudices, a tightly-closed corporation until you qualified by their measure.

In combat, many men suffered emotional breakdowns of such severity that they were no longer able to function and had to be removed from battle. It was a traumatic effect the men could neither help nor resist. Most would have avoided this if they could have, many on the verge of a breakdown for some time, trying courageously to hang in there before finally caving in. There were a few malingerers who pretended to this in order to escape from battle, and between the most severe cases and the few fakes was a fairly wide spectrum of degrees of disability. Many men could, after a period of rest, return to battle, some even to later serve heroically. Many more were able to rest for a time and return to less arduous service, something away from the battle. Some were disabled to a degree that left them unable to perform any meaningful service and were sent home for more intensive treatment.

This phenomenon was called "battle fatigue," a term intentionally chosen to avoid the implication of cowardice or weakness. Studies made after the war suggest that no person can endure past a certain point. Some men, of course, were able to last longer than others, but there were only a very few who seemed to have no limits. Even some of them pressed on in a near zombie-like state.

Dr. Judith Herman, Professor of Psychiatry at Harvard Medical School, published results of several studies of troubled combat veterans suggesting that the trauma of combat can produce disorientation which prevents the sufferer from continuing to function in the traumatic situation which produces it. The victim may physically collapse, or may lose control of bodily functions. Removed from battle, the trauma leaves torturing memories. She found that alcoholism was a frequent result and reported that two researchers, Grinkler and Siegel, "found that uncontrolled drinking increased proportionately to the combat group's losses; the soldiers' use of alcohol appeared to be an attempt to obliterate their growing sense of terror."[7] Ominously, they also found that of men who suffered battle fatigue only seven percent had an alcohol problem going into battle but eighty-five percent came out with an alcohol problem. Many such men came home and had a serious problem.

During the fighting in Normandy, and thereafter, it was reported that men suffering this breakdown were regularly removed from combat for seventy-two hours, then returned to duty. Thirty percent actually returned to combat, another sixty percent to less stressful duty. By the end of the war it was assumed that nearly all the men who broke down and were temporarily disabled would return to normal functioning. Dr. Herman disputes this and wrote, "though the survivors may make a rapid and dramatic return to the appearance of normal functioning, the systematic stabilization should not be mistaken for full recovery, for the integration of the trauma has not been accomplished."[8]

The custom of helping victims heal by retrieving memories, reliving them in their minds as it were, done with sodium amytal, is of limited use. The effect of combat, Dr. Herman wrote, "is not like the writing on a slate that can be erased, leaving the slate as it was before. Combat leaves a lasting impression on men's minds, changing them as radically as any crucial experience through which they live."[9] In other words, once the damage is done some effect is permanent. Once in combat, no one is left unaffected.

Some men quickly went into a sort of sensory overload, suddenly exposed to violent action, rendered unable to make sufficient sense of their experience to deal with it and became paralyzed. One just-arrived GI, James Lingg, a private in Item Company, 26th Regiment of the First Division, later admitted that during fighting in the small village of Ste. Anne his company was overrun by a large column of Germans. He decided not to participate and just crouched down in a ditch and waited for the fighting to cease. As the fighting continued, he turned to a friend and said "Let's get the hell out of here and go back to the beach." The two of them pondered this for a moment, then decided that would be desertion, so they just waited for the firing to stop. That was not at all unusual as newly-arrived men were sometimes stunned by events and rendered unable to function. Lingg and his friend later performed satisfactorily and only told their story much later.[10] Men like this soon managed to adjust on their own.

In determining how to prevent breakdowns for most men, given that the stress of combat is universal in any fighting unit, Dr. Herman reports that the researchers "observed that the strongest protection against psychological breakdown was the morale and leadership of the small fighting unit."[11] This fact, learned much too late for World War II, helps explain why so many men became victims. Rather than do as the British did, replacing losses with men who knew each other, we were sent in piecemeal, often one or two mystified kids arriving and bluntly told, as I was, "dig in." Knowing none of the experienced men of the unit, many new men felt rejection and coldness from the veterans; only if they performed satisfactorily in combat were they accepted and finally made to feel part of the team. By that time much psychological damage was sometimes done. It was all further exacerbated by the realization that there was no end in sight other than death or physical injury. In other words, there was nothing to hope for. If you survive today you'll do it all over tomorrow, and tomorrow, days without end. I think this coldness warmed up a bit as time went on, and those of us who had felt it on arriving were a little more understanding when other new kids arrived. Still, though, until the newcomer had been "blooded" as they used to say, he wasn't really one of us.

Another little-examined factor closely related to the terror factor is an ethical one. Within a short time, because of heavy casualties among the older combat troops, the replacements came in and we were almost all kids. Nearly all my friends were eighteen or nineteen years old. As people so young, we were still totally the products of our homes. Swiss psychotherapist Paul Tournier puts it this way: "A child cannot receive his first lessons in morality directly from God: he receives them from his parents to whom he then ascribes a divine authority." In other words, we were basically products of family values taught in the home, and that influence had about it the will of God. If we came from good, decent homes, as most of us did, we'd been taught personal values, such things as honesty, kindness, love thy neighbor, respect other people, make me proud of you. Not all were so raised, of course, but most of us were. Well and good. At our ages we had never experienced the real world in such a way as to have this set of values seriously challenged. To young untested minds, they came from God, in the form of Dad and Mom, and were not to be questioned.

Some teenagers had been sharply warned of severe consequences for the violation of any of these moral precepts, and were prone to guilt feelings. Now we found ourselves in an environment which demanded that we abide by an entirely different value scheme. No one there cared what kind of record we had at home. Now we were to be killers, men who ruthlessly deceive, denigrate, hate and otherwise act in destructive ways toward people who, but for the uniforms, looked like us. That was fine with us in theory. We'd all been raised on cowboy movies, the rural kids hunting with .22s, the city boys with BB guns, so we knew the theory. But to actually shoot someone? Kill a man? That was to court a profound trauma and the effect of such a conflict of values is inevitably guilt. Either we failed Mom-Dad-God, or we failed Lieutenant Whoever, and right now that's the person whose admiration and respect we most desired. Either way, we must betray something important and valued. So we tried to do all those "bad" things, knowing that while Mom and Dad wanted us to be good soldiers, we also knew they hadn't the slightest idea what that required. Mom (God), at least, would be horrified at what we were now trying to do. Our highminded selves submerged in our psyches, seeking always to escape to the conscious mind, and we pressed on in the course of a demonic undertaking. Just imagine the clean-cut kid next door, or your cousin, or the president of your church youth group, being taught to kill other young men. Imagine the psychic/ethical transformation they'd go through, and what they'd be like after carrying out their new lifestyle.

An example of this dilemma is the story in *Huckleberry Finn* by Mark Twain in which Huck is forced to tell a lie in order to protect his friend, the runaway slave Jim, from pursuers. Huck, forced to choose between loyalty and honesty, struggles with his conscience. "It don't make no difference whether you do right or wrong," he complains, "a person's conscience ain't got no sense and goes for him anyway." Huck speaks for all of us when he decides, "If I had a yaller dog and he had no more sense than my conscience I would poison him. It takes up more room than all a person's insides and ain't no good nohow." He clinches his argument with this: "Tom Sawyer says so too." So it is when we have to choose between two conflicting alternatives, neither of which is entirely right nor entirely wrong. The more crucial the choices, the more painful the dilemma.

Most of us struggled with this inner conflict and had to live with the results. Some men could not. Karen Horney, whose studies of neurosis are primal, explained that in situations like ours we were internally confronted with two radically opposing sets of expectations, those of God as received through parents, and those of military authority which determined our very being at the time. For some men the conflict was intolerable. Horney wrote that "there are quick retributions if we do not measure up. In the case of the inner dictates, this means violent emotional reactions to non-fulfillment - reactions which traverse the whole range of anxiety, despair, self-condemnation and self-destructive impulses."[12]

This conflict can generate a seething hatred of one's own self as one seems to be in an inescapable trap of unacceptable behavior no matter what we do. "We may hate ourselves with an enervating and tormenting hatred," warns Horney. And "the hatred...results from the discrepancy between what I would be and what I am. There is not only a split, but a cruel and murderous battle."[13]

Those men whose personal value systems were too brittle were prone to be examples of this. The result was sometimes a form of personal paralysis, and such men who were not overcome by the terror of battle were overcome by the terror of the inner battle. They too, like the first mentioned, could be rendered nonfunctional.

However high flown this may sound to those who have never endured such inner battle, it was all too true for many, and never more so than for the loving, gentle, perhaps one must sometimes say neurotic men who were pressed into service and armed to kill. A complete history of warfare is incomplete without taking account of the inner warfare which battle precipitates, something which in many less disabling ways was true for us all. Many a man was denounced for cowardice whose disability grew, not from cowardice, but out of a sensitive, troubled mind faced with the shattering psychic experience of trying to survive on the field of battle, while enacting violence against other men. While most of us solved this turmoil in our own minds, or at least found a way to come to terms with its effect, a tragic number of men could not and had to be hospitalized excepting, of course, the ones who took their own lives. Hushed up as this casualty rate was, it was monstrous. Many men must have engaged in heroic psychic conflict within themselves, quite in addition to the dangers of the battlefield. Perhaps all of us did in some measure.

To indicate the gravity of these problems and their effect on the progress of the war it's worth recording that according to historian Max Hastings, not long after the campaign had begun, "temporary or permanent losses from 'battle fatigue' had reached an alarming 10,000 men since D-Day, around twenty percent of all casualties. Finally, a staggering twenty-six percent of all American soldiers in combat divisions were treated for some form of battle fatigue." Hastings reported that 929,000 men experienced some degree of battle fatigue in the U.S. Army in the Second World War.[14] If true, that's an astounding figure. Even today there are very elderly men who dread the memory of their World War II days, and they may be numbered among those who prefer not to talk about the war.

There was a large sub-group of men who were unable to deal with the stress of battle: men who shot themselves. I later learned there were many such men in the hospitals, "SIW" on their hospital records. General Eisenhower was horrified to learn of one hospital with over a thousand such men. Historians have documented a large number of cases of such wounds by men who simply couldn't stand any more. Incredibly, one man in the 319th Infantry Regiment literally killed himself to escape combat. His commander remarked that "that was going too far." Private Gerard Ascher told of witnessing a new arrival who took one look at Normandy, said "This is no place for me," walked away and was never heard of again. These, too, were men whose emotional limits were exceeded, and they could find no other way to end the ceaseless torment of battle in Normandy.

One day I went for a walk to see if I could find any friends in other companies and came across a young corporal with whom I stopped to converse. We began talking about the coming attack and the number of cases we'd heard of, men intentionally wounding themselves to escape combat. Maybe most of us had briefly toyed with the thought of sticking one leg out of the protection of a slit trench during a barrage hoping for a minor wound. But no one I knew ever actually did this. Still, it happened. We talked of this for awhile, my momentary friend expressing disgust at the very thought of doing such a thing, then I said a "see-you-later" and climbed over a nearby hedgerow. I heard a shot, ran back, and found that young corporal on the ground, a terrible wound in his arm, his pistol lying beside him. I watched as he was bandaged, then placed on a stretcher in a jeep and driven away. I wondered how he'd make his way through life when people back home asked about his war wound. Surely he would later wish he'd faced battle honorably. Poor kid. I realize now he was terrified at the thought of the impending battle and desperately wanted to live.

It's a sad commentary on a certain segment of American troops that not all of us faced up to our duty. Historian Max Hastings has recorded the distasteful fact that "by July, the rear areas of the Allied armies were generously populated with deserters, whom Americans treated with much greater forbearance than the British."[15] Adding these to the malingerers and the men who were guilty of self-inflicted wounds, it certainly takes away something of the aura of the heroic Greatest Generation. However, it's necessary to keep in mind that many of those men had reached their limits and have since had to live with the silent knowledge of their failure. It's also fair to try to imagine the devastating effect warfare can have on anyone's psyche. Still, it's also only fair to those who didn't flinch, who stayed the course and bore the wounds and in so many cases died that the truth be told. We can also keep in mind that for all the sadness at facts such as these, the truth is these men who failed in the trial were a small minority of men who were called to serve. We won the war because most of the American young men who were pressed into combat service served faithfully and well. And, as already acknowledged, many of those who failed gave it their very best in an effort their psychic strength could simply not survive.

The Army leaders had completely failed to anticipate the tactical problems to be faced in hedgerow fighting. General Omar Bradley,

First Army commander, described the hedgerow country this way: "Across the neck of the Normandy peninsula, the hedgerows formed a line of natural defense more formidable than even Rommel could have contrived. For centuries the broad, rich, farmlands had been divided and subdivided into tiny pastures whose earthen walls had grown into ramparts. Often the height and thickness of a tank, these hedgerows were crowned with a thorny growth of trees and brambles. Their roots had bound the packed earth as steel mesh reinforces concrete. Many were backed by deep drainage ditches, and these the enemy utilized as a built-in system of communication trenches. To advance from pasture to pasture it became necessary for us to break a path through those ramparts in the face of savage and well-concealed enemy fire. Not even in Tunisia had we found more exasperating defensive terrain. Collins called it no less formidable than the jungles of Guadalcanal."[16]

Historian Stephen Ambrose added this: "Undertaking an offensive in the hedgerows was risky, costly, time-consuming, fraught with frustration. It was like fighting in a maze. Platoons found themselves completely lost a few minutes after launching an attack. Two platoons from the same company could occupy adjacent fields for hours before discovering each other's presence...seldom during the first week of battle did a unit as large as a company go into an attack....In the early days of battle, many GIs were killed or wounded because they dashed through the opening into a field...only to be cut down by pre-sighted machine gun fire or mortars."[17] General Dwight Eisenhower echoed this sentiment in his book *Crusade In Europe*, writing that "In almost every row were hidden machine gunners or small combat teams who were in perfect position to decimate our infantry as they doggedly crawled and crept to the attack along every avenue of approach...our tanks could help but little."[18]

A visitor to Normandy today would gain only a general idea of what it was like in 1944. Following the war, modern farming techniques were introduced requiring much larger fields and most of the hedgerows were plowed over. Fighting in this maze was constantly confusing as leaders could become disoriented. Confusion reigned during an attack by the 506th Infantry of the 101st Airborne Division on June 8.

The attack, seeking to capture the town of St-Comte-du-Mont beginning at 0445 was preceded by an artillery barrage fired by the few guns which had survived the initial invasion. In no time the highly-trained men of the 506th Regiment were becoming hopelessly confused by the hedgerows. The attack later became known as "the Snafu engagement" as units soon became mixed together, commanders lost contact with their men, and "they mixed together in a confusing jumble of clumsy, uncoordinated attacks along the eastern and southern fringes of St-Come-du-Mont."[19] "For most of the attackers," wrote historian John McManus, "the day was a blur of random engagements with groups of Germans who were defending buildings, intersections, or hedgerows."[20] By day's end the ground was littered with the bodies of Americans and Germans intermixed.

In the early going newcomers failed to understand the risks of bedding down among the hedges, each field an opportunity for ambush. One unit, the 2nd Battalion of the 115th Infantry newly committed to the fighting, exhausted and short of men, bedded down in a hedgerow near the town of Carrefour, and they failed to post enough guards. Survivors told what happened next. A large German force had spotted the men as they settled in and waited for the exhausted Americans to fall asleep. At 0230 the Germans opened fire using every weapon in their possession: rifles, machine guns, self-propelled cannons, hand grenades. "The enemy could scarcely have imagined better circumstances," John McManus reported. "They slaughtered the 2nd Battalion troops with impunity...everyone ran to the edge of the fields to seek protection in the ditches along the side of each field, at the base of each hedgerow. This field, unfortunately, had no ditch on any side, and the men just piled up as they threw themselves in the dark into what they hoped would be a ditch."[21] Before long 50 dead Americans and many more wounded littered the fields before the Germans moved on. So it went, one of dozens of similar battles throughout Normandy as the just-arrived Americans had only begun to learn hedgerow fighting.

One captured German soldier reported that before the invasion they trained for fighting in the hedgerows. "The lines of hedges played tricks on your eyes. We trained to fight as individuals; we knew when the attack came we'd probably be cut off from one another. We let them come forward and cross the hedge, then we blew them apart. That was our tactic..." He also said they had pre-sighted mortars to land where they wanted and dug holes in the hedgerows small enough to stick a machine gun barrel through, which remained unseen from the other side.

We had to quickly master the art of climbing over a hedgerow. All that training in scaling high walls proved priceless now as a man trying to conceal himself while climbing over a hedgerow presented for a moment an easy target for an enemy rifleman. The quicker you could vault across, the safer you were. I guess General Bradley best summed Normandy up with this observation: "It's the damnedest country I've ever seen."

CHAPTER FOUR

THEN THE FIRE

SERGEANT BREWER LED US TO A HEDGEROW, AND LOOKING OVER IT
I saw a line of men standing along another hedgerow on the far side
of the field between us. They were firing M1 rifles at enemy soldiers
dug in just beyond them. We were ordered to cross the field and join
those men. I started jogging across the field. Hearing return fire from
the enemy, I ducked low, hit the ground halfway there, slipped out of
my pack, and detached the small pocket on the front which was used
to hold my mess kit. I tossed the mess kit, tied a strap to the pocket
so I could carry it over my shoulder like an Italian gigolo's purse, and
left everything but my toothbrush, a fork, and some spare socks and
underwear, which I put in the "purse." That would be the sum total of
my possessions in addition to my rifle and cartridge belt for the next
several weeks.

Just then our men along the hedgerow began shouting, the air crack-
led with the sound of automatic gunfire, and they started running in
my direction as something apparently went terribly wrong. There was
a horrendous burst of rapid fire. German automatic weapons fired at
a significantly faster cyclic rate than did ours and we quickly learned
to tell instantly when hearing automatic fire whose it was. Now it was
German, their Schmeisser machine pistols which fired nine-mm pistol
bullets from a 32-round magazine sounding like ripping cloth. Our
men were retreating. Two men dashed past me and, having no idea at
all what was happening nor what action was necessary, I joined them.
We all ran back across the field, into the next one, some by running
through the small opening in the hedgerow, some by scrambling over,
and on into the next field. There a few men faced back toward the

enemy who had apparently decided not to pursue us, and I took up a position in the far corner of the field where we set up our machine gun. That was our introduction to combat. I wasn't afraid because I had no idea what was going on. The whole situation was only just a confusing, mind-numbing introduction to the real world of Infantry combat.

Floyd Lainhart, standing some twenty feet from me, started digging a slit trench and I decided I'd better do the same. Then I heard a rifle shot and Lainhart grunted, pitched over, hit in the leg by a sniper's bullet. As he dived into his shallow trench, another shot slammed into Lainhart's arm. It had come from the second floor of a small outbuilding on the other side of the hedgerow where I was standing. Two of our men dashed up the small outside stairway, kicked in the door and killed the sniper. So began our first day in combat. Lainhart would be able to tell his kids he served in combat for twenty minutes and then earned the Purple Heart. I'm not proud of my initial, shocked reaction to seeing a man I knew get shot: I was grateful the sniper had chosen Floyd rather than me.

That sniper was the first German I saw killed, and it became shockingly real to me that that's what we were here for. Maybe that sniper was not a bad person really, just the product of a society gone wrong, was probably some respectable German family's kid. How quickly we all found ourselves able to cast enemy soldiers in our minds as sub-human role players, tools of evil, something to be destroyed. Somewhere, that sniper grew up with a family teaching him right from wrong, was pressed into serving a system he had no capacity to criticize, probably demonstrated exceptional courage in hiding where he was, doing what he did, surely knowing he wouldn't live long afterward but serving something in which he believed. An admirable young man. I guess that's part of the tragic cost of war that we young men learn not to love our fellow men but, rather, to hate them and worse yet, devalue some mother's beloved son as "just one less Kraut." Only thus can wars be won.

Today the History Channel features movies recording the excesses of the German Third Reich with their candle lighted rallies, 100,000 hypnotized voices shouting "heil," hero-worshipping women clamoring after the cartoonish-looking Adolf Hitler high on his pedestal while statue-like storm troopers stand at unflinching attention, lined up as far as the eye can see. It is shocking. We see young boys exercising in preparation to go die for the fatherland, smiling young women offering themselves for the breeding of the new supermen. One can easily visualize the Germany of the thirties and forties as a nation struck by collective criminal insanity. In truth, while all of this did happen and God must recoil at the vision of those days, a high percentage of Germans were decent people. Their nation had undergone generations of poverty, runaway inflation, depression. Surely many of them thought they were reaching out to a genuinely godly man who could lead them back to their days of prosperity. By the time most German citizens realized that the godly man whom they trusted was a devil, it was too late. Deluded, hypnotized, brainwashed, call it what we will, a nation was firmly ensnared in the grip of Evil. Many protested. They were soon silenced, some disappeared. By the height of the war to publicly protest in Germany, or even to criticize Adolf Hitler was suicidal. Yet man by man, woman by woman, many were decent human beings. Some I met.

Sometimes we sat around and discussed the idiocy of the German nation. How could they have become what they were? How could a civilized, self-proclaimed Christian nation have allowed this man to lead them? Professor Fritz Stern, who grew up in Hitler's Germany, wrote of the German people that "They weren't blind, they were lied to, and it is a measure of Hitler's evil genius that he was able to deceive not only the Germans and many German Jews, but much of the rest of the world as well."[1] "Hitler rose to power legally, through votes" Stern wrote. "He was propelled into office by a population that was both polarized and exhausted, one that had lost faith in the idea of democratic capitalism and was still traumatized by the Bolshevik terror."

We didn't know much about German history, how the people had suffered terribly, their own fault to be sure, from economic ruin following World War I. "It is fair to say that had Hitler died in 1938," concluded Stern, "he would have been regarded - at least in Germany - as the man who restored his country to its place in the sun."[2] Had we known this we would still have argued that the people were responsible for their own misery and deserved what they were getting, but we could at least have understood it. As it was we decided they were all crazy criminals.

I suppose there's a more sympathetic way to view the Germany of the thirties and forties. Following the first World War, despite some efforts by the Allied nations, Germany had fallen into desperate economic ruin. A few American dollars could buy what was literally a foot-high stack of German marks. Unemployment was colossal. Historian Richard Evans writes that "despondency got worse the longer people went without a job...people put off marriage plans, married couples put off having children, young men roamed the streets aimlessly, sat listlessly at home, spent the day playing cards, wandering through public parks, or riding endlessly round and round on the electric trains of Berlin's Circle Line. In this situation, action often seemed better than inaction, boredom turned to frustration."[3]

Professor Stern recalls, "The pageantry of Naziism, like the pageantry of Italian Fascism, a secular amalgam of Church and Army rituals, continued to appeal to a defeated, deprived self-flagellating people. Hitler, the man of violence, rhetorically dissolved political complexity into a Wagnerian battle between the pure and the impure, between German heroes and Jewish, Marxist traitors." To some small degree one might understand how young men of Germany felt during those times. On the other hand, America also faced difficult economic times with high unemployment, millions of men on the dole. But our president pushed for economic solutions, the NRA, the Civilian Construction Camps, other means of involving young men far more constructively. But this is hindsight. In the later 1930s young German men flocked to the siren voice of the man who was absolutely certain he could lead the people out of their darkness into his own marvelous light.

Psychiatrist Karen Horney described Adolf Hitler this way: "Hitler is a good illustration of a person who went through humiliating experiences and gave his whole life to a fanatic desire to triumph over an ever-increasing mass of people. In his case, vicious circles, constantly increasing the need, are clearly discernible. One of these develops from the fact that he could think only in categories of triumph and defeat. Hence the fear of defeat made further triumphs always necessary. Moreover, the feeling of grandeur, increasing with every triumph, rendered it increasingly intolerable that anybody, or even any nation, should not recognize his grandeur."[4] This meant that Hitler was immune to any suggestions regarding his course of action in Normandy, as elsewhere, which he saw as leading anywhere other than to total victory. No price was too great to pay, even his own life as it would turn out, certainly no other lives, to ensure that victory.

From a Christian perspective, theologian Reinhold Niebuhr in 1937 wrote prophetically, "The degree to which the mighty have deified themselves from the days of the earliest priest-kings and god-kings to the contemporary Hitler is an illuminating indication of the temptation to which the mighty invariably succumb. The perennial sin of man is his rebellion against God, his inclination to make himself God. All men are tempted to this sin; but the mighty are particularly subject to it."[5] Thus Hitler would discover there's but one God, and it wasn't Hitler.

Later I reflected on the fact that the sniper I'd just seen killed must have had a choice between Lainhart and McGriff. Maybe he'd seen a German version of a film we were shown at Camp Blanding which demonstrated that when you see two enemy soldiers, one closer than the other, you shoot the one farthest away, thus increasing the chances of also being able to shoot the other man who would not have time to hide. That was the theory. I knew I could have been shot right there and if I hadn't gotten the idea before, I certainly knew now that I was in a war and could die. That sniper was just doing his job and he paid the price.

We formed into a very ragged version of the kind of formations we learned in basic training and began moving back in the direction of the Germans, the "Krauts" as they would henceforth be known to me. Also, we were learning that most of what we'd been taught in training was irrelevant to Normandy. I would learn more in the next twenty-four hours than in seventeen weeks in Blanding.

"Watch for snipers," Brewer ordered, and I kept my attention focused on the trees we were passing, and wondered how anyone could want to be a sniper if he didn't have to. I supposed someone could remain hidden in any of the trees we were passing then shoot one, maybe if he were quick, two of our men - their rifles were all bolt action rather than semi-automatic like ours - at which point he'd be shot. Sometimes snipers were captured. If they hadn't shot anyone they had a fair chance of becoming a prisoner of war. However, if they'd shot anyone and our men knew it they were often shot on the spot. Yet apparently some German soldiers were willing to do it. Ernie Pyle told about them when he visited Normandy. "There in Normandy," he wrote, "the Germans went in for sniping in a wholesale manner. There were snipers everywhere, in trees, in buildings, in piles of wreckage in the grass. But mainly they were in high, bushy hedgerows that form the fences of all the Norman fields and line every roadside and lane."[6] I was an early believer.

My first day in combat was pretty much a matter of dumbly following the person in front of me. Other than Lainhart's wounding we had little contact with the enemy. That night we moved into a field and I walked past a dead man. No one seemed to pay any attention to the body and I assumed someone would later gather the poor guy in. In retrospect, it's disturbing to recall how quickly we found ourselves able to look at dead bodies and, provided we didn't know the man, feel very little emotion. That was a terrible realization, and yet to have reacted otherwise would have quickly drained us of the will to go on. Today I think back to that moment, the placid face of death, a kid, someone who had loved ones waiting at home, who had friends, not long out of high school, a kid with hopes and dreams, a person who that very day had smiled, had laughed at some childish joke, maybe written a reassuring letter to his mom. Now he was dead, lying uncared for along a nameless country road as one by one we walked by and turned quickly away. Now, shrouded in darkness, unknown, he lay there. No one should die that way. These are the photographs of the mind which dispel any idea of the romance of war.

Our objective was to cross the Merderet River at La Fiere. Unfortunately, though our junior officers were courageous, most of them had little idea where they were going. Leadership from the regiment and division was inept. Heavy casualties were the result as no one had a comprehensive view of the battle and each only tried to move ahead with no clear objective in mind. Other units were doing the same and the result was an aimless milling about of small units. Nineteen-year-old Private Elvir Magnuson told of getting lost, along with a friend. They tried to make their way across a field by guesswork but were soon caught by mortar fire. Every member of their squad was killed or wounded as the two of them hid out until the firing stopped. All over the area in which Germans and Americans met similar melees were enacted, no one able to relate what was happening to any kind of coherent purpose.

My second morning we were ordered to begin crossing a field and were soon caught in a barrage of 88 mm cannon fire and that's when I learned about artillery. The Germans had two guns which did most of the damage in Normandy. The most dangerous was the 88 mm artillery, often loaded on a mobile stand, usually a tank. It could fire overhead, or direct fire. Officially the Flieger Abwehr Kanone or FLAK, it probably gave the nickname to anti-aircraft artillery, though it was far more effective against ground troops than against aircraft. It was terribly accurate and all we'd hear was a shriek and an instantaneous bang. *Shriek bang, shriek bang.* Its extremely high velocity was so great it has even been estimated that the sixteen-pound shell was 300 yards ahead of the sound and if fired from nearby, it was more *bang shriek, bang shriek.* A British soldier called it "the deadliest bastard to come out of the war."

Then there were the mortars which lofted a rocket-like shell in a high arc, dropping in at a steep angle. We'd hear a distant thump and knew an explosion was soon to occur. Most German artillery fire we experienced in Normandy was one or the other, though they also used a little number called the Nebelwerfer which fired a salvo of rockets, screaming with such frightening crescendo as to receive the nickname "Screaming Meemies." Because the Germans were retreating in a mostly organized fashion, they used mainly highly mobile artillery which could be fired, then quickly moved.

Our artillery was varied, with the huge 240 mm guns some twelve miles behind us, their ninety-five pound shells huffing overhead sounding like departing freight trains. The 155 mm Long Toms were about as noisy, fired from five or six miles behind us. Men in those units were safe from German direct action since the Luftwaffe, the German Air Force, was all but kaput. We also had 105s which were closer, maybe a couple miles behind us, more available for tactical fire on short notice. One of our meanest weapons was the 4.2-inch mortar which could loft a 27-pound shell almost soundlessly. The shell took 60 seconds to reach its target; it's said seven rounds could be fired before the first landed, leading the Germans to believe we had automatic rapid-fire artillery. It was designed as a chemical weapon but we had, through the Geneva Convention, agreed not to use chemicals as weapons, so it was now the carrier of deadly explosives. We had both 81- and 60-millimeter mortars, the larger ones safely positioned at least 2,000 yards to the rear, the little mortars almost up with us. New men hit the dirt either way when the firing started, while experienced men laughed when our shells went out and the new men dropped flat. We soon learned when to duck and when not to.

That second day I learned what it felt like to be caught in the middle of an open field when enemy 88s were landing. As we crossed the field the first shell exploded, almost surely an 88. It landed some distance from me but was quickly followed by another, closer, then one nearby. I followed the example of the more experienced men which was just to fall flat and pray. There are no adequate words to describe the terror one feels when subjected to artillery fire. The imagination visualizes each incoming round. We'd flatten ourselves and experience the ultimate sense of isolation and helplessness. If a man in terror jumps up to run, the odds of survival are nil as slashing, hot steel rips through the air, tearing everything in its path. The ground vibrates, throbs, soon accompanied by cries of shock, calls for "medic, medic." Only because the enemy can't really see where his shells are hitting it finally stops. This day Roy Buchanan left his carbine hanging on a tree limb and when the barrage ceased, he found it cut in two pieces. We quickly got up, looked around to see who was hit, then hurried out of the area. Captain Rod Taggart, a regimental chaplain, wrote in his diary "When these 88s open up it is the nearest thing to hell on earth."[7]

People who watched newsreels of artillery barrages probably had a better idea of what they looked like than did those of us who were there. A combat soldier, hearing incoming artillery, immediately hits the dirt and buries his face in the ground. Holding one's head high enough to see what's happening could get one killed.

Actually, combat soldiers knew least of all about the progress of the war. We were utterly uninformed about how things were going. Other than rumors (usually wrong) we didn't even know what was happening in the next infantry company down the road. For all we knew we could be losing the war, or it could be nearly over. We did, once or twice, receive a field copy of the Army newspaper *Stars and Stripes*, but that was carefully controlled by the generals to see that we learned only what they wanted us to know. It occurred to me that if we didn't have any idea at all how the war was going, neither did the average German soldier. That may help explain why they fought so fiercely later when they were almost finished.

On June 13 it was hot, a clear day. The Germans were close, just beyond the next hedgerow. Our platoon leader, Lieutenant Dick Harvey, ordered our section forward, German rifle and machine-gun fire ahead. One man came running back through an opening in the hedgerow, face pale, blood streaming down his right arm. Another man ran to him, appeared at first to offer aid, but only grabbed the wounded man's pistol, a most desired and virtually unobtainable weapon, then let the man run to the rear. I especially watched the wounded man's face as he walked by me. He was the first man I'd seen face to face who had just been hit. He appeared to me to reveal a combination of pale-faced shock but relief as well. Everyone watched for a moment with envy as we realized the man would sleep in a bed this night; maybe if he was lucky and the bullet hit a bone, he'd be out of it for good. "The million dollar wound" that every man hoped for.

We moved into the next field, fell prone in a line, facing yet another hedgerow from behind which Krauts were firing at us. Our light machine gun was needed. Germans were firing at us with burp guns, their highly efficient counterparts to our clumsy Tommy Guns. They'd crouch down out of sight and reach up with the machine pistol firing blindly, but spraying the field. The Germans had the best machine gun, their air-cooled MG-42 which was capable of firing 1,500 rounds per minute, more than double the number of rounds fired by our Browning machine guns. It was also easier to carry than ours and was every way a more effective weapon. They also had about twice as many machine guns per man as we did. Ours were so clumsy to carry I suppose we couldn't spare that many riflemen to be machine gun squad members.

I didn't know then but learned later that much, probably most of their firing was unaimed, random noise-making designed to scare us, keep us from advancing. Three or four Schmeisser pistols going at once, several rounds a second each, could make a frightening racket.

A major ordered us to attack the hedgerow. None of us moved. The frightening crescendo of explosive noise kept a line of us firmly pressed against the ground which was slightly depressed close to the hedgerow so we felt fairly safe as long as we didn't get up and expose ourselves. The major strode out in front of us, the air alive with the crackle of small-arms fire, drew his pistol and ordered that every man get up and rush the hedgerow, further threatening to shoot any of us remaining. That was leadership. We all got up and ran to the hedgerow, firing. The Germans fell back to the next field. Huey plopped our air-cooled machine gun in a corner of the next field but by that time the enemy soldiers had retreated.

Being an officer in combat is a terrible responsibility - for two reasons. One, of course, they're more exposed to being wounded or killed because of the necessity that they show fearlessness to their men, officers suffering half again as many casualties percentage-wise as did enlisted men, and, two, because they must sometimes order men to their certain deaths. I have since been glad I wasn't a couple years older, maybe been an officer in Normandy. Sadly, many officers failed in all of this. But most did their duty and the cost was high. I've thought about that Major since then. He stood up straight with firing going on around him. I never saw him again.

In truth, though, many officers were just as scared as we were. Major Randall Bryant, a battalion commander, told of one captain, a company commander who stepped up to him and said "I've had it. You can do anything you want. I won't go back." Bryant, telling this recently, said he could understand the man's breakdown, but he was angry many years later to see that captain at a reunion of combat soldiers.[8]

We crossed the hedgerow, crouched down. A medic came by leading a man who was drooling, shambling gate, a case of total emotional breakdown. Just as they passed a shell exploded nearby and they dropped down beside me. I vaguely recognized the patient as a man who'd come in with my group. He trembled relentlessly, eyes staring at something I couldn't see.

The Germans attacked supported by a heavy mortar barrage. They had our field zeroed in, which was what they routinely did. Our officers ordered us to fall back. We turned and ran toward the rear as shells exploded around us. One man next to me began hopping on his right leg and I realized his left ankle was nearly blown away, his foot hanging by a shred. Another man picked him up. Two men carried another man I knew from the night we were assigned to our units. He'd been shot in the stomach, his shirt now open, blood streaming down his sides. Other men suffered lesser wounds, one man ahead of me barely able to run, apparently hit in the back. I was fortunate to remain uninjured.

We made it to the field behind our original position, then we began firing toward the German position and they remained out of sight. I was learning this was typical hedgerow fighting. Back and forth, fight all day, capture a field, only to face another field, then another. Of the eleven months required to conquer all of Europe, the capture of Normandy would require about two and a half of those months. The Germans had an overwhelming advantage as is usually true of defensive units. While fighting us as we tried to advance they could set up a new line of defense behind the present one, sight in mortars and artillery pieces, place machine guns in the corners of the fields, carefully aim them where attackers were most likely to appear, then withdraw and wait for us. Only if we could get our own mortars and artillery zeroed in on their positions and, if at all possible get a Sherman tank to precede us, which rarely happened, could we usually get and hold a hedgerowed field. After seven weeks of murderous combat the farthest inland the Allies had advanced was some 25 to 30 miles on an 80-mile front. In the early going men would rush into a seemingly empty field, only to be shot down as they reached the middle, unseen machine guns tearing them to shreds. We soon learned you don't just rush into an unoccupied field.

The fighting broke off. All of a sudden my friends and I were veterans, we were the "old" guys. The next day some new men came to replace our losses. One was Paul Casteel, a nice young guy no more than eighteen. Another was Roscoe Hoppes, a kid who looked about sixteen and was just as odd as his name sounds. "Hoppy" was short and skinny. How he got in the Army I can't imagine. He couldn't have weighed more than 120 pounds. I didn't even think the Army would accept someone that small. His hips were so tiny his cartridge belt kept slipping down toward his knees. He seemed utterly mystified at his present situation but he never complained. I have noticed that combat soldiers in the movies are usually actors in their twenties pretending to be teenagers most chosen for their brawny physiques. Some of the kids I saw looked like they were sophomores in high school. One book about the campaign by Paul Fussell carries the very descriptive title of the men I saw, *The Boy's Crusade*. He was a combat officer himself and wrote that "these infantry soldiers, if they weren't children, weren't quite men either, even if officers commonly addressed groups of them as such."[9]

Most people base their ideas of infantry combat on movies and television, few of which are realistic. The movie *Battleground*, filmed shortly after World War II, was accurate. *To Hell And Back*, the exploits of Medal of Honor winner Audie Murphy was authentic, probably because he himself was the star and knew exactly how it really was.

Pieces like *Saving Private Ryan* and the series "Band of Brothers" are cinematically excellent but present an exaggerated idea of combat as experienced by most men. They are depicting highly-trained professionals; that is, men who spent some two years in preparation, trained in such demanding ways as to weed out the ordinary man, as compared to the rest of us who had three or four months of training and everyone passed. They are probably accurate but still, it wasn't very often like that. Basic infantry units, the great majority of fighting men, were nothing at all like those units. We were barely trained kids really, with virtually none of the attitude that made those elite fighters so effective. By the time of the Normandy campaign most of us were much younger and not even close to being motivated like they were, and our battles were rarely as close quarter as shown in the movies.

Today's movies leave viewers with the impression that World War II Infantry combat was a constant process of running and shooting at enemy soldiers, of carrying off the wounded. There was more than enough of that to be sure, but just as inherent in combat is the endless moving, digging, struggling with heavy equipment which had to be constantly carried along. There was the anxiety of wondering what's next, the cold nights, the sweltering days. I had to choose between carrying enough clothing to be warm at night while being burdened all day in the heat, or getting rid of those burdens so that I could move quickly and freely in the daytime, only to nearly freeze at night for lack of warm clothing. I had chosen the latter. There was no one around to take care of you, to help carry your clothes and equipment.

Then there was guard duty. I probably had slept no more than three hours a night for my first several nights in Normandy, yet I had to stand guard duty as did everyone. To be awakened at two in the morning after no more than three or four hours of sleep to stand for two hours, quietly, so the enemy, were he sneaking up on us, wouldn't know we were there, to shiver in silence, struggling to stay awake, responsible to protect our friends from surprise attack, was mind numbing. To be alone, exhausted, peering into the night, listening intently for any slight sound, yet your body screaming for rest is every bit as memorable as battle.

One night a private, a man with whom I had trained in Florida and who had been in trouble several times there, was caught moving the hands of the watch ahead to shorten his duty. A day or so later he disappeared and presumably was assigned to a different unit. In a rifle company he would have been made a scout, the man who precedes the body of troops moving toward the enemy, thus increasing the odds of being rid of him early. He could never again have had any friends in our company.

Another night Sergeant Elbert Hallman was on guard duty and heard a slithering sound on the other side of the hedgerow where he was assigned to stand. He tried to see into the darkness but saw only a vague shape. He fired and scared the daylights out of the rest of us who were sleeping. The next morning a dead German soldier lay where Hallman had fired. We then understood that guard duty was more than a mere formality.

There were many times when I found it almost impossible to stay awake on guard. We were just too exhausted. We each tried to find ways to be sure we didn't fall asleep. I tried to stand away from anything so I'd fall down if I fell asleep. Other times I'd hold my rifle directly over my feet so that were it to slip from my hands it would bang my toe. I'd guess every one of us at some time or other simply dropped off while standing there and, hopefully, one or another of our little safety devices rescued us in time. After all, you could be shot for falling asleep, though I never heard of that being done. The old joke was about the sergeant checking on a sleeping guard, who wakening at the sound of the sergeant's presence, looked up toward the sky and said "amen." I still recall how miserable it felt to be shaken awake and told in whispered tones "time to take over." If anything, remaining awake was aided by the constant trembling from the cold. We were soaking wet most of the time, then were required to stand quietly for two hours. Apart from actual combat, guard duty was the worst part of war for me.

CHAPTER FIVE

PRELUDE

WAR IS COMPOSED OF PART TERRIFYING BATTLE BUT ALSO SOME sheer boredom and exertion. Famed war cartoonist Bill Mauldin, in his classic book *Up Front* wrote, "Many people who read and speak of battle and noise and excitement and death forget one of the worst things about war - its monotony... the endless marches that carry you on and on and yet never seem to get you anyplace - the automatic drag of one foot as it places itself in front of the other without any prompting from your dulled brain, and the unutterable relief as you sink down for a ten-minute break, spoiled by the knowledge that you'll have to get up and go again - the never-ending monotony..."[1] Units were moved here and there depending on what was happening nearby. We might walk for great distances over hedgerowed land, only to turn around and head back where we came from, always carrying heavy equipment - machine guns, ammunition boxes, our own equipment - never with any sense at all of where we were in relation to anyone else. Only some commander in a rear area office with a map had any sense of the relationships of units to each other. Able to see only a couple hundred yards in any direction, one did indeed feel like being lost in a maze. It's amazing to remember how strenuous a day well-conditioned teenaged boys could endure, then with a few hours' sleep do it all over again the next day, and the next, never seeming to wear out. Most of us who survived would probably never be as fit again as we were that year.

A vivid memory shared by anyone who experienced Normandy was the scattering of dead cows and horses in every field, most hideously bloated by the hot summer sun. The stench was omnipresent. I recall more than once being called to a halt by our leader and told to "take ten" and eat, so, thirty feet from a dead, bloated cow, I'd eat a K ration. Once I saw a cow virtually explode from the gases generated by death. For some time after my return home that scene would flash before my eyes as I sat at dinner on some formal occasion. I couldn't help feeling sorry for the French farmers. Life under Nazi occupation was hard enough, certainly it offended their French sense of manhood. But now, as I saw the carnage, the smashed homes, the dead cattle, the violated fields and hedgerows, I thought they must surely have wondered whether the price of freedom from the occupation was worth it. Surely one of the most lucrative post-war businesses in France must have been the building and installing of church steeples. It was automatic for the artillery folks to blow steeples off every church in sight, knowing that's where German observers were stationed. That, and replacing farmhouse roofs.

So it went until it all seemed second nature. The stench, the weariness, the cold at night, the drenching night rain from which there was rarely any relief, the excruciating effort to stay awake, the blistering midday summer sun as you'd run, stop, dig rock-hard ground, then move on. The nagging hunger for a genuine meal, the search for a place to relieve oneself in the midst of a crowd, the frequent chatter of rifle and machine-gun fire, the constant strain to listen for the thump of a mortar or the scream of an 88, the all-too-frequent cries of "medic, medic," this was war. All the movies with their special effects well document those brief, cataclysmic moments of close combat, but they can never depict the context of war day by day. Napoleon once wrote "The first quality of a soldier is constancy in endurance, fatigue, and hardship. Courage is only the second. Poverty, privation and want are the school of the good soldier."

It's a wonder we ever got any sleep, that our night-time imaginings didn't keep us constantly on edge. In combat we were lying on cold, often muddy ground, and we had nothing to place between ourselves and the muddy ground. Many nights it was raining. Normally we were in a depression in the ground for safety's sake, no pillow except a metal helmet, the only "blanket" a damp field jacket. It was cold, it was miserably uncomfortable, it was anything but a calming environment. And we knew we had only two or three hours before we'd be awakened for guard duty. We had to banish floating visions of dead faces, men whose names we knew. I have since wondered how we managed to banish the ever-present realization that we could and very likely some of us would be dead or mutilated before the next day's end, threshing endlessly in mortal fear. This didn't seem to happen. Somehow we were rarely troubled by sleepless nights. I guess we were always exhausted. Sometimes I dreamed I was home and my parents were crying because their children were gone. They couldn't hear me as I tried to explain that I had been sent home. When I awakened from this dream I would be in shock, disoriented, trying to remember for brief seconds why I was dressed and cold.

I was curious about the fact that we had retreated twice in my first few days in combat. Obviously, men at my level had no control. I was a teenager, a private. The 90th Division got off to a rocky start. First Army Commander General Omar Bradley wrote that while the 90th became one of the Army's outstanding divisions, the 90th turned out poorly in its starting attack. "For three days the division floundered," he wrote, "so exasperating was its performance at one point that the First Army gave up and recommended that we break it up for replacements." Then the commanding general, Jay McKelvie, was sacked on June 13, my fourth day in combat.

McKelvie was an incompetent flake. He began by firing his best regimental commander, highly capable John Sheehy of the 357th Regiment, replacing him with another incompetent, Colonel P.D. Ginder, right before the invasion. Ginder was described by those who served with him as "full of boast and posturing...a classic loose cannon." "He was quite obtuse," one commander observed, "and almost constantly made the wrong decisions." Ginder had no understanding of infantry tactics and sent men needlessly into attacks to repeat what had just failed. He caused untold numbers of unnecessary casualties before being relieved of command a few days into the campaign.

General McKelvie, our division commander, was described by his assistant commander, General Williams, as "uninspirational." Willliams told of finding McKelvie in a furrow hugging a hedgerow for dear life during a battle. He yelled at his boss "Dammit General, you can't lead this division hiding in that damn hole. Get the hell out of that hole and go to your vehicle. Walk to it or you'll have this whole damn division wading in the English Channel."

Corps Commander Lieutenant General Lawton Collins fired McKelvie and replaced him with Major General Eugene Landrum, his own deputy. That proved another bad choice. Landrum was described as "short, fat, slow-moving, no demonstrated spark or drive." He sat in a wicker chair in the cellar of his Command Post, "unsympathetic and pessimistic in outlook" and "showed little confidence in his subordinates." He was all but useless but remained in command until late July. Finally, Major General Raymond S. McClain was placed in command, and under his leadership the division earned this comment from General Omar Bradley made many years later: "In the end the 90th became one of the most outstanding in the European Theater."[2]

We can compare that leadership with men like Major General Charles "Uncle Charley" Gehrhardt who led the 29th Division onto Omaha Beach on D Day. On June 8 he'd ordered one of his regimental commanders, Colonel Paul "Pop" Goode, to take the just-arrived 175th Infantry Regiment into the small town of Isigny, an important roadblock. The Colonel decided to hold up and wait for artillery support. While he was hesitantly waiting in his Command Post for reinforcement General Gerhardt drove up in a jeep, slammed on the brakes, dashed angrily into the CP and yelled "Has the attack on Isigny begun yet?" Goode assured the general that he was making preparations for it. "There's nothing in your way," Gerhardt yelled, "get into Isigny." Goode protested, arguing for artillery support. General Gerhardt lost patience, snapped at his regimental commander "Never mind the artillery, get those tanks rolling. I'll get in that jeep of mine right now," he said, "and roll right into Isigny. There's nothing there. Now get the hell in." With that he whirled around and strode to his jeep, heading toward Isigny. That was leadership, and that was why that division was outstanding from the beginning.[3] It proved what General Bradley wrote, that one division differed from another only by the leadership skills of their commanders. When General McClain was asked to take command of our division, he said OK, but he wanted to be allowed to get rid of incompetent officers. Bradley agreed, McClain put together a list of sixteen senior officers, they were sacked, replaced by good men, and the division became one of the best in the European Theater of Operations, the "ETO."

One of the problems which would plague us throughout the war, and which probably besets every army, is that commanders who don't actually take part in the fighting itself have no real idea what's going on in combat areas. Brigadier General James Gavin, a decorated combat officer who commanded the 82nd Airborne and jumped with them in Normandy, told of going to Corps headquarters after leading what he considered a useless attack in the Huertgen Forest, preparing to challenge the commander. He told of being ordered to wait and standing, listening as the commander pored over a map with a newly-arrived division commander who was being instructed before leading his division. After overhearing what he recognized as faulty advice, Gavin later wrote, "I realized how remote they were from the reality of what it was like up where the battalions were."[4] It clearly takes certain particular skills in order to lead large numbers of people in combat and there is probably no way to discover who has those skills until they are put to the test. All of this makes me wonder if the same dynamic was true in the recent past when our men landed in Iraq.

Colonel Ginder was relieved of command of our regiment on June 14 and replaced by the man who'd been fired from the job earlier, Colonel John Sheehy. At the time we were trying to capture the town of Gourbesville, and we were failing, suffering heavy casualties. On June 15 Colonel Sheehy, a good commanding officer, decided to do something about the failure. He jumped in a jeep and drove through the night to reach the front. His jeep was driven into an ambush and Sheehy was killed. His friends grieved that this fine officer, so misused by an officious self-important superior, had died so soon after being restored to his command.

This all makes one wonder how men are promoted in a peacetime army as it's apparent that many so-called leaders of key units are incapable of leading under wartime conditions. I guess there's no way to know. No man or woman of any rank can know how he or she will react when the shooting starts and mutilation or death are immediate possibilities, perhaps likelihoods. Many generals and colonels had to be relieved of their commands before the campaign in Normandy began to succeed. It appears that the qualities that make a man a peacetime general are quite different from those of a good combat general. Using current psychological jargon, the peacetime general must be left-brained, a good organizer and administrator. The good combat general most be right-brained, able to go with constant, unexpected change, making on-the-spot decisions of far-reaching effect without the peacetime luxury of appointing a committee. Many successful peacetime commanders proved incapable of fighting a war. Historian Max Hastings, assessing American leadership in the early portions of the Normandy campaign, wrote "The roll call of senior American officers found wanting and sacked was astonishing."[5] It seems the armed forces need both kinds of men to maintain a strong fighting force. Getting the right man in the right place at the right time is the hard part.

One day we heard a rumor that our battalion commander was missing. The very next day I was with a small group sneaking through a barnyard and we rounded a corner and came upon several dead Americans, one wearing the silver oak leaves of a Lieutenant Colonel. Then I knew what had happened to our commander. Little wonder the men of the 90th were struggling in the early going. In just a few days we'd had three division commanders, two regimental commanders and two battalion commanders. We would eventually get organized but those first few days were exceedingly expensive in casualties of fine young men. There it was. Navy Captain Butcher had been right in his apprehensions about the qualities of many of our officers.

Whatever the failures of the generals, the men I knew were doing their best. I learned that some of the men who had trained with me in basic training were casualties. Warren Hale was killed, Rex Kramer whom I liked was killed with K Company, Wally Goulet was badly wounded, with L Company I think. On the 16th of June Fox

Company of the 2nd Battalion was supporting us, coming in from our flank when they were suddenly pounced on by a German parachute unit. It was a fierce battle. Several Germans went down from Bill Duling's light machine gun, then a shell landed nearby, killing the gunner and inflicting a light facial wound on Duling. He grabbed up the gun and dashed to the rear, one of the few to escape as thirteen Fox Company men were killed and fourteen were wounded. Most of the rest of the company, sixty six in all, were forced to surrender. I ran into Bill a day or so later and he showed me his Purple Heart. His wound was so slight I was amazed to learn he'd received the medal. It seemed to me there ought to be several degrees of Purple Hearts. I also learned that our own First Sergeant Herb Woodward was hit in that battle and carried off, along with two other men from M Company.

This was how it was for M Company for awhile, a war of attrition. On June 13 Ed Lopinski was killed and Virgil Story was wounded. On the 14th Chris Self was killed and Ed Medina, Keith Hinsman, and Frank Foley were wounded. On the 15th Jarrel Moores was wounded, and two days later we lost Marion Chapman. Two days after that Staff Sergeant Elmer Madrone and John Cherich were wounded. The constant shelling was slowly but surely taking my M Company.

We were to attack and capture the town of Gourbesville, which we then began calling "Gooberville." I suffered a painful ankle injury. Someone called a jeep and they drove me to a nearby medical unit where a medic there started caring for my ankle, but when I saw the men of my Company march by, I asked him to hurry and wrap it up. He did, and I dashed out without permission to rejoin the company. Since I'd been registered as a patient I was technically breaking the rules; I didn't care and apparently neither did they. I didn't like the thought of ending up with a different unit. Those were my friends walking by and painful ankle notwithstanding, I wanted to remain with them. I heard no more about it and limped for the next ten days.

First Sergeant Joe Huddock had arrived to replace Sergeant Woodward. He called us over and showed us some heavy machine guns. So far we'd been using air-cooled light guns. Huey and Duey McMillion were assigned to carry the new gun which was heavy and Huey and

Duey were the big, "strapping" as my dad used to say, men of the squad. Actually, Duey, the largest, and I had gotten into a wrestling match in England and I threw him to the ground. It ended there and we became friends. The McMillions were brothers from Kentucky. I was content for those two characters to do the heavy lifting.

We turned in our M1 rifles and were issued Carbines, which fired the same caliber cartridge, but one much less powerful. It held fifteen rounds and originally replaced the old 45-caliber pistol. I also picked up a trench knife which I strapped to my leg. Its main purpose, while I hoped it looked lethal to the Germans, was to open K Rations easily. Sergeant Smith, who liked to swagger a lot and always carried a Thompson sub-machine gun, elected to keep it. I was impressed by Smith who was constantly ready for action. He was good looking, dashing, frequently striking a heroic posture. I remember him as looking like Robert Redford. Other men tried to look like Smith, a real leader. Those heroic types were important in setting a style for the rest of us.

We also got rid of our bayonets. I never understood why we carried them anyway. General Patton contended that German soldiers were afraid of bayonets because Americans were better than the Germans in their use, though where he got that idea I can't imagine. I'm guessing Patton made that up. I'd learned how to use one in training. In fact, for awhile I had been an instructor of some of the men who couldn't get the hang of using one. You didn't just run up to someone and stick them with it. There was a lengthy routine: short jab, long jab, horizontal butt stroke, slash, vertical butt stroke, butt smash, and so forth. I thought at the time "I hope I never have to use one of these things." Actually, I have known many combat men and have yet to hear of anyone who ever who used a bayonet. Combat psychological researcher David Grossman concluded that "in bayonet charges one side or the other invariably flees before the crossing of bayonets occurs."[6]

Author Paul Fussell, who also commanded Infantry troops, wrote that "During their infantry preparation, American troops had been trained in killing with the bayonet...but the boys never took to the training very well. They seemed too good-natured to imagine themselves such vicious killers. Bayonet drill sometimes left them weak with laughter. It seemed they did not enjoy even simulating hatred, and they thought the whole thing rather comic." Fussell also observed that this lack of hatred on the part of young infantry soldiers very much troubled General Eisenhower.[7]

Sergeant Huddock told me I was promoted in rank to Private First Class.

CHAPTER SIX

CAPTURE OF GOURBESVILLE

ONE DAY WE HELPED PUSH A GERMAN BATTALION ACROSS THE Merderet River and were dug in on the outskirts of a small village. All the houses in the town seemed to be badly damaged by artillery fire. There was, however, one undamaged house near where we were dug in. Sergeant Brewer came along and told us to stay where we were, not to do any looting and, when he'd made his way along the line, he came back to me and we decided maybe we'd see what we might find in that one undamaged house since it was obviously deserted.

Duey McMillion and John Mowrer came along and we broke a window, reached around and unlocked the door to the home and in we went. It was a neat place with Catholic symbols indicating the people were devout. We didn't damage anything, merely filled our pockets with a few souvenirs, then went to the kitchen. We were all in a permanent state of near-starvation, existing exclusively on K rations. We found some butter and a fairly large supply of beans. It was decided we had the makings of a pot of soup, so we left the house and took our newly-acquired food down to a small out-building fifty yards from the house. Someone started a fire, we emptied some canteens into an upended helmet, dumped in the beans, tossed in some vegetables we'd also found, chopped in the meat portion of a K-ration, and waited for the concoction to turn itself into soup.

I decided we should refill our canteens, and while the others who seemed to know more about cooking than I did watched the soup, I carried several canteens up to a well I'd noticed near the house. Just as I was starting to pump some water I thought I detected a sound. I whirled around and saw a dark figure pass through one of the rooms of the house. Realizing some Germans may have been hiding there, I jacked a shell into the chamber of my carbine and slipped over to the front door. I saw the doorknob turn. I waited. As a man stepped out I shoved my rifle into his stomach, only to find myself confronted by an extremely large Roman Catholic priest clad in black robe and starched clerical collar. I spoke no French, he spoke no English. We each stared in shock at the other for a brief moment, then I wordlessly turned and dashed back down to the building where the soup was in progress.

"What do we do now?" I asked Sergeant Brewer, who clearly had no idea what was appropriate. Despite our extraordinary situation, we were still civilized enough to know you don't break into a man's home and steal his food and other possessions without consequences, particularly since you've just robbed a priest at gunpoint.

As we discussed our options, the priest appeared carrying some butter in a large leaf of fresh lettuce. He smiled and offered us what remained of his food, of which he probably had possessed less than we did. All of us were embarrassed and ashamed. I looked to Brewer as the ranking man to manage some sort of apology. Meanwhile, I asked the others to give me whatever they'd stolen. In preparation for the invasion we had all been issued newly minted invasion currency to be used we knew not where and I also collected all that invasion currency. While the conversation was going on with the priest and my embarrassed sergeant, I slipped back up to the house and put everything we'd taken, adding in the currency, through the window we'd broken.

We hurriedly consumed some watery soup, bid the priest adieu with as much grace as we could muster, and mercifully learned that our unit was just now moving on. As I marched from the town, I realized I still had one item I'd taken from the house, a small silvered box containing several ancient coins. On the inner side of the top of the box was the word Lourdes. It was a souvenir of the priest's pilgrimage to that sacred place. I still have that box and those coins, and to this day I cannot be sure whether I only forgot to return it or whether I intentionally kept it, making me a thief. Shades of *Les Miserables*.

On June 13 our regiment crossed the Merderet causeway at LaFiere through heavy artillery fire and progressed one and a half miles. It was night as we moved toward Gourbesville, a small village near Amfreville. We were facing one of the enemy's crack divisions, their 77th Infantry. It was late as we reached the outskirts of the town. My squad members and I were moving quietly in almost total darkness when a German machine gun suddenly opened up on the other side of the hedgerow where I was standing. One of the guys tossed a hand grenade over and it was silenced. It was an eerie feeling, walking silently in deep darkness devoid of starlight, knowing we were only yards away from other silent men whose lives were presently devoted to killing us. It's amazing how our minds can adapt to danger in ways we could not imagine under normal, civilized, conditions. A cold, icy resolve takes over.

A terrible mistake had occurred because of the just-relieved Colonel Ginder. After being relieved of command, he'd gone to our battalion Command Post and talked the commander into moving us 150 yards forward of the originally designated jump-off point, probably thinking to show last-minute tactical genius. Meanwhile, 90th Division artillery had been called for on a pre-chosen location - exactly where we had been moved and told to dig in. The first rounds began exploding in our midst causing several casualties. We assumed it was German fire and took cover, our attack totally disrupted by the foolish mistake. Several wounded men along with a couple dead men were evacuated, then we fought all night but failed to capture the town. Thank goodness that was Ginder's last act as our regimental commander.

It was hard to get any sense of progress. I presumed someone somewhere was looking at a map and knew what was going on but for the guy with the rifle our world was circumscribed by the hedgerows around us. We did what we were ordered to do and saw the entire war in terms of defeating the force which opposed us in the next field, sometimes no more than platoon size, and surviving one more day. Not every field was zeroed in by enemy artillery and we could slip up on them just as they could slip up on us. Riflemen threw grenades, our mortars pounded them while we closed in, and they either ran, fought, or surrendered. If we won we could tell by the equipment left behind, and by any signs of men having been wounded and helped away as a means of knowing how well we'd done.

Eventually we became more wily. A sergeant armed with a carbine and three fifteen-round magazines was caught out in no-man's land when several Germans took him under fire. He began firing back with his carbine. Just as he fired his last cartridge and ejected the magazine for reloading a couple Germans dashed closer to him, then took cover before he could get ready to fire. He figured they had counted his shots and knew that when they heard that fifteenth shot he would require a few seconds to reload. So he fired six rounds from his second magazine then very quietly exchanged it for the third magazine. As soon as he had fired nine more rounds, sure enough, three Germans dashed toward him, at which point the sergeant with six more bullets ready shot one of them and forced the other two men to dash headlong behind a tree. That gave the sergeant a few seconds himself, which he used to dash to safety.

When possible the enemy did as we did and took their dead with them. Often that wasn't possible and both sides were reasonably respectful of the dead. I hear stories today about the Marines and the Navy Seals assuring men that no man will be left behind. Admirable to be sure, but I don't know how they expect to pull that off without unnecessary additional casualties. Wounded men, yes. As for the dead, both sides often had no choice but to leave their dead. Take them along if you can, to be sure, but it would be crazy to suffer more casualties just to carry away a dead body. There was pretty much an unwritten agreement that enemy dead of both sides would be treated with respect, and I certainly have never heard of anyone despoiling a dead enemy soldier once the battle had subsided, though it is true that their possessions were stolen. That was true of both sides. Sadly, at times even our own dead were treated by our retrieval people like so much cord wood and, while that sounds heartless, it wasn't possible for the people who collected the dead to feel grief for them. That would have made the job intolerable. One author did, however, report that one young Lieutenant just back from the front saw some graves people, those unfortunate fellows whose jobs were to gather up the dead bodies from the battlefield, unceremoniously tossing dead Americans on to a truck. He jumped from his jeep, dressed the men down in no uncertain terms and ordered them to treat the bodies with respect. I feel sorry for those men. I'd almost rather be in combat than spend my time collecting dead bodies.

As we were moving through Gourbesville, firing at a group of Germans behind a hedgerow, they suddenly yelled "kamerad," German for "surrender." About a dozen of them threw down their weapons and stepped out with their hands up, then were lined up to be searched. Looking at their faces, I saw that they were not unlike my own friends. I didn't see any of the heroic defiance we sometimes see in movie versions of the war. They revealed more of resignation, of let's just get this early part over with. I didn't see fear so much as a grim recognition of the fact that their war was over and I'd guess that some, perhaps most of them, didn't think that was very bad. If anything, they were just happy that they hadn't been shot. My group moved on as the prisoners began trudging back toward our rear area. I wonder if those kids had any idea what was happening to the cities where they lived, where their loved ones resided, or perhaps had died. What must it be like to fight a war knowing the people you love are under fire back home?

Two days of raging combat were required to drive the Germans out of Gourbesville with a wide flanking movement to the north. That proved costly. Our Carl Perry was killed, as were Rocky Locciasano and Charley Jones of L Company. Sergeant Merle Welfare's mortar squad was taken under heavy machine-gun fire and every man, including Welfare, were wounded. Welfare risked his own life to drag his wounded men to safety and later received a Silver Star medal. Technical Sergeant Norman Durandt was credited with plugging a hole in our lines with such courage he was given a Silver Star and a battlefield commission as an officer.

Dr. William McConahey was in charge of the 357th regimental station hospital. He reported that "the casualties poured in at an alarming rate, and many of them were bad ones too. Our litter bearers were having a real workout bringing in the wounded, and the aid station was working at top speed." The attacks continued. It was bitter fighting, especially for the rifle companies whose men were being hit by enemy artillery and by the merciless fire of hidden machine guns raking the small fields as our men had no choice but to enter the hedgerowed fields. "It was brutal up there," McConahey later reported, "and what a slaughter. The wounded poured back in dozens and I've never seen such horrible wounds, before or since - legs off, arms off, faces shot away, eviscerations, chests ripped open and so on. We worked at top speed, hour after hour..."[1]

Men did cry, but not from pain. They cried from the realization of their own approaching death, sometimes, just as depicted in movies, calling for their mothers. Germans did this too and could once in a great while be heard in a guttural voice calling out in the terrible realization that death was near, and sometimes they'd cry out "mama, mama." I found no satisfaction in this. I'm not sure very many of my friends took any satisfaction in the death of an enemy soldier though it was essential that many of them die if the war was to end. I confess it's hard to recall the emotions of those moments. I guess we were inured to the deaths of others after awhile. Certainly today it's heartbreaking to think of young men trading bullets, falling in the mud of Normandy, their life blood flowing, none with any understanding of why they aren't home instead, surrounded by loved ones.

All told, on the 15th of June our battalion lost 30 men killed and 66 wounded. Second Battalion lost 18 killed and 18 wounded. The worst loss in this engagement was that 99 men of the two battalions were captured. We did inflict significant casualties on the Germans units and they were finally driven out of the town, but our Regiment's losses that day totaled 231 men. In the end our battalion was credited with capturing Gourbesville. The next few days would be spent fighting in the hedgerows from Orglandes to Le Ham, protecting the northern flank of the advance to the west coast.

That night we dug in along the edge of a field as the rain which had been drizzling all afternoon became heavy, cold, and constant. That night I scraped out a slit trench maybe seven or eight inches deep and it soon had an inch of water pooled in the bottom. The temperature had dropped into the high fifties Fahrenheit. I had no choice and laid down in the mud and water, used my helmet as a pillow, put my soggy field jacket over me, portions of it floating on the surface of the water, and I slept. I discovered a psychological trick by which I would divorce my mind from my body, refusing to acknowledge how miserable I felt lying in cold muddy water and that plus extreme tiredness served to let me fall asleep.

The next day Duey McMillion and I headed out to check on an isolated farm building in a hedgerowed field in the middle of so-called no-man's land. That kind of place could easily house a German sniper, and we were to make sure that wasn't the case this time. When we got close we could see that the building had been damaged by artillery fire. We could, of course, have lofted a hand grenade in the front entrance which would have discouraged an enemy soldier but there was always the slight chance that some innocent French farmer, frightened at our approach, was hiding within. Instead, we shoved our carbines ahead of us and jumped inside. The place was empty. We prowled around for awhile, then went back outside to make sure that no one was nearby, then headed back to rejoin our unit, which we realized had continued moving on leaving Duey and me out in the middle of a field all by ourselves. We also realized we hadn't paid sufficient attention to the direction from which we'd entered the building. And the fact was that neither Duey nor I were very good at directions. We weren't absolutely sure which way our friends had gone, and we couldn't just remain where we were.

I didn't like that feeling. Surrounded by your friends there's a feeling of security. Being alone and lost was an eerie feeling. We knew we could easily run into a Kraut patrol if we went the wrong way and worse, even as we stood there we could have been in the sights of a German soldier, his finger already tightening on the trigger. We were completely disoriented, and there were no markers to suggest the correct way. Hemmed in by hedgerows on all sides, we had to make a guess and go for it. It was a lesson for us in what some of our officers who were charged with leading the way must sometimes feel, and it helped me understand how easily units were led into ambushes. It was like one of those dreams in which you are looking for someone or something, but you're not just sure who or what it is, you just search feeling lost and deserted. And strangely, I find that while far more memorable events easily merge into blurred memory, this one remains vivid with a kind of mythical symbolism of our individual lives in Normandy. It made me more than ever aware of the importance of the companionship of men in battle. Only a few heroic souls were comfortable being out there all by themselves and I wasn't one of them. Duey and I heard firing in the distance and headed at right angles to the sounds of battle which reunited us with our platoon.

Within a couple days the rain increased. By nightfall it was gale proportion and became the worst storm recorded in the area in the previous eighty years. It began on June 19 and lasted four days, forcing the port facilities on Omaha Beach to shut down completely and cutting off the supply of much-needed ammunition. General Bradley then ordered that no artillery piece fire more than twenty-five rounds a day unless under direct attack. It became necessary to cancel an attack by the 9th Division on Cherbourg. The port director on Omaha Beach later said he'd rather have faced the German Luftwaffe at full strength than have gone through that storm. Two artificial piers called Mulberries had been constructed in England, then floated across the Channel to enable unloading of supplies. The one at Omaha Beach was destroyed, the other, at Arromanches, survived but was badly damaged by the storm. An estimated 800 ships and boats of various sizes were sunk or beached and damaged by the storm so that needed repairs would have to wait. General Bradley said the ammunition shortage continued throughout the campaign. For me personally, it meant being soaking wet for days with no way to get dry. Like most of the men I'd discarded my raincoat and there were never any replacements of clothing. The rain rattled down on our helmets, endless, drenching everything. The first night I crawled under an armored personnel carrier parked near a hedgerow. Just as I was drifting off to sleep I awoke with the realization that someone could drive the thing away suddenly and, not knowing I was there, run over me, so I gave that up and with no alternative laid down in the mud and pounding rain. You endured in what you had. At night we froze. Worse, the rain also prevented our planes from roaming the skies in search of German tanks and other road traffic. Rainy weather was their friend. It most assuredly wasn't ours.

What went on in the mind of a combat soldier who spent seemingly unending days in battle or the immediate threat of battle without relief? What thoughts occupied one throughout the waking hours? Our individual personalities and earlier life experiences of course dictated this, and no two people were exactly alike. But there were some broad generalizations one could make. A few men lived in constant fear, every moment preoccupied with thoughts of death or serious injury. Every loud noise made them jump. Conversations about home and loved ones brought tears to their eyes. They viewed every wounding of another either with horror, or with profound relief that they weren't that man. These men were often destined to become battle fatigue cases. Their sensitive natures simply made them ill-equipped for battle. Only a few were cowards. Most were good men with active imaginations, easily picturing the frightening possibilities of personal disaster. Some were highly creative people, constantly exhausted from inner stress which rarely let up, and the sooner they were retrieved from combat the better. Maybe men like this should not be forced to serve in combat.

Some men were angry. "What in the hell am I doing here, what bunch of idiots did this to me?" they might rage. They tended to be outspoken, defiant, sometimes attention-getting enough that they were promoted, or, if they directed their rage at a superior, punished. Usually, their rage was directed at the enemy and they were often courageous fighters. A very few were sadistic in their attitudes toward the Germans and could act in ways the rest of us would consider inhumane. Historian John McManus told of one man watching a young German soldier strolling in what he apparently assumed to be a quiet sector. The GI marveled at the German's long golden hair. Leisurely, he drew a bead on the man and shot him. The German fell on his back and the GI watched as the German arched his back in pain, gasping in the death throes. The GI, telling the story, later said he could easily have put the German out of his misery but enjoyed watching him struggle in pain to see how long he'd take to die. Once the man finally died he decided to go scalp him and take that head of golden hair as a souvenir. He regretted that a mortar barrage prevented him from acquiring his gruesome souvenir.

Sometimes their rage was directed inward, producing illness, depression, and hopelessness. Many seemed to have a permanent chip on their shoulders. These latter personality types could also end up as emotional casualties. There were a few men, and I would guess they were extremely few in number, who were just plain killing machines. Maybe General Patton was their patron saint. He was quoted as looking out on the smoking ruins of a tank battle, dead bodies still visible, and pensively remarking to another officer, "War, I love it...love it with all my heart." These men didn't seem to be troubled by the feelings most of us experienced in battle. They could run great risks to get at an enemy soldier and could pull the trigger remorselessly. They were in their element. I could never decide whether people like this lacked the imagination to envision consequences, whether they lacked any inclination toward empathy, or whether they just had a rare ability to suspend all normal human sensitivity while going about their jobs with cold calculation. This doesn't mean they weren't good people. They probably won more than their share of battles. Some were heroes in the fullest sense of the word and I suspect they, more than any others, love reunions where they can relive their glory days. Those who survived, that is.

Let's face it, a few men were criminals. I don't know what percentage of American males were criminals and sociopaths in 1944 but presumably that percentage applied to GIs as well. Crimes were committed by members of the United States armed forces - rapes, murders, thievery – and the rest of us hated it. The guilty were quietly punished, and the rest of us were left with our honor unblemished. People today who express shock at revelations of such crimes by members of the armed forces in places like Iraq and who cite World War II as the "good war" might be surprised to know that these things happened then too but were generally hushed up.

Those nut cases were out there. A few bad apples stole from other GIs, raped French women, and murdered captive soldiers for no reason other than sheer sadism. I know these people were there. I'm not sure, however, that I ever met one.

The greater number of us managed to achieve some form of emotional tunnel vision in combat, keeping our minds on the immediate situation, finding a certain amount of relief in our day-to-day relationships, making maximum use of rare periods when we were far enough back from the face-to-face with the enemy situation to actually rest. Many drank, but I do not recall ever seeing anyone drunk on the front lines during the fighting. I suppose there must have been times when men would uncover a cache of wine or booze, in which case it didn't last long. But if there was drunkenness in combat I never saw it nor heard other men mention it. It would have been a good way to get killed, and to get a friend killed. Behind the lines was, of course, a different story. Basically, we clung to our sanity and a basic sense of common decency, and tried to be faithful to our mission.

We didn't talk about home much, not because it wasn't dear to our hearts, but because the contrast between those memories and our present reality was almost more than we could bear. Some people might say that we were into denial, unable to fully accept our unhappy situation. Of course we all fervently wished we were somewhere else. As Fussell wrote, "Ninety percent would have escaped if there had been any non-shameful way out. It was only the buddy system...that kept the boys honorable." Only in quiet, almost intimate moments, with men to whom we felt close, men whom we trusted, did we share much about our former private lives.

What about religion? That was a private matter for nearly all of us, except, perhaps, for the few fundamentalists who could be very verbal, sometimes preachy. It was just a subject one didn't bring up except to ask "do you believe in God," or "where is God in all this if He's so loving?" such phrases often spoken not in sincere seeking but in exasperation at the entire situation. Most of us, whether we'd attended church or synagogue or not, had never struggled with the life-and-death issues related to a faith. We may have confided to a friend or two that we were believers, but we also noticed that the casualty rate among believers seemed about the same as that among the rest of the men. Whatever part God cared to play in our lives it was obviously not to protect us from harm. Certainly if God was put off by the taking of the divine name in vain then we were all in trouble. Every fourth or fifth word was profane or obscene, though of course there were a few men excepted.

I think of one conversation between two men on the subject of religion. As I recall, it went something like this.

Bill: "Tom, do you believe God helps people when they pray?"

Tom: "If He does He sure hasn't been listening to me."

Bill: "How do you know? You're still alive aren't you? Maybe God has helped you."

Tom: "I doubt it. If he wanted to help me I wouldn't be here in the first place."

Bill: "Good point."

Tom: "I wish I could believe what Harry says about God, that He loves me and wants me to be happy. Harry's a Southern Baptist and says that if I accept Jesus Christ as my Lord and Savior it won't matter what happens to me. I told him I'd already done that. I attended Sunday School in a Presbyterian Church at home and we all were taught to accept Jesus. Harry didn't seem very impressed. He said I had to stand up and actually say and mean it. Harry's a good man but he's too damn religious."

Bill: "Yeah, well, maybe so. I went to a Methodist Church and like you I'm a believing Christian but I still don't know what to believe. I guess God won't be too hard on us young guys when we die. I sure hope not. I'll still keep praying but I know darn well God's not going to get in the way of the next 88 shell. When it's my time I'll go like everyone else. Besides, what about the Jews? If God loves us he must love them as much as us Christians. After all, they started the whole thing. Jesus was a Jew himself, so I don't believe God rejects everyone who doesn't believe like Harry does."

Tom: "I suppose you're right. Still, it can't hurt to pray in Jesus' name. At least I've been doing that since I talked to Harry and I have to say I sleep a little better at night."

I believe every one of us thought about God. Those who were true believers found comfort in the conviction that God would find some way to at least guarantee a desirable outcome if only a trip to Heaven, though preferably a safe passage home. Most of us were not so sure about that. Some men actually worried that something they may have done was a cause of divine anger, that God really might choose this all as a form of deserved punishment. For them there was a strong element of superstition. Others played it safe and said their prayers in a kind of in-case-you're-listening spirit, not expecting much. Still others began to suspect that whatever else we can say, God is not a God of love. Either that or He's powerless. Otherwise this whole mess would cease or, better yet, it never would have happened. But it was a rare man who never considered the matter at all, certainly during an artillery barrage. Christian psychotherapist Paul Tournier, who spent his life helping troubled people, wrote that "the supreme and universal need of men is to find God."

A few men really believed God actually intercedes in the physical world for those who pray. They still tell the story of the time General Patton -- who for all his blathering was a complete believer in God and the life hereafter, apparently in the form of reincarnation -- was so irate at the intolerable weather during the Battle of the Bulge that he called in the chaplain of the 3rd Army and ordered the poor man to write a prayer for clearing weather. The chaplain, a highly-trained and thoughtful theologian, demurred on the grounds that God did not usually interfere in things like that. Patton chastised the man, reminded him that he, Patton, gave the orders around there, and sent the man off with his assignment. The man hurriedly turned out a very generic prayer asking God for goodness sakes to do something about this awful weather as General Patton found it a total nuisance. Copies were run off forthwith, distributed to all the men, and a day or two later the weather cleared. Patton, seemingly not at all surprised, eventually awarded the chaplain a Bronze Star medal.

One of war's tragedies is that they're fought by young men who have not yet learned a faith sufficient for the trial. The great German theologian Helmut Thielicke, who was ostracized from his university in Heidelburg because of his opposition to Adolf Hitler, wrote that "The New Testament and the hymns of the Church show us that we all - even we mature, rational, intellectual and even highly polished people - have moments when we are nothing more than a heap of misery, when we no longer speak rationally, and with sensible grammar, but when we can only groan." It was in this way that we experienced our faith. In the end, no answers, only the anguish of not knowing whether God even cared. Theologian Paul Tillich said, "Life in the Spirit is ebb and flow - and this means whether we experience the present or the absent God, it is the work of the Spirit." We know now that God was always present with us even though many men experienced him as the absent God.

I've learned a lot since those days, learned a lot about God. The noted Russian writer Nikos Kazantzakis told of two men standing together under the night sky discussing the tragedy of a broken world when suddenly a shooting star flamed across the sky. One man turned to the other and said, "Look, did you see that? A tear just rolled down the face of God." That's the only answer that makes sense to me now. God could not be faithful to His creation and interfere with even the most nefarious actions of His children, not if we are to have free will. Goodness, moral faithfulness, honor and integrity, all would be meaningless in a world in which we have no choice between good and evil. And yet, if evildoing is one of our choices, then once chosen it quickly infects the entire of creation and God, now faithful to that creation, must wait and not interfere. How His great divine heart must have broken in those days as, indeed, it must remain broken throughout human history, as we again and again inflict suffering upon those whom He called us to accept as our brothers and sisters. And each German young man wielding his schmeisser pistol was as much the recipient of God's redeeming love as was I, an inconceivable thought at the time. Instead we were trying to kill each other, brother against brother, while God wept.

What I did discover was that when I prayed I seemed to find within myself the inner qualities of courage, energy, and the ability to go on doing what I was required to do. Now, long years later, I recognize in that remembrance the evidence that God was at work in me. However, other men prayed as well and too many of them died. I have only been able to conclude that death is part of the larger continuum of life with God and that to die is not to cease to exist, it is to go on with life in ways not yet revealed to my tiny mind.

You can't stay scared for weeks on end and remain functional. One way or another we had to find some inner emotional strategy for survival. Each man was unique, though we nearly all fell more or less into one or another of these categories. Those who could not move beyond their fear were the ones who turned and ran or, more often, suffered emotional failure and had to be relieved of duty. The more we possessed denial skills, blocking out thoughts of home and Mom and apple pie, the longer we lasted. It was all intense, scarring in many ways, life changing for all. I suppose everyone had a breaking point but for some it was much sooner than for the majority of us. Men who lasted for long periods of combat reported that the longer you're in combat the more you begin to fear you won't live long. The myth of seasoned troops fighting heroically because they've learned superior combat skills isn't true for most men. Historian Robin Neillands writes of such men that "inevitably, their determination wanes, too many terrible sights eventually sap the will to fight. Rest is essential to keep soldiers going even this far, but eventually the will for battle declines."[2] The British discovered this when their elite units which defeated Rommel in Africa were transferred to France and immediately began to complain "Why us?" We've already done our part."

Most of us didn't have serious girlfriends, though it was customary to pretend that we did. Some men actually did though, and they sometimes worried that the girls would soon forget them. Once in awhile someone would receive a "Dear John" letter from a girlfriend who had found someone else. The movies usually made this seem like trag-edy, young men thereafter heedlessly risking their lives as though life was no longer worth living. That may have happened once in awhile, but actually some men were relieved, glad they no longer had to go home and honor commitments made when they were a hundred years younger experience-wise. Other men were sorry to hear such bad news, but the piercing reality of the present moment usually shoved that sadness to the backs of their minds. Though the girls left behind were occasionally the conversational topic, we really all lived in the present. Of course some men who had left serious girlfriends behind built exag-gerated images of that perfect person. In most cases they'd go home and end up marrying someone else.

Since having children was a ticket out of combat there were very few married men among the enlisted men. Truthfully, we realized that for teenaged girls to wait a year and a half, two years, for someone for whom they'd felt a long-since dulled infatuation was unrealistic anyway. The woman I finally married was engaged to a friend of mine serving on an LST in the Pacific and both were glad to call it off when he returned home. Some young men were more in love with love than in love with a specific girl. In any event, since we were gone from home at a significant time in our lives as we transitioned from youth-fulness into manhood, our girlfriends were doing the same thing back in the real world, and, for most, it would have been asking too much for them to retain those early romantic love feelings which were almost always mere infatuations. Plus, of course, none of us would be the person they knew when we went away. Once in a blue moon a young fellow would actually go home, marry the girl he left behind and have a happy marriage. But that was rare.

A few men were newly married, had impulsively tied the knot just before leaving. Movies of the day featured this scenario a lot, and it was all very romantic. I fear that for many a wife at home whose new husband never returned there followed a lifetime of fantasy, "Oh how happy we would have been, what a perfect marriage we would have had," and meanwhile, those who did return discovered that as often as not they'd made a terrible mistake. One truth we all discover in life is that opposites attract but likes stay together. Compatibility is the basis for a good marriage, and those impulsive kid decisions of the early 1940s were made without any real idea at all of the qualities needed for happy marriage, nor of the qualities, the likes and dislikes, the inner life, of that other attractive person they really had never had time to get to know. After all, how could two kids wildly in love have any slight idea what life is like when the grand adventure of wartime settles down to the give and take of everyday life, of job, and kids, and a mortgage?

Some conversation about girls was totally fictitious stuff, boastful claims of conquest that few of us believed. It was important, though, to be perceived by comrades as a real ladies' man, and men who'd hardly ever had a date told grand stories of romantic adventure.

One reason for this sex-related conversation was one about which most of us were totally naive: homosexuality. I for one was only dimly aware that there were men who were gay. I'd heard all the jokes in high school, but I was not aware I'd ever actually known a gay person. Only in modern times have we realized that an unknown but probably larger percentage of gay men than we would have guessed were in the Army in 1944, and given the unenlightened attitudes of the time such men found it of crucial importance that no one know. They surely found it very important to report boy-girl relationships, imagined in most cases, as a way to divert any speculation about their orientation. Men showered together in large groups in the Army, and for a gay man to be discovered would have had consequences that were brutal, conceivably even fatal. That was one of the hidden tragedies of the war. When we were medically examined for entry into the service every man was asked whether he liked girls. For a man to have replied that no, he preferred boys, would have gotten him a deferral, but it would also have labeled him at a time in history when this would have also guaranteed tragic consequences socially and at home. No sane gay man came out of the closet in 1944. Such men probably felt they had no choice but to enter the service.

CHAPTER SEVEN
ON TO CHERBOURG

ONCE GOURBESVILLE WAS CAPTURED OUR DIVISION WAS ORDERED to turn toward Cherbourg, the main port of Normandy needed to supply the eventual push toward Germany. It was General Bradley's primary objective apart from Caen and Saint Lo. We were sent to a position near the town of Portbail, our mission to prevent a German breakout while the 9th, 4th, and 29th Divisions would attack the port. We were also tasked to prevent any German reinforcements from behind us making their way through to Cherbourg. We would receive some more replacements to be trained, and damaged equipment could be replaced. We were loaded on trucks and as we rode east we began to see dead Germans along the road. Our graves people had apparently gathered the dead from an earlier battle, and in the course of a couple miles we passed at least 200 dead Germans. It's a gruesome memory these many years later to recall how heartwarming we found it to see so many of them.

Suddenly, I saw two American fighter planes approaching from the direction of the German lines. They were descending, and as they drew closer I saw that they were P-51 Mustangs and one was trailing smoke. As they headed toward our line of trucks it began to look as though they were planning to strafe us, but at the last moment one plane pulled up. He'd been escorting his friend, trying to reach an airfield. The second plane dropped into a steeper dive and within a hundred feet of the ground a parachute began to blossom out as the plane crashed and exploded a short distance from us. We watched in horror as the pilot, momentarily visible in his half-open chute, disappeared into the flames.

The next few days were a relative relief from the fighting of the past several days. We had time to dig in deep enough to afford some real protection from the more or less constant shelling by the Germans. We'd been in combat for two weeks and were ready for a rest. It's amazing, looking back, to realize how little it took to constitute comfort in our world. A fairly warm night, a dry slit trench, a lull in the fighting, and it felt better than a trip to Florida in the winter feels today. Sometimes two men would room together, one man digging deep the other searching for limbs and boards with which to create a roof over the hole. We'd even dig little openings in the side of the hole for such things as boots, canteen, or a hand grenade. It could get pretty homey given enough time. Of course the officer who then decided to move his platoon a hundred yards closer was exceedingly unpopular, though someone else was then supplied with a well-deserved break.

Everything was relative in war - a few men sitting around knowing we were too far back to be hit by artillery fire, lighting up a cigarette, kidding around with insults and jokes flying, speculating on the probable strategic situation, cleaning weapons in a leisurely way. There were many moments when the world actually looked pretty good to us. Some inherent optimism could break through in times like that and make it all OK. But just for brief periods of time. Then we'd grab our equipment and start moving out, back into that other terrible world.

Because we were in a defensive position our part of the battle was limited to patrols by riflemen and all-too-frequent artillery and mortar barrages by the Germans. They needed to dislodge us as our 90th Division was blocking the only viable escape route from the peninsula of the Cotentin.

One day our division artillery fired a salvo of shells loaded with leaflets calling for the enemy soldiers to surrender, and 99 Germans traipsed in to give themselves up. This was rare, though. Not many enemy soldiers would quit without a fight, at least until the waning days of the war. Most seemed ready to fight to the death. Also, SS officers were legally allowed to execute a man on the spot, and this happened many times. By war's end thousands of young German soldiers, wanting to survive the approaching holocaust, refused to fight and were promptly gunned down by their own officers.

This brings to mind the battle-experienced GI's idea of humor. The things we thought excruciatingly funny may have brought, at best, an amused smile to anyone else. Bill Mauldin told of the crew of a 105 mm howitzer battery which found a large supply of leaflets designed to encourage the Germans to surrender. What we all knew was that when those leaflets were fired in artillery shells, they scattered over a wide area and it was then customary to hold fire for awhile so the Germans would come out of their holes, read the leaflets and, so the theory went, decide to surrender. It was also known that the Germans welcomed this, knowing they could safely answer nature's call, take a smoke break, reinforce their positions and just take a stretch. For them it was a welcome respite from the firing and was a kind of agreed-upon rule of war. But this particular fire team fired some shells filled with the leaflets, counted ten while the Krauts left their cover, then sent in a salvo of the real thing, chortling to themselves at the thought of the casualties they must have inflicted. Back then this was funny to everyone except the people who counted on leaflets to bring in prisoners.

Then there was the time a large unit entered a French town and the leaders, especially a not very popular colonel, were surrounded by cheering, celebrating French people who showered the jeep carrying the colonel with flowers, handing in some fresh fruit and a bottle of wine as gestures of appreciation. But in the jeep behind the colonel some of the men were tossing items less delicate, the occasional piece of fruit, aimed to land on the back of the colonel's helmet who assumed he was merely being hit by well-intentioned French people. That, of course, brought great joy to the few men who knew the truth.

Another story making the rounds concerned my friend "Meejy" who had insisted that he had nothing against the Germans. We all kidded him about that, and the McMillion brothers and I sometimes made a big deal about Meejy's passive attitude. Then one day as we were more or less resting in the sunshine, we heard a distant series of bangs announcing the imminent arrival of 88 shells. Unfortunately, Meejy had just climbed over a hedgerow and dropped his pants preparatory to relieving himself. A shell exploded close by and Meejy, terrified, came climbing over the hedgerow, trousers trailing behind him as he frantically scrambled toward his trench. As another shell landed closer Meejy shook his fist in the direction of the enemy and uttered an outburst of obscenities as he disappeared into his hole. We later asked Meejy if he still didn't have anything against the Germans, and he grinned and admitted "Yeah, now I hate the bastards." The story of course made the rounds of the battalion. This kind of black humor was typical of men living in combat. In fact, nearly all verbal communication was in some degree laced with our ideas of humor. Insults which could get one in real trouble anywhere else were received with a comparable retort and this continued until someone couldn't think of a comeback.

Incidentally, that event of Meejy's almost wasn't funny as I casually strolled to the hole I had dug and, as I climbed in, I heard the shriek of incoming. I hurriedly dropped down just as an 88 shell exploded immediately behind my head, shearing a small tree at the base and depositing it within inches of my trench. I later estimated that the shell had passed where my head would have been had I waited half an instant longer. Also, we heard an anguished cry for "medic." Some kid whose name I didn't know was squirming, holding his leg which had a piece of metal driven into the side of it. The wound was ten or twelve inches, the shell fragment still sticking out. A medic ran over and removed the metal after sticking him with a hypo of morphine. Litter bearers ran over and carried the kid off as the rest of us watched enviously. He'd walk in a month or so, run two weeks later but no doubt be able to hang around the hospital for another month. Then, the bad news was he'd probably be back.

On a still more somber note, and back to the capturing of prisoners, regrettably, many Germans were killed trying to surrender. This wasn't publicized until several years after the war ended, but the tragic truth is that in the heat of battle some American soldiers could be every bit as ruthless as could some Germans. A lot depended on the personality of the individual American and on his particular experience in combat. After an especially vicious and costly battle, after seeing several friends killed or badly wounded, some men did things they would never have considered doing ordinarily. There are former World War II infantrymen alive today who admit to agonizing guilt for doing what they would, now, consider war crimes. Other men, watching this, were sometimes appalled to witness these actions, but the bond between them prohibited reporting a man to his superiors. Nor were officers always free of guilt. We may have done as much of this as did the Germans. One man from the 4th Infantry Division said he once watched an officer "shoot a wounded German who asked him for water, took out his pistol and just shot him in the head; he said 'water, hell', and just fired." The 4th Division man then said "Nothing we could do about it, just keep moving."[1]

Another GI, Lindley Higgins, told of the capture of a German who had just set off an explosion under a bridge, causing several American casualties. Higgins said he was about to lead the German to the rear when a lieutenant walked up, said "you're going to take that man to the rear?" then pulled out his pistol and shot the man in the head. Historian Max Hastings, reporting this, wrote that "it is difficult with hindsight to draw a meaningful moral distinction between the behavior of one side and the other on the battlefield."[2] Having interviewed many former combat men Hastings reported, "Among scores of Allied witnesses interviewed for this narrative, almost every one had direct knowledge, or even experience of the shooting of German prisoners during the campaign...many British and American units shot SS prisoners routinely."

It wasn't an easy choice sometimes. A unit moving in an attack, suddenly confronted with a surrendering enemy soldier, couldn't very well stop the attack in order to look after the man. Nor, frequently, could they afford to detach a much-needed rifleman to escort the prisoner, and possibly suffer their own casualties because of the loss of a gun. Neither could they just tell the surrendering man to head on back behind our lines. No telling what he might do once roaming free. Sometimes the only rational solution seemed to be to kill the man. It happened on both sides all too often, and we all knew that the chances were better to keep on fighting than to quit alone under fire. Some men who did shoot a surrendering enemy soldier suffered aftershock. Many didn't sleep well for a long time. One former officer told of meeting a member of his unit fifty years later and asking the man about the rumor that he had killed an unarmed prisoner. The man broke down and cried uncontrollably. He'd carried remorse throughout his life. Not many men could bring themselves to execute an enemy soldier, but there was nearly always someone around who could and would.

On both sides, once a man survived the first hour or so of captivity, he was fairly sure of surviving. It is true, however, with not many exceptions, once safely past the front lines German prisoners were well treated by American captors whereas in many cases, American prisoners suffered, some terribly. Sometimes this was not so much inhumanity as it was the conditions in which the Germans were existing at the time. There were, however, cases of intentional mistreatment of American prisoners by German captors, and I know of no such cases on the American side once the immediate capture has been survived.

Former Major Robert James, then executive officer of a company of the 114th Infantry of the 44th Division, tells of watching a group of men from a sister company surrender to a German force and later finding the men dead, executed. John McManus told of Sergeant Don Foye, a member of our 358th Regiment, who was leading a patrol searching for stragglers when they were ambushed by a team of German paratroopers. Forced to surrender, Foye and his men were disarmed and lined up along a hedgerow. Suddenly, the paratroopers opened fire, shooting all of the men. Foye was shot in the back of the head but survived. Eventually a medic found him and Foye spent years in reconstructive surgery for damage done to his face, finally recovering completely.

Most of us recall the infamous execution of some 107 captured Americans at Malmedy by the Germans at the outset of the Battle of the Bulge. It happened too often on both sides, but I know of no such mass executions by Americans. Nothing is more reprehensible than to mistreat an enemy captive when the man is helpless. Understandable as these executions may seem, they are still crimes. It leaves us facing the terrible maxim of General Sherman that "war is hell."

Deep down, most of the men I knew were just too tender-hearted to kill a man in cold blood no matter how angry we might be. One day I walked into an aid station and saw a young German boy no more than eighteen or nineteen lying on a stretcher in the middle of the room. The poor kid looked scared to death. They'd just brought him in off the battlefield and no doubt he'd had his head filled with awful stories of what would happen to him if he fell into our evil hands. He held a hand out to me and said "wasser, wasser." He was thirsty. I went to the lister bag and drew a small cup of water. As I was about to give it to the boy a doctor yelled at me, told me not to give him the water. I glared at the doc and he explained to me that the boy had a stomach wound, that he would receive medical attention right away, and water was the worst thing for him at the moment. There were a few men who would have argued "why not shoot the SOB and save our medics all that trouble." Thank God those people were extremely few in number. This kid would receive excellent medical care and hopefully, went home to his family one day.

Many men felt delayed remorse for all sorts of misconduct during the fighting. It's hard today to recall the feelings of those days. There were still rules, of course, but tracking everyone's conduct, and holding men to account for misconduct was frequently impossible. Most of the rule-makers and enforcers were safely back behind the lines, and one unbreakable rule above all others was that you don't betray a friend, not one who has shared battle with you and on whom you may look as the man who might just have to save your life. It was often a matter of one's individual conscience which determined how we acted. Many men then and, I would imagine, in today's Army, became complicit in such crimes though they themselves would never do such things. The bond joining men together in battle is well-nigh unbreakable.

Studs Turkel told of a GI named William Thomas who was helping escort a line of newly-captured prisoners to the holding area. He was walking with his thoughts elsewhere when suddenly a young German soldier dashed out of line and jumped Thomas, trying for his rifle.

Thomas managed to shove the other man away long enough to unsling his rifle, and as the enemy attacked again, he hit him with his rifle butt, knocking the man down. Before the German could scramble to his feet Thomas turned his rifle, jacked a shell into the chamber, pointed it between the other man's eyes and squeezed the trigger - not enough, though, to fire. He stood there, looking into the flaming eyes of a kid no more than seventeen years old. Every fiber of his being wanted to kill the Nazi on the spot. It would have been legal. But something, some shred of decency, stayed his hand. Slowly, he lowered his weapon as two older Germans hurriedly dragged the kid to his feet, and as they hustled him back in line, one German stepped close to Thomas and whispered "danke." Thomas would go home eternally grateful that he'd done the right thing.

I look back at this now and can only conclude that we, as Christian people, and I include Judaism in this observation, believed that to kill an unarmed man was a crime against God, and one which most of us could never commit. I do, however, have a friend whom I admire who does today admit to killing two German soldiers who had thrown down their arms and were offering to surrender. It was in the heat of battle at the Siegfried Line, and those of us who were not there cannot presume to judge. It was a situation in which many other enemy soldiers were attacking and he had no way to deal with prisoners.

On June 22 a large flight of American bombers and fighter planes went over us flying low, heading in to bomb the Cherbourg defenders. General Collins, commander of the army attacking Cherbourg, had arranged for a major attack to be preceded by air support but we later learned that, as was nearly always the case when bombing preceded infantry advances, the air attack killed many Germans and several Americans. Smoke markers drifted with the breeze, and communications between ground and air were poor, preventing the ground commanders from calling off the bombers. Later evaluations judged the air attack as somewhat helpful but extremely costly. The Air Corps was great at destroying tanks and other enemy vehicles, but they weren't much good at close infantry support. Judged by today's technology the mistakes seem criminal, but close support was a relatively new tactic, communication capabilities were primitive compared to current technology, and pilots did the best they could (which was pretty good considering everything). Ground commanders also played their part, not always realizing how difficult it was to fly at several thousand feet, at a couple hundred miles per hour, and hit the bullseye which is about what they had to do to avoid our own troops who were hidden, not only from the Germans but also from our planes.

German General Von Schlieben, commander of the German forces in Cherbourg, had received direct orders from Adolf Hitler reading "Even if the worst comes to the worst, it is your duty to defend to the last bunker and leave the enemy not a harbor but a field of ruin." Von Schlieben obviously ignored this order but sent word to General Rommel asking for reinforcements. Rommel sent word back that he had tried to do so by sending troops by water, but the American Navy had the port completely blocked, which meant that the forces of Cherbourg were on their own.

On June 23 elements of the three American divisions entered the city limits. By the 25th most of the defenses had fallen. Still, some 6,000 German troops refused the order to surrender. Fort du Roule still held out, keeping the American attackers under direct machine-gun and rifle fire. A squadron of P-47s carried out a bombing raid but missed. Finally, Lieutenant Carlos Ogden, realizing he would soon lose all his men if the attack continued, grabbed an M1 rifle with a couple bandoliers of ammunition, plus a grenade launcher, and single-handedly advanced on the fort's defenders. He launched grenades at the fort, emptied his M1 again and again at the machine-gun positions and, though shot in the head, continued his attack until the fort's defenders surrendered.

Men like this are hard for the rest of us to understand. Why he wasn't killed in the first two minutes is amazing. What could have gone on in his mind as bullets missed him by inches while he pressed his attack only he knew. To me such colossal heroism goes way beyond mere courage. Not many men could have done that. He more than deserved the Medal of Honor which was eventually awarded to him by President Truman.

Meanwhile, back at the 90th Division, another senior officer joined the exodus of the disgraced, as Lieutenant Colonel Homer E. Jensen was fired as commander of the 1st Battalion, 357th Regiment, and replaced by Major Ed Hamilton, a younger man who had shown himself a capable leader under fire. I have wondered since if he was the major who drew his pistol on us a few days earlier. Jensen was yet another example of a man who'd been steadily moving up the career path but lacking that one quality so essential in our circumstances.

On the 29th Cherbourg officially surrendered, and the next day an engineering appraisal of the extensive damage done by the Germans to the port facilities was possible. Only then could reconstruction begin.

Incredibly, given the extensive damage, the port was working at full capacity only three weeks later. It was desperately needed. By that time the Navy had disgorged some 850,000 men and nearly 150,000 vehicles onto the beaches of Normandy. The need for food, ammunition, equipment, fuel, clothing, and other supplies was tremendous. A great battle had finally been won, the first time we'd won a major amount of territory on European soil, and it was all because of the heroism of the men of the 4th, 9th, and 29th Infantry Divisions. Those three divisions, along with elements of other units, suffered 22,000 casualties, and captured 39,000 German soldiers. General Eisenhower was ecstatic. Finally, we'd won a significant battle.

This brings to mind the whole issue of heroism. There were several ways to view this. A few men, very few, Audie Murphy the supreme example (America's most decorated hero), actually combined the killer instinct with a complete disregard for their own safety and could attack a machine gun head on, or race across a field exploding with artillery to destroy an enemy position, as Lieutenant Ogden did. Then there were those men who would, under special provocation, risk themselves to save another man, or to perform some admirable act of heroic achievement, sometimes because it would save their own skins. But the most common heroism was that of the many men who, while not inclined like the others, did their duty. They stayed the course. Scared at times, clearly aware they might never see their loved ones again, they obeyed their orders, they stayed at their posts, they faced the enemy to the death if necessary rather than run and live the rest of their lives knowing they were cowards. These were the men who finally won the war. Good people mostly, they would return home knowing they'd done their duty, would go to school, get married, work at responsible jobs, one day restore a nation, a world, raise children who could be proud of their parents. These young men with whom I was living and fighting would one day be celebrated in their country as The Greatest Generation. Maybe that title is too grand. Most are embarrassed to hear it. But they faced the worst a demonic enemy could bring to bear and they won, they came home, they rarely complained, and most barely mentioned their exploits except when some were gathered over a couple of beers to talk about old times.

Some men received medals. Most were richly deserved, some were not. Many medals were deserved and never awarded. So much depended on who was there and who lived to tell about it. To be recommended for a medal a man must have the witness of an officer preferably, or a ranking non-com. Often, however, a heroic act was performed when no one was looking, or when the potential witness was killed.

It occasionally worked the other way. Friends who admired each other have been known to exaggerate actions to qualify men for decorations. The story was told to me by one man in the hospital who said he'd been there, of a lieutenant who was notorious for staying behind his troops, for hiding when at all possible, but who managed to have his actions depicted to a high-ranking officer in such a way that he was one day awarded a Silver Star for gallantry. The man's troops were lined up to witness the award and as the medal was pinned on the man's shirt, the men turned and faced the other way.

Post-war reports told of several generals who received Silver Stars for merely getting closer to the actual fighting than usual, doing what the rest of us did every day. Officers varied in what they considered to be heroic action. A man named Harrison Summers killed an estimated 100 Germans on or near Utah Beach, and was said by one biographer to be almost single-handedly responsible for the successful landing on Utah, yet never received the Medal of Honor due to a clerical error. Somehow, when those things happened as they frequently did, no one wanted to be inconvenienced to go back and correct someone's mistake. General SLA Marshall in commenting on this miscarriage wrote, "Homeric happenings go unreported. Sometimes the bravest meet death with their deeds known only to heaven." One commander in North Africa as reported by biographer Don Graham "stopped recommending his men for decorations because too often the wrong men got the medals while the real heroes did not."

Some commanders wanted lots of medals for their men, while other commanders were strict about them. Sometimes the person writing the recommendation lacked writing skills and failed to adequately describe an event, thus it was refused. Others with vivid imaginations and generous hearts would add a machine gun or two to the casualty report and get their man a higher award. The most serious problem was simply that in the heat of battle with everyone up to his ears in crises no one had time to watch what others were doing, so many acts of bravery went unrecognized and unrecorded. Someone had to see and make a believable report, substantiated by someone else who also saw.

Captain Franklyn Johnson, a company commander, wrote shortly after the war, "It is always a struggle to extract deserved decorations from Regiment, which usually seems reluctant to reward enlisted men and low-ranking officers with medals and promotions. Regiment also places much stress upon how well-written the recommendation is." Probably most awards were granted or denied by men who had never been in battle.

Major Robert James, then a company commander in the 114th Infantry, told me that after a particularly bitter battle during the Battle of The Bulge fighting, he wrote several recommendations for medals for some of his men who fought heroically. They were refused. Later, James re-wrote the recommendations and submitted them again; again they were refused. He got in touch with someone at Regiment and asked why the refusal and was told "the General doesn't believe in giving a lot of medals." Much later, James reported that when it was learned that his regiment had fewer medals than other units, the same commander reversed his position and there was a period in which James said "you could almost win a medal with a stubbed toe." He felt that as the war progressed medals were more easily handed out.

CHAPTER EIGHT

CRISIS

BY JULY THERE WAS MUCH PESSIMISM AS THE SITUATION IN NOR-
mandy threatened to become static. We'd already suffered 37,000
casualties, the British and Canadians another 25,000. The Germans
had lost 80,000 men. Historian John McManus wrote that "in sum,
the strategic situation in the West was still in the balance at the end of
June. Only an Allied breakout in Normandy, led by the United States
Army, could tilt the balance in favor of the Allies."[1]

The Germans, on the other hand, were equally depressed over their
inability to throw us out. It was stalemate for sure. On July 3, Hitler
learned that when General Keitel had asked the German commander
Field Marshall Von Runstedt what should be done about the inability
of the Wehrmacht to oust the Americans from Normandy, Von Runstedt had instantly replied that they should surrender. Hitler fired him
and replaced him with Field Marshall Von Kluge, which added energy
to the German cause as Von Kluge was determined to refuse the Allies
breakout from Normandy.

July was to become the crucial month of the war in Europe. Behind
the scenes, the British and the Americans had disagreed on the best
strategy to defeat Germany. Churchill had wanted to pursue the Mediterranean campaign and had been, at best, lukewarm about Overlord.
Roosevelt, however, had given in to Stalin's insistence and approved
the invasion of France as agreed in their November 1943 meeting in
Tehran. General Montgomery, Britain's premiere general and the British choice for supreme command, had instead been made commander
of the Allied ground forces, but was now stalled at the city of Caen
which was considered to be the key to any breakout from the Cotentin

peninsula. The capture of Caen had been the objective of the British 3rd Infantry Division on D Day, but now, a month later, Caen was still in German hands. It was the route by which it was hoped tanks and other armored vehicles could escape the hedgerowed peninsula with its soggy ground and make a run for Paris.

Things were not harmonious at the top of the command structure. Sir Arthur Tedder, British Air Chief Marshall, was Deputy Supreme Commander and did not like Montgomery. They'd been friends earlier but had soon fallen out over differing ideas about strategy. Tedder also shared Eisenhower's personal doubts about Montgomery's willingness to be aggressive enough to carry the day at Caen. Montgomery, for his part, was a masterful excuse maker, often changing his plans then later insisting those changes were, in fact, what he'd had in mind all along. The newspapers in England had fastened on "Monty" as the hero of the war in Africa and hence in Normandy also, and played along with Monty's explanations for his failures at Caen. This put public opinion in Britain solidly on Monty's side and meant that Ike had to be careful not to disparage Monty lest he lose his carefully-gained reputation for diplomacy in leading a mixed-nation command team. To relieve or demote Monty would be disastrous public relations-wise. Eisenhower had been chosen for, among other things, his ability to keep the English people behind American leadership of the war effort. Eisenhower decided Montgomery had to remain in command at Caen.

Behind those scenes Eisenhower was faced with frequent conflict with our own General Bradley and some of the other American generals because Monty remained in command in what they believed to be a losing battle, everyone believing that breaking out of the Cotentin Peninsula required victory at Caen. They all felt that Montgomery's style, a so-called "set piece" battle in which every element is carefully in place and all is carefully in readiness arranged to incur a minimum of casualties, would require endless fighting to defeat the Germans. The Americans, more willing to incur those casualties, wanted the British to attack far more aggressively. Later, when General Patton would arrive with his hell-for-leather style, there would be real fireworks. But that was later. Eisenhower's solution was to change the plan for a breakout at Caen and instead use the British forces at Caen as a magnet for the strongest of the German Panzer forces which drew them away from other Allied forces enabling progress in the west, then south toward Saint Lo. It worked in that ten of the twelve German Panzer divisions were defending Caen, thereby weakening the Germans elsewhere.

Had Montgomery taken Caen by now, from that point east it was open country, ideal for armored divisions to operate. It would have been a straight shot for 120 miles to Paris. But that was not to be. Obviously, if we knew that Caen was the key to a successful campaign the Germans knew it too. Whatever else, they had to stop us there. It was time for Eisenhower to force the issue. Winston Churchill later was reported to have said, "Up to July 1944 England had a considerable say in things; after that I was conscious that it was Americans who made all the big decisions."[2] Eisenhower's patience with the seeming stalemate was about at an end.

General Bradley made the decision to keep the pressure on at Caen to hold the Panzer units and to aim for a breakout at Saint Lo. All the roads from the beaches ran to and through Saint Lo and from there it would be possible to move out into open country in Brittany, enabling the Allied Armored divisions to do what they did best, to move in massed formations south through open country and from there east toward Paris. That became the new strategy. However, planning it was one thing; doing it was something else.

General Eisenhower wrote of this period, "Late June was a difficult period for all of us. More than one of our high-ranking visitors began to express the fear that we were stalemated and that those who had prophesied a gloomy fate for Overlord were being proved correct." He made a trip to the front to get a better picture of the overall situation and later wrote: "It was difficult to obtain any real picture of the battle area. One day a few of us visited a forward observation tower located on a hill which took us to a height of almost 100 feet above the surrounding hedgerows. Our vision was so limited that I called the Air Force..." He then ordered an observation plane to take him on a flight over the territory. "Even from the vantage point of an altitude of several thousand feet," he wrote, "there was not much that could be classified as helpful." Again the hedgerow country had stymied the planning for the necessary breakout. Ike concluded this report by recording that "it was dogged 'doughboy' fighting at its worst" and "the battling all along the front involved some of the fiercest and most sanguinary fighting of the war."[3]

The pressure was clearly on to get out of Normandy. A recent reviewer of the campaign bluntly put it this way: "By the beginning of July, the Germans had succeeded in sealing off the Allied lodgment area so effectively that when Bradley began his great offensive to take the key town of Saint Lo, the battle of the hedgerows became what the Allies feared most - a slaughter yard."[4] As historian Robin Neillands described the situation, "There would be no sudden victories in Normandy, no great advances along the front, no early and entirely fortuitous German collapse. This was going to be a grinding battle."[5]

In early July Allied planners were preparing for the crucial battle. General Bradley's breakout plan was to penetrate the German defensive line by capturing La-Haye-du-Puits, a crossroad village south of St. Sauveur-le-Vicomte. He hoped to turn the German flank, forcing them to retreat as far as Coutances. Three divisions of VIII Corps commanded by Major General Troy Middeleton would lead the attack. The 79th Division would attack on the west flank against the Mahlman line, so named after the German general commanding the defense force, with the objective an area called Montgardon Ridge. The 90th Division would attack on the east with the objective of capturing a small village, Beau Coudray. The 82nd Airborne Division in the center, limited because of heavy casualties, was to capture Hills 131 and 95 just north of La-Haye-du-Puits, then stop there. Hopefully, the 79th and 90th would join up around Lessay which would pinch out the 82nd and open the way to Saint Lo.

Overlooking this territory was high ground marked on the maps as Hill 122 in the Mont Castre Forest. Throughout the campaign this hill had been a thorn in the American side as it enabled a clear view of our formations at a great distance. To break out of the hedgerow stalemate necessitated the capture of Hill 122, sometimes referred to as "the eyes of the enemy." The official history of the 90th Infantry division records, "From this observation post the Germans were able to observe almost at will with practically unlimited visibility. Until it was taken every move made by the American divisions was subject to the closest enemy scrutiny." The 90th Division was assigned the task of capturing the hill. Another historian recorded, "By far the toughest initial objective was the 300-foot height of Mont Castre (Hill 122), dominating the Cotentin Plain."

On July 3 we were assembled in a reserve position with the 358th and 359th Regiments scheduled to begin the initial attack, then the 357th to move through the 358th and try to take the hill. We were issued extra ammunition and grenades and had a few hours to rest in preparation.

I wrote a letter to my parents when we heard that the major attack was imminent. I thought there was a strong probability I wouldn't survive the coming battle so I told them in the letter how sorry I was for the ways I felt I had disappointed them, how wonderful they had been to me, how I regretted never actually saying "I love you" to them, but assuring them that I loved them dearly. I then included the letter in another letter to my brother, asking that if I should survive he destroy the letter but if I did not survive, he give it to them. He and I never talked about that letter after the war. I have a suspicion he gave it to them anyway. I hope so. By the time I was finished writing I was crying and had to go off and compose myself before rejoining my friends.

It had begun raining again, drizzling for awhile, then increasing in intensity and we were soon drenched to the skin. Any hope that the Air Corps would assist the attack was now gone. Nor would there be observation planes, which meant our artillery would be firing blindly. None of this boded well for the attack.

In making preparations for the battle for Mont Castre, General Middleton, commander of the VIII Corps, seriously underestimated the strength of the German forces. "Intelligence estimates suggested that the Germans in La Haye were no longer capable of much resistance," read one review of the battle, "and the advance began with a great air of confidence. This soon evaporated; the enemy struck back fiercely, aided by low cloud and heavy rain which curtailed Allied air support for the U.S. divisions."[6] An elite German unit, their 5th Parachute Division, was waiting for what they knew would be an all-out assault on the promontory, an essential objective for us to hold if we were to succeed in capturing Saint Lo.

In the initial stage of the attack we moved into position for the jump-off. We lined up against a hedgerow, our officers assuring us that our unit would be preceded by three Sherman tanks which would follow in behind an artillery barrage. It was July 3. The seemingly endless rain, very heavy at times, had us plodding through mud. "Day after day," wrote Professor McManus, "storms blew in from the sea across the Cotentin Peninsula and all along the American lines, pelting the soldiers making them wet, miserable, and muddy."[7]

The artillery pounded the German lines for awhile, General Bradley having suspended the limitation on use of artillery shells, then the Sherman tanks -- which I could not see but we were told were in place -- began to move forward. Horrendous shelling from both sides followed. When we finally crossed the hedgerows, the three tanks were burning, destroyed. There must have been one of those 64 ton King Tiger tanks in the vicinity with its hellish 88 gun which could cut through a Sherman like a hot knife through butter. In one battle near Caen a single Tiger tank destroyed sixteen Shermans without being seriously damaged itself. Our attack failed. We returned to our former position. Tanks were still of limited use in the hedgerows.

Stopped again. Historian Paul Fussell wrote, "The month of July was profoundly discouraging for the Allies. After more than a month, their ground troops had not broken through the heavy crust confining them to little more than a beachhead in Normandy, and the planned breakout was far behind schedule. The main problem was the landscape of the *bocage* country of Normandy."[8] The whole world was involved in the war in one way or another, yet we who were fighting it couldn't see beyond the next hedgerow most of the time. Burial grounds were jammed, hospitals were full and getting fuller. Young men from the states were flooding into England, then on to France as replacements, yet for a time it must have seemed to the generals that it would all never end. It was probably just as well that men at the front had virtually no idea of the overall situation. At least we more or less assumed we were winning. Thank God the German Luftwaffe had been put out of commission. When it wasn't raining, though it seemed to do so constantly, our planes were at least destroying enemy tanks at a rapid rate, otherwise we might still be in Normandy today.

Also on July 3, badly depleted of men, the 82nd Airborne Division attacked the high ground north of La-Haye-du-Puits and faced stiff resistance. The battle was itself another chapter in their heroic history as they lost hundreds of men but inflicted heavy losses on the Germans. They killed 500 of the enemy and captured nearly 800 of them.

July 4 was memorable for many reasons, for the Germans as well as for us. It was the day of TOT. General Omar Bradley described this in his book *A Solder's Story*. TOT - Time On Target. It was an artilleryman's trick to blow the daylights out of enemy positions. It was too costly to do very often, but when it worked it was devastating. It consisted of having every piece of artillery from the big 240s located a dozen miles behind the lines, through the 155s five or six miles back, the 105s much closer, the cannons, 4.2 inch and 81 millimeter mortars back behind us, and the little 60 millimeter mortars nearby. All of them, calculated to land at the same instant, would fire simultaneously, saturating enemy positions with explosive death.[9]

We crossed a country road and passed two dead Germans, young boys our age. One was splayed out in a wheelbarrow, the other lay between the handles. The man on the ground had apparently tried to rescue a wounded comrade and someone had drilled them both. It was one thing for me to see many dead Germans laid out like so many mannequins, but it bothered me to see a couple kids like that lying dead even though they were Germans, especially since it was obvious one had been trying to save his wounded friend. For some reason I have never been able to erase an occasional remembered vision of those two boys, sightless eyes unseeingly open to the sky. What a waste.

In came the TOT and it was memorable indeed. From the rear we heard the boom of the heavy stuff, then the 105s, then mortars, and the air was filled with the crescendo sound of a dozen freight trains going overhead, then the upheaval of what seemed like half of France. Years later General Bradley reported that the Germans suffered terribly as a result. Histories quoting survivors among the Germans revealed the devastating effect this tactic had on morale. Many a young German boy grew to manhood permanently effected emotionally by the force of that barrage.

The 358th and 359th Regiments preceded us by pushing up the lower slopes of Mont Castre. The Germans were ready. They knew where we were, what route we'd necessarily use, and they had zeroed in artillery with pinpoint accuracy. MG-42 guns were emplaced all across the front each ready to spew 1,500 rounds per minute into the faces of our forces. Anti-tank weapons were carefully placed where they could observe crossroads and the rare open spaces where our tanks could maneuver. One battalion of the 358th was stymied by a small contingent of German self-propelled artillery pieces which slowed their entire attack. The Germans had sewn the surrounding ground with mines, forcing the infantrymen to move slowly. At one point an officer scolded one of his men who was picking his way very carefully for suggesting there were mines in their path. He threatened the man with court martial and told him to get moving, and while the confrontation was taking place a muffled explosion caught their attention. Soon two men came by carrying a third man whose legs were gone, victim of a mine explosion. The officer then unapologetically told the man to carry on in his search for mines. The 359th Regiment lost 600 men, the 358th lost 500 in the effort and failed to get to the top.

Our 357th Regiment was now assigned to replace the sister Regiment 358 and capture the little village of Beau Coudray, then take the heights. The 358th people made one helpful contribution as reported by Major William Falvey, a staff officer, when they captured a German captain and, in the interrogation, found his pay book. It listed his family's names which included those of his wife and four small children. It also contained a photograph of the captain wearing no clothes and happily embraced by a bevy of four prostitutes all sitting around a table in Paris. Major Falvey, unable to extract any helpful information from the man, solemnly informed him that they felt it necessary to send the photo to the address listed in the pay book. The captain suddenly became cooperative and "sang like the proverbial canary." He revealed the locations of several observation posts on the hill which were promptly eliminated by 90th Division artillery.[10]

Hill 122, known as Mont Castre, was some 300 feet high and overlooked the surrounding area for miles, the invasion beaches even visible from the top. Its identifying landmark was a small stone structure built 2,000 years ago by Caesar's legions to repel an angry Gallic enemy. Its capture was crucial to the effort to make any progress toward Saint Lo, and it was obvious that we would be visible to the enemy while scaling the approaches to the summit. To the east it was infested with bushes and brambles, heavy brush, growth which could contain enemy snipers and machine gunners. We could stay to the west side which was fairly clear but would require movement with very little cover. Even those of us not privy to the planning of the attack could see that the effort was going to be extremely costly, our other two regiments having already been stopped with heavy losses.

VIII Corps commander General Joe Collins realized it would be necessary to attack from the marshy area near Carentan. He ordered the newly arrived 83rd Division to attack in support of the stalled attack on Hill 122. On July 4 they attacked. In the beginning there was a light-hearted mood, the new men watching a murderous American artillery barrage of German positions convincing the inexperienced troops that no one could possibly survive such a holocaust. Then they jumped off. The tanks of their supporting 746th Tank Battalion promptly proceeded to run over the division telephone lines, cutting all communications between General Macon, the division commander, and his regimental and battalion commanders. The division floundered. Macon had earlier distinguished himself as a regimental commander but was over his head now. As the division advanced piecemeal they were cut to pieces by the Germans who had survived the artillery barrage, emerged from their holes, and begun the slaughter with 88s and machine guns. Mines added to the toll. Before long the men of the 83rd had to retreat having suffered a horrifying 1,400 casualties. General Collins was furious. He ordered the men of the 83rd to go back again on the 5th of July. Once more they went out, one over-anxious battalion commander quickly killed. Professor John McManus recalls that "the July 5 attack was, in essence, a carbon copy of the day before - more terror, more hopelessness, more gruesome bloodshed, more young men shattered beyond repair or maimed forever."[11] General Collins was furious with General Macon, relieved him of command, withdrew the division and prepared the 4th Infantry Division to take their place. The 83rd had just lost another 750 men. Casualties of more than 2,100 men in two days out of some 8,500 combat men was devastating. The division would have to reorganize and wait for replacements. Before the campaign was over the 83rd would lose another 3,000 men.

Meanwhile, the 79th Division was fighting its way toward La-Haye-du-Puits down the west coast of the Cotentin Peninsula with extraordinary heroism. On July 3 they attacked the German strong point of Hill 121, winning that battle on the 4th of July but at tragic cost. By July 7 they had drawn enemy troops away from us by capturing Montgardon Ridge, at which point they were blindsided by an attack by the 2nd SS Panzer Division and were driven temporarily off the ridge. The Americans counter-attacked, regaining their ground and knocking out four German tanks.

Pfc Bill Thurston, seeing his company blocked by a German machine gun emplacement, single-handedly attacked it head on, firing his M1 rifle killing the enemy gunners, enabling his company to advance and regain the ridge. He was later awarded the Distinguished Service Cross, but the battle had cost the Americans another 1,000 casualties. Nonetheless, the division maintained their attack for three more days losing another 1,000 men. Exhausted from the fighting and drenched by the endless rain which discouraged us as well, they had to halt their attack. La-Haye-du-Puits was still in German control. The Germans were also suffering heavy casualties and were feeding in other available units to fill their ranks.

General Collins realized the 79th Division was no longer battle-worthy and ordered the 4th Division to move through their position and take the lead in the attack. Unfortunately, the 4th had fought in on D Day, then battled through to Cherbourg, and now was called to attack where other divisions had lost thousands of men. They pushed through in an effort to fight to Perrier a few miles to the south. General Raymond Barton pushed his division relentlessly as the fighting raged back and forth. Now their heavy casualties began to increase as more hundreds of young kids soon littered the landscape soaking the Norman ground with their blood. Hundreds of Germans did so as well.

CHAPTER NINE

DESCENT INTO HELL

FINALLY, THE ELEMENTS OF OUR DIVISION'S TANK BATTALION ARRIVED to help us, only to have four of their tanks knocked out. A German tank destroyer was dug in, hidden, able to nail the American tanks as they showed themselves. A Sergeant actually named Rambo managed to destroy one enemy tank before having to leave his own burning tank and dive into a marsh. Five of his tank crew were killed, five more wounded. The other tankers had to retreat. A German panzer grenadier, Helmet Horner, kept a diary of the fighting at the time and wrote "Counter attacked, against U.S. lines near La Haye-du-Puits. My eyes witness the usual picture of devastation as we break through the enemy without much resistance...a machine gun nest with its dead, there a soldier lies who took a splinter while already in retreat. Two U.S. tanks are now smoking ruins on the landscape. A dead American bends out of the turret."[1]

Ideally, tanks would have been essential to infantry combat. Advancing troops could remain partially protected behind them as they approached enemy positions. In the *bocage,* however, it was necessary for a tank to mount a hedgerow exposing its soft underbelly and a well-placed rocket from a *panzerfaust,* a much-improved German copy of our bazooka, would kill the entire crew. The Germans had sewn Teller mines in the hedgerow openings which were the only alternative way from one field to another, so either way, tanks were completely vulnerable. Many days later a Sergeant Culin would rig a cow catcher affair on the front of a tank using metal pieces from the traps built to stop gliders and fashioned them in such a way that a tank could, moving quickly, break through a hedgerow. This proved to be effective, but came much too late for most of the hedgerow campaign.

Private Bob Slaughter told of watching several men follow a Sherman tank as it started through an opening in a hedgerow. "Unexpectedly," he wrote, "the monstrous tracks rolled over a hidden Teller mine. It blew the tracks off the Sherman and killed the occupants. It also blew the men using it for protection to smithereens…it was sickening. After that," Slaughter said, "I kept my distance from road bound tanks."[2]

Despite the heroic efforts of the men of both divisions, the German defenses were carefully and skillfully positioned and progress was slow. Because of the losses suffered by the Germans in fighting the men of our 83rd Division, and the fact that General Raymond Barton was an experienced division commander, the 4th Division made some progress but, like the others, suffered heavy losses. "General Bradley was having no luck piercing the enemy line in western Normandy, indeed, his July offensive was little more than a World War I style bloodbath with hundreds of men being sacrificed for minimal gains."[3] It was into this discouraging situation that our 357th Infantry Regiment was to move against their elite 15th Parachute Regiment.

Back on July 3 we had started at the base of Hill 122, stopped and dug in briefly. I scraped a shallow ditch, then sat waiting. A tiny, bedraggled looking puppy wiggled over to me and licked my hand. I felt sorry for the little fellow who seemed starved for attention. His little tail wagged happily and it was a moment of simple quiet for me. I just sat staring at the heights ahead. Our machine-gun platoon had been transferred over to L Company a few days earlier, and I was amused to call that crowd of potential killers "Love Company." Next to me now as we reclined in the brief, infrequent appearance of the sun for a break was a kid named Doyle Morgan of Love Company. It was the world in microcosm: innocence personified in a tail-wagging, bewildered little puppy, two teenagers sprawled on the ground on a summer day, a momentary quiet amid the maelstrom of battle, and for awhile it was the way things should be. The scene was one of those snapshots of reality we all keep stored in some deep recess of the mind.

It's funny in a way, of all the confused and frantic memories of that shattering day - I remember it now like a video played at triple speed when one presses the pause button and a blurring scene is suddenly clear, frozen in time. So, now, just maybe the terrible day was finally ended.

A heavy barrage of 88 artillery exploded in our midst. I heard the oncoming shriek and managed to flatten myself in my shallow trench. The firing lasted for a minute or so, a chance battery fired by the Germans who had no idea where their shells would land. When it was quiet again I looked over and saw Morgan lying peacefully, partially outside his trench. He was dead, blood flowing down the side of his head, his young boy's face tranquil in death. On the edge of my trench lay the puppy, dead, and for a moment I wanted to cry. It was the death of innocence. There lay Morgan, no older than I. There'd be no college for him now. Somewhere back home his mother may have been fixing an early breakfast, summoning the family to get ready for the day, all of them joining in prayer that their beloved Doyle would be safe. I knew better and I hated everything I was feeling. Then there was that innocent little puppy.

Ed Perry of M Company also was wounded in that barrage along with others of my platoon. I walked away and saw our Sergeant Hasler being carried off on a stretcher, his jaw badly injured by a shell fragment. Now our section sergeant was gone. I ran into platoon sergeant Gregg who said we were low on ammunition and he would be back shortly, as he was heading to the rear for supplies. I wasn't sure whether Gregg was running out on us or whether he really tried to bring up more ammo. I never heard of him again.

I saw two aid men stooping low, scurrying across the road nearby, carrying a stretcher on which lay a blanket-covered man. The blankets were shaking, the man was trembling violently. A case of battle fatigue. I watched as the stretcher bearers headed toward the rear and saw the mottled face of the disabled man whom I remembered, especially because he had once produced a Colt .32 caliber automatic pistol he'd somehow managed to bring with him into combat as a backup weapon.

Much earlier I'd heard another officer remark that of eleven lieutenant replacements in our incoming group, all but two were either dead or wounded. Now one of those two was gone.

We advanced into the small village of Beau Coudray, many of the village homes in flames, roof tiles crackling and popping, dead Germans lying in the middle of the street. Beau Coudray has been described as "a cluster of buildings nestled along a road between grassy meadows at the foot of Mont Castre in the west, and swampland in the east...it offered little room to maneuver." It was, however, a strategically important crossroads necessary for American troops to swing toward the Germans in the effort to encircle their nearby units and, hopefully, move toward Saint Lo.

Lieutenant Harvey signaled us on through the village and out into an adjoining field. Sergeant Brewer and I decided to share a slit trench. Two men would often dig a trench together so that one man could dig while the other was on guard or, as in Brewer's case, overseeing the men. Brewer and I had become friends. I dug, he helped.

I heard a plaintive cry for help as a badly wounded German soldier crawled from under some protective undergrowth and approached me for help. He'd been wounded in the legs and buttocks and held a wallet up to me revealing photos of a woman and a child. Speaking no English, he clearly was pleading for medical aid. I called for Don Cerulli, our medic who yelled back that he was overwhelmed caring for wounded Americans. I hated my own sense of helplessness. I'd won an Eagle Scout badge a hundred years earlier which required some knowledge of first aid and I wanted to help. But what could I do for a man so badly wounded? He needed to be in a hospital. I stared at his face, his anguished fear of never seeing those loved ones again. I still see his face. There was nothing I could do and he soon gave up on me and crawled away. A couple of my friends stood with me and we pondered what we might have done. Our hearts went out to him, he was such a sad-looking man.

Just then there erupted the most devastating artillery barrage we had ever experienced. The ground exploded in an earthquake of bursting heavy shells as I jumped into our hole, grateful that I'd dug deeper than usual. Brewer piled in on top of me and we lay there, pressed together, both of us shaking with something beyond fear, beyond terror. The ground shook and pulsated, I just mentally crawled within myself, went into a state of suspended animation and waited. Shells were pounding in on us, exploding in a deafening crescendo of sound, thousands of shards of jagged steel tearing at the air, pieces of dirt, rocks, torn trees and metal raining down on us. It lasted several minutes but seemed like hours. Finally the barrage ceased. Brewer and I just lay there for a long moment recovering from emotional shock. The terror of those minutes alone was psychically scarring for us all. The landscape had become a moonscape, trees shredded, ground torn open. Leo Buchanan of my squad lay dead. Our other platoon leader, Sergeant Story, lay badly wounded. Hoppy, the little guy who couldn't keep his cartridge belt up without my help, had been wounded. I hoped it was a million-dollar wound and that he would go home and lead a happy life. I never heard of him again.

One foxhole was filled with the trunk of a huge tree blown in two by an exploding shell. It should, by rights, have killed the two men who owned the foxhole but by some godly chance both had been too far from their hole when the shells landed and they'd both dived into someone else's place. Major John Cochran wrote of this barrage that the "shelling was intense, blasting men out of their holes, shattering buildings, blowing up lines of communication...The fighting in that thick undergrowth," he wrote, "will never be forgotten by those of us who went through it." A Sergeant Lutz had panicked, turned and run back toward our lines, and a German shell exploded nearby and killed him. "How any of us survived the intense concentration of artillery fire will never be understood," wrote Cochran.[4] I have no idea how many more dead and wounded lay nearby, men whom I did not know. The Germans had pulled out all the stops trying to blow us off the hill.

"The 90th was dealing with the best German troops and the toughest part of the Mahlman Line," wrote historian John McManus, and "throughout the day the fighting raged between the 90th and its adversaries as both sides attacked and counter attacked."[5] As the Germans began an encircling movement, tanks of our 712th Tank Battalion arrived and were engaged by German Mark V Panther tanks and by their infantry using panzerfausts. Lieutenant Jim Flowers' tank destroyed a German anti-tank gun in a duel, then he led his three accompanying tanks toward a linkup with the 359th Regiment which was renewing the attack. This, however, meant we would be left without tank support, one Sherman having been destroyed as it approached our position.

Whoever was in command of us ordered us to move back into a nearby field where we would set up a more secure defensive position. As we prepared to move someone called out, "what about that wounded Kraut?" I heard someone yell, "shoot him." I was unable to believe anyone could really do that. It was some sort of miracle that he was still alive. Surely, now, he deserved to live. I recall that now with shock, but in the confusion of battle with our own men dying, someone may very well have killed the man. I heard a number of shots but those could have been only the firing at the enemy. To this day I see that man with his pleading arms held toward me and am troubled by the memory of my inability to help him.

We gathered what we could carry and followed Harvey, everyone frantically running to the next field through a wide opening in the hedgerow, Huey and Duey running a lopsided gait as they tried to run with a 150-pound machine gun, including a cartridge belt. I followed bumping along with two metal boxes of machine-gun belts. A long, deep drainage ditch bordered the next field. Some 80 yards long, it was five feet deep, V-shaped from top to bottom, the top opening a good five feet across, narrowing to some two feet at the bottom. We all jumped in. Huey set up our machine gun facing the open field. Our ditch extended vertically, like the leg of a T from the alleyway we'd come through earlier which bordered Beau Coudray. Just offset from the end of our ditch was a barn. My squad was in about the middle of three similar parallel ditches, like the Roman numeral III.

A six-foot-high hedgerow bordered the edge of each ditch and, because we were five feet down in the ditch, we could only see in one direction, the one from which we had just come. Though L company was no more than 80 yards from K company to one side, I Company to the other, we couldn't see each other because of the hedgerows. On the bottom of our ditch a few feet from me lay a dead man, Technical Sergeant John Kemper, fatally wounded as he got to the ditch. We'd have to step over him to move down the line. There were probably some 120 men in our ditch, a few less in the other two because our M Company platoon added to our L Company numbers.

It had begun to rain again. Some paratroopers of the 15th German Parachute Regiment had hidden in basements while we moved quickly through Beau Coudray, then had come out and attacked from our rear while we were pinned down by that hellacious bombardment. Several Krauts had worn American blouses and helmets as we'd passed through town. We didn't know it yet but we were now completely surrounded by German paratroops with some SS officers.

The clanking sound of a tank could be heard by the men in the I Company ditch some eighty yards across from us. Captain John Scott hurriedly called over several of his officers as he realized the tank, a Mark V Panther, was grinding toward them. Second Lieutenants Eulus Scoggin and Don Oliver and First Lieutenant Hugh Talbert joined Scott in a staff meeting, a hurried, probably frantic effort to deal with the tank. They obviously needed a bazooka but apparently in the frantic dash from the area of the artillery barrage no one had brought one. The Panther ground its way closer as I Company men poured machine gun fire against its impervious front. The Germans opened fire, their 50-caliber gun sweeping the edge of the ditch, killing Scoggin, Talbert and Oliver. Only Captain Scott, seriously wounded, survived.

Sergeant Bill Cantwell and Pfc Joe Larvie of our platoon were wounded during the afternoon, along with several other men in the other companies. I began to miss Sergeant Smith of the Tommy Gun. No one seemed to know where he was. Finally, someone pointed to a most impressive foxhole there in the ditch. Smith had spent every moment of his time digging deeper and deeper, then covering the hole with limbs and dirt. It seemed impregnable. He was safe; safe, hiding with his Tommy Gun deep in his hole in the ground. I guess he'd reached his limit. Sadly, Smith apparently just couldn't face the hell of battle.

During the next several hours the Germans crept around our positions while our men fired at anything they saw. That night the Germans set fire to the barn near our ditch, then threw an occasional grenade in to keep the flames high which made enough light that we had to remain concealed as much as possible. Why they didn't just throw the grenades in on us I can't imagine.

Private Leonard Lutjen, a machine gunner in the L Company weapons platoon, saw a group of Germans moving toward us. He placed his light 30-caliber machine gun to spray them but was shot through the face, the bullet exiting under his chin. Members of his squad carried him to a nearby farm building and left him there. For a time he heard American voices, then silence, then German voices. He managed to crawl behind a cabinet, find a blanket and pull it over himself hoping to become invisible. A party of German paratroopers burst into the building and quickly spotted Lutjen. One of the troopers pulled the blanket off him and he fully expected a bayonet to the heart. Instead, the trooper put the blanket back over Lutjen and they then went into another room where they found the bodies of six dead German soldiers. Apparently, the building was also being used as an aid station for the Germans. A German medic walked over to Lutjen and offered him a shot of morphine which he refused, fearing it might be fatal. Later, he was placed in an ambulance and transported to a makeshift hospital in Rennes, where he recovered, was finally rescued, and was later able to relate his strange adventure.

Tankers from our division tank company tried to make their way to us. Jim Flowers, the Lieutenant and commander of the platoon of Sherman tanks, started around Hill 122 and encountered heavy opposition from German tanks and panzerfausts. A shell penetrated his tank, igniting ammunition and blowing off his right foot. He managed to extricate himself and all but one crew member who was killed in the initial attack. Two other Shermans had also been set on fire, and nine of his twenty-man platoon were dead. He and a crewman together with a wounded infantryman saw a German patrol approach and opened fire, Flowers firing two magazines in his Tommy Gun, then he put a tourniquet on his leg as the Germans departed.

Flowers and his gunner were both badly burned and they lay in a ditch as a German patrol passed by, looked at them briefly, then moved on. A German medic wearing a red cross stopped and gave each of them first aid, making sure Flowers' tourniquet wasn't too tight. They asked for water and the German opened his canteen, turned it upside down, showing that he had no water. Then he went on.

The three men, hoping to be rescued, found themselves in a field occupied by some attacking German troops who saw but ignored them. Suddenly an American artillery barrage shredded the field and the air was filled with the cries of wounded Germans. One shell blew off Flowers' good leg below the knee. He sent his gunner who was still able to walk to look for help. The Germans saw the gunner walk by their machine gun but only laughed and let him go. Flowers was rescued and eventually received the Distinguished Service Cross.[6]

We had been out of food and water for more than a day. It rained that night and I used my helmet to capture a small quantity of water in which I swirled a couple halizone tablets for purification purposes. The water was muddy but I drank a few bitter swallows. I dug a slight depression in the side of the ditch, as did most of the others, for protection if grenades were thrown in. The night seemed long but the Germans made little attempt to disturb us. Of course we didn't dare fall asleep.

Morning of July 7 dawned dreary but the rain had stopped and in the distance we could see the remains of one Sherman tank that had been destroyed earlier. Enemy machine-gun fire was coming from the area of the tank, and we decided the Germans were using it as a firing position. Sergeant Brewer thought we'd better do something about it. We had a bazooka with two rounds remaining so I wired one in and John Mowrer fired it. It was a direct hit but nothing happened. I'd forgotten to remove the firing pin. We fired the second round which missed. This was undoubtedly the stupidest thing we could have done. A German Panther was roaming nearby and had already killed or wounded most of the officers of I Company, and we used our last bazooka rocket to fire at a damaged American Sherman tank. I have no idea where Lieutenant Harvey was at the time, probably no more than fifty feet away. Our only excuse was that we still didn't realize the Panther was still out there, though we should have expected one.

Truthfully, I don't think our officers had much idea what to do. The Captain commander of L Company was nowhere to be seen, his First Lieutenant Shaver now in command. Lieutenant Harvey was a nice guy but that didn't count for much now. Our batallion commander was back where the living was safe and easy, and we had no radio communication with anyone. Presumably, our officers didn't know much more than I did about our actual situation, which obviously wasn't much. Though we didn't know it yet the officers of I Company were dead or wounded, and we had no idea what was going on in K Company. Our chances were pretty slim without direction from a senior officer who had access to information of our situation relative to the Germans.

We were pretty certain some Germans were using the destroyed Sherman tank as cover. Someone then came up with a hand grenade and a small blank cartridge designed to be fired in a carbine to launch the grenade from an attachment to the carbine. I loaded the blank, affixed the grenade, pulled the pin, placed the butt of the carbine on the ground, aimed where we thought the Germans were hiding and fired, but the grenade just dropped off the end of the carbine, the handle flipped off and we had four seconds to save ourselves. We all dived into the ditch and the grenade exploded harmlessly. It was our last grenade. That seemed to me to cap the whole situation, incompetence by all of us. I have no idea why the grenade launcher failed.

Our M Company mortars had poured in heavy fire for awhile, but the Germans were too close to us now for that. We didn't have communication with the mortar people so couldn't control their fire. It was later confirmed that our M Company mortars had earlier fired 6,000 rounds, killing or wounding hundreds of Germans, and for a time the artillery of Lieutenant Colonel Ken Reimers' 343rd Artillery Battalion pounded the German positions keeping them at bay, but the battle had become so confused and fluid by July 7 that they had to cease firing for fear of hitting our men.

One sergeant from L Company led several men on a combat patrol. They soon encountered the German lines, were immediately involved in a firefight and reported inflicting ten casualties on the Germans. By then they were near our own lines and went on through instead of returning to our position. Another group tried the same thing but soon returned and reported that the way was now hopelessly blocked.

As the morning of July 7 wore on we became a little bolder. In early afternoon there was a hiatus, as quiet reigned briefly and several of us sat talking about home and our hopes for the future. I think the quiet fooled us into thinking the battle had ended. Actually, Baker Company had been sent to try to relieve us, and the main body of Germans were doing battle with them. I stood outside the ditch and fell into conversation with Jimmy Lynch, an L Company rifleman. I had found an unopened dinner K ration so we sat down together and divided it. It was the cheese ration which I gave to Jimmy. We ate while we discussed our prospects for relief, which we decided were not very good. Jimmy got up, walked away, a distant rifle cracked, Jimmy spun around with a bullet in his chest. I hurried back to the ditch, unable to see where the shot had come from. Another L Company man had also dug a shallow slit trench twenty feet from the main ditch. He too was shot and we could hear the heaving sound his breathing made as he tried to breathe with a chest wound. He soon quit breathing.

We were running out of ammunition. Sergeant Gregg was right, though he never showed up with any new supplies. Maybe it was too late by the time he reached the rear area. Lieutenant Harvey was concerned that we wouldn't have enough to last much longer, and we thought the men of K Company were still positioned along the hedgerow across from us and hoped they might have some to share. I had held the record for the obstacle course in our basic training company at Blanding, mainly because I was able to fly over the eight-foot wall while everyone else got hung up on it, so I took a deep breath, ran eighty yards across the field and leaped over the hedgerow, hoping to find some spare ammunition or food and expecting to find the men of K Company. There was no one there, only several packs which had been tossed aside. Somehow in the night, the men of K Company had managed to slip back to our lines. Why this information wasn't communicated to us being close as we were I never learned. Nor have histories of the action ever explained it. However, they'd lost six men killed and eleven wounded, including two officers killed and one wounded, probably in the earlier artillery barrage, so evacuating those wounded probably was the right thing to do.

I sat down with my back to the hedgerow and wondered where everyone had gone. There was supposed to be a company of infantry there and it began to dawn on me that if K Company was gone, then L Company was now exposed and the Germans must already be moving into the position where I was sitting. I could hear the ripping sound of a "burp gun" (a schmeisser) on the other side of the next hedgerow. I hurriedly opened a couple of the packs and found some D bars but no ammunition. Where the Germans were at that moment I wasn't sure, but I knew they would soon be where I was standing and it had become apparent to me that I'd better get moving if I was to have any chance of getting back to our position without being shot. I took a deep breath, said a little prayer, then dashed back across the eighty yards to our ditch, muttering something like "please God, let me get there without being hit." It felt to me like 800 yards, as though it was taking me minutes to arrive, like I was running through water up to my neck, the feeling that I was the target of a hundred aiming rifles. I made it safely, leaping in to be met by friends who were anxiously waiting for the ammunition which I didn't find. Jim Lynch was lying in the bottom of the ditch, Cerulli doing what he could. I then learned that Dick Harvey, our platoon leader, had just been killed.

We would learn much later that our regimental commander had ordered Baker Company of the second battalion to try to break through to us. They had tried heroically. They still had three lieutenants and nine sergeants. In the course of the next few hours, as they tried to reach us, the three lieutenants and five of the nine sergeants were killed. All told, eighteen men died and thirty-two were wounded, including all four sergeants who remained, and the two Sherman tanks which accompanied them were both driven off.

L Company riflemen kept firing at whatever Germans they managed to see, though an entire regiment was out there we rarely saw anyone. Huey was on our gun and fired several bursts in the direction of the hedgerow where we'd thought K Company was dug in and now knew they were gone. Sergeant Huddock came along and had us break down the next-to-last machine gun belt so we could fill expended M1 clips. We had no more grenades. Then L Company commander First Lieutenant David Shaver was shot and killed, and shortly after that Sergeant Phil Sharp was killed. It was still a matter of us using covering fire, unaimed fire laid down in volume which, while scoring few hits, forces the enemy to keep his head down and affects his morale. It's expensive in ammunition and we were running low, hoping against hope for relief from regiment.

I looked out and saw a German paratrooper moving toward me wearing a camouflaged helmet and holding a machine pistol, not having seen me yet. Behind him were several other Germans wearing squared helmets, some with twigs in them to break up the outline of their helmets against the sky. I ducked down, loudly whispered "here they come," then stood back up, raised my carbine and started firing; the nearest man dropped to the ground, either hit or just ducking. Then my carbine jammed from too much mud. Other Germans crouched low, moved toward us, the machine gun fired, several rifles fired. I saw a flag bearing a red cross move through the grass, a German medic moving toward a wounded German. Huey opened up with his machine gun again, but we stopped him, pointing out that the man was a medic. It didn't matter anyway as Huey was shooting too high, his tracers arching ten feet over the enemy's heads. They were coming from the direction of the town. Some of our riflemen fired, one German went down, then another spun and dropped. I heard the clatter of ammo clips ejecting, then our men quit firing.

Someone yelled that there was a German tank moving toward us, one of those monstrous tanks nearly twice the size of our Shermans, probably the Panther that had shot the I Company officers. Many

Germans were now approaching from in front of us. John Mowrer pulled a plastic-wrapped package from his pocket and produced a clean, ready-to-fire service pistol. Just then someone ordered us to surrender, probably one of the remaining sergeants, maybe Brewer. Lieutenants Harvey and Shaver were dead, there were no other officers around our end of the ditch, we were almost out of ammunition and grenades. A German soldier jumped into our ditch and raised an automatic rifle pointed at us. Paul Casteel whirled around, the two stared at each other for a paralyzing moment, then Casteel shot first and killed the man. A German potato masher grenade landed in our ditch next to me, and as I dropped into my shallow depression it exploded and did no damage, but we all knew a rain of grenades would soon follow.

With my carbine being jammed, that was it for me. Several men tossed empty weapons out. Mowrer argued, saying he was ready to fight on with his pistol. I told him he was nuts, that if that tank were to pull up to the end of our ditch it could execute all of us with one long burst of its 50-caliber machine gun. The thought flashed through my mind that there was swaggering, Tommy Gun toting Sergeant Smith hiding down in his specially deep foxhole while quiet, unpretentious John Mowrer was ready to take on an entire enemy parachute regiment with a 45-caliber pistol. Anyway, John saw that I was right, so he agreed, dropped the pistol in the mud and kicked more mud over it so no German would get a souvenir, then we threw our weapons out and yelled "surrender, surrender." We were surrounded, hopelessly outnumbered, almost out of ammunition, our supporting tanks destroyed, our battalion commander safely back in his command post, a German tank rumbling toward us, our junior officers dead. We had no choice.

One historian, departing from his coldly factual report of the battle describing the German effort in this engagement, wrote "They gave the 90th Division one hell of a beating." He then added this: "...whatever was wrong with the 90th Division, it was not lack of courage."[7]

Sadly, later records revealed that our regimental commander had ordered the battalion commander to send yet another company to try to rescue L Company, and to send a patrol to us to inform us of its arrival. On the official 357th regimental morning report of July 8 was included this entry: "About two hours after daylight it was found that the attack ordered for daylight had never jumped off and that the patrol had not been sent through to contact Company L as ordered. Lt. Colonel Kilday was relieved of command." Colonel Barth, regimental commander, had been suspicious of Kilday for some time, later stating that an officer had told him that Kilday spent a lot of time sitting around doing nothing. He wrote that "I relieved Colonel Kilday realizing that his mental and physical condition was such as to make further command on his part impossible."[8] It was probably just as well the effort wasn't made. B Company had already taken terrible losses and to send another company of men into that meat grinder may very well have been a case of throwing good money after bad. As for Kilday, he was another in a line of successful peacetime officers who couldn't lead in combat. We could only wonder what the outcome might have been had we had a courageous batallion commander with us.

The bocage consists of small, irregularly shaped fields, measuring only about 200 by 400 meters, enclosed by ancient, overgrown hedges that grow from earthen mounds flanked by drainage ditches. The hedgerows grow up to 15 feet high, limiting visibility to one field at a time, and they are impenetrably dense — even for tanks. They form a thousand square miles of tough patchwork terrain, connected by a network of dirt roads sunken far below field level by centuries of use. The towering hedges shade these lanes, further decreasing visibility. Using the ideal camouflage and concealment of the bocage to best advantage, the Germans dispersed small, heavily armed antipersonnel and antitank units through it, dug in at the bases of the hedgerows and nearly invisible to the oncoming Americans. In these ideal defensive positions, small German units sometimes repulsed attacking forces five times as large.

(Photo and text from www.skylighters.org)

Another shot of the endless fields bordered by hedgerows. As soon as the troops fought through one, another lay ahead with the enemy ready behind them.

The infamous "Hill 122"

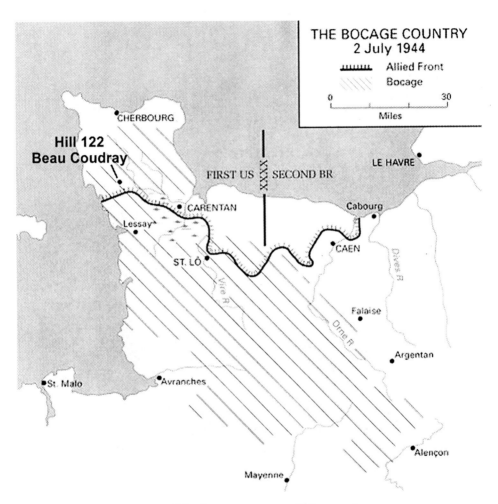

Map of the bocage country of Normandy.

(Map courtesy of www.skylighters.org)

Carver's wartime pals George Schickler (on left)
and Jim Haigh (on right).

The French resort town of Etretat ("a swell little town" as Carver calls it) where he spent a brief time during his recuperation.

The building next door to where Carver stayed in Etretat.

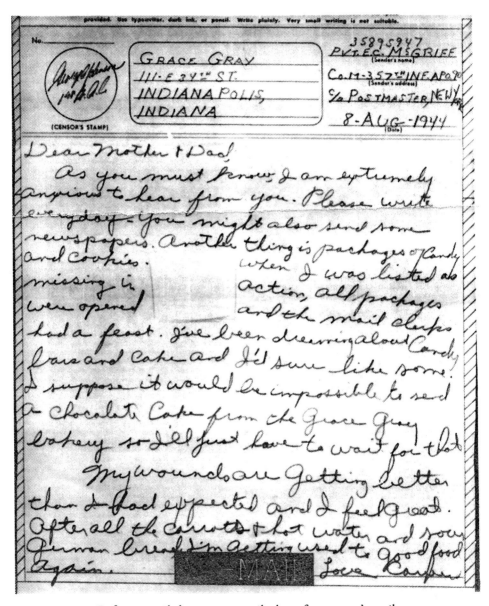

Before e-mail there was v-mail, short for veteran's mail.
This v-mail from Carver to his parents is dated August 8, 1944.

From a 1947 reunion. Pictured left to right:
Bruce Wiegel, Jimmy Haigh, George Schickler and Carver McGriff.

Aged by war. Carver after fighting in Normandy, 1945.

Fifty-five years later: Carver in 1999 visiting the site of the fighting
of the 90th Infantry Division in Normandy.

CHAPTER TEN

CAPTIVITY

WE STOOD UP, HANDS IN THE AIR, AND WERE QUICKLY SURROUNDED by a crowd of German paratroopers, several with burp guns pointed at us. This was always a crisis moment for anyone being captured. It only required one angry Nazi to take a notion to begin shooting and others could join in. Many of their men were lying out there too. I knew enough not to make eye contact which could be interpreted as defiance.

They made three of our men carry the body of the trooper Casteel had shot, and I was surprised they paid no special attention to Casteel, probably not knowing who had shot their friend. We were herded a short distance and were then able to watch across the next field where the men of Item Company were battling just as we had done. I watched as though it were a movie as one of the Germans stepped to the edge of the other ditch and emptied his rifle at them. When those men saw us standing with our hands in the air, they, also nearly out of ammunition and most of their officers dead or wounded, yelled "surrender" and dutifully joined us. We were ordered to form a straggling marching formation and were marched back into the main street of Beau Coudray where we were lined up and the Germans began to search us. We left quite a number of dead and wounded out on the field of battle, and I have never learned of their fates.

Then all hell broke loose. Someone had ordered artillery fire on the town. No one knows for sure to this day whether the Germans were firing at attacking Americans who were trying to rescue us, or whether one of our officers had somehow found a way to call down artillery on the town before being killed. In any event, a devastating barrage began exploding in our midst, wounding and killing Germans and Americans alike. I turned and headed across the street, glancing to my left and saw George Waggett, a man I knew from Love Company, double over as he was hit. I was running directly toward a German paratrooper whose machine pistol was trained on us, he looking confused, probably wanting to run for cover as we were doing. Then suddenly, I saw the machine pistol fly from his hands and he pitched over backward.

The world went blank. I felt a brief sensation of floating in air, my next conscious awareness that of lying flat in the middle of the street, shells exploding around me. I tried to get up but could barely move. I felt no pain (that would begin later), only numbness, and I began calling for help. It happened there were some Mexican American soldiers in our company whom I did not like, one in particular. They refused to be friendly with the rest of us, or so we thought, preferring to keep to themselves, singing sad Spanish songs, often talking among themselves in a language we didn't understand. They were noisy and stayed up at night; all in all they came from a culture I found very strange. Of course, this many years later, I know they were homesick. To be quite honest, I had rejected them as being somehow inferior to the rest of us though I had never learned that kind of prejudice at home.

As I lay there in that street, half paralyzed, calling for help, I felt myself being picked up gently like a baby in a mother's arms. I looked up into the face of the man saving me. He was the leader of that group of Mexicans, the man I didn't like, the man I treated like an outcast. He carried me to relative safety alongside a nearby building, then went back out into the midst of the exploding shells for someone else to save. I learned that day a lesson I would not forget. It defines for me a form of love that has nothing to do with sentiment and valentines. It's the kind one reads about in the Bible, something you do for the undeserving. I was the undeserving one. It also was a case of a man deserving a medal he would never receive. It was also a lesson for me about prejudice, one I would never forget.

Someone dragged Earl Brewer next to me. The shell which had hit me in the legs and one arm had torn his chest open. My friend and Sergeant looked up at me pleadingly. I was in shock and could only stare at Earl, only half comprehending what was happening. He tried to say something, then his eyes rolled back and he died. He and I had stood side by side moments before. We'd been comrades for a month, eating together, having long talks together, facing the most significant month of our lives together. Now I watched his face as he died. I knew I should cry but I couldn't. I didn't feel anything. It would have to wait. Sergeant Jackson, who led the other section, was next. They laid him beside Brewer. He too breathed heavily for a moment, looked at me questioningly, then was dead. The street was littered with dead of both nations.

I have thought of Earl many times in recent years. We shared the most significant, traumatic month of our lives, enduring countless artillery barrages, struggling against the sheer misery of life on the battlefield, and then our final battle, the artillery falling among us. Earl and I were side by side until that fateful instant in which the shards of steel hit me in the legs and Earl in the chest. Just like that, I to survive the Great Adventure and live a long and productive life, Earl to die. This raised for me a theological issue I have never fully resolved. I never cried for Earl until the Sunday morning following 9/11. That morning I was presiding over a worship service in a suburban church. Suddenly, a flood of grief caught me by surprise, all for Earl Brewer. I couldn't tell whether it was for Earl alone or whether Earl was a symbol of all those innocents who died in the World Trade Center, or for all the men who'd been my friends in France and never came home. I had to stop for a moment to get control of those suddenly volcanic emotions. It required all the emotional control I could muster to keep from sobbing in long-repressed grief.

Since that time I have observed other men who served in World War II. We all find that long-buried emotions often come flooding forth as we look back at what we have had and what those old friends lost. Many people have visited the cemeteries at places like Omaha Beach and Bastogne, and felt this very experience. When we see elderly veterans interviewed on television documentaries, they frequently appear suddenly overcome with grief at ancient memories. It's all buried in there, triggered to the surface when least expected. We discover as I did that all of those days of battle and the costs they incurred are forever with us, on rare occasions flaring up when we are least ready.

Finally, things grew quiet. Someone carried me into the nearest building, a small café, and laid me on the table nearest the window. My legs began to hurt. I stared at them and saw gaping wounds in one leg, small penetration wounds in the other, and my arm was hurting. Soon, the room was full of groaning wounded Americans. Don Cerulli, our medic, had escaped injury but had been allowed to remain with us though he was able to do little but examine the room for anyone bleeding too much to live. Sergeant Roy Hidecker died there that night. Sergeant Larson and an old friend of mine from Blanding, Jesse McKinney, were there among the wounded, as was sergeant Elbert Hallman.

A German sergeant soon came in and stood over me. Now we would begin to learn our fate. I was surprised to see compassion in his eyes. I asked for water and he handed me his canteen which was full of hard cider. I drank my fill and, having little experience with alcohol, was soon roaring drunk. The German sergeant waited patiently, smiled, gently retrieved his nearly-empty canteen, and departed. After awhile I fell asleep, waking in the early night darkness believing I was bleeding to death, and I started complaining. Don Cerulli examined me, assured me I was not bleeding to death and I soon fell back asleep. When I awoke it was pitch dark, the room heavy with the sweat of wounded men. Artillery was still exploding nearby and I decided I should try to escape. Since I couldn't walk I concocted the idea of sliding along on my backside in the direction of our lines. I guess I was still inebriated. I soon fell asleep and when I awoke, it was daylight.

The official 90th Division history written from records of the time and interviews of veterans who took part, described the events of those two days this way. "July 6 and action flared to new heights of violence. Elements of the first battalion, 357th, forced their way into Beau Coudray, later to be reinforced by the 3rd Battalion. But this was the hinge of the German line, and the Boche (Germans) entertained no thought of allowing it to fall. Into the breach came the 15th German Parachute

Regiment attacking their outnumbered opponents (three companies) with hitherto unequaled ferocity. One company was forced back out of the town. Two remained to face the onslaught and found themselves cut off.

"The two companies of the 3rd Battalion fought stubbornly against the mounting, hopeless odds. Those few who escaped the trap and made their way to friendly lines told harrowing tales of the 'Lost Battalion's' heroic stand. Every effort was made to relieve the isolated defenders of Beau Coudray, but every effort was hurled back with heavy losses. In one such attempt every officer and non-commissioned officer in the attacking force was killed or wounded. On the evening of the 7th the last word came from Beau Coudray. The gallant defenders, weakened and ravaged by the most intense fire, exposed to continuous armored blows, hemmed in on every side, had been run over. The Mahlman Line, though threatened, remained intact." [1]

Historian John McManus wrote, "The very name Mont Castre soon equated with blood, horror, and exhaustion." In our three-day battle our three companies B, L and I with some 400 men when the battle began, lost a total of 74 dead, 144 wounded, plus over a 150 listed as missing in action, most of them prisoners of war, some of them also probably walking wounded. Two days later a group of 35 enlisted men and one wounded officer, men of I and L companies, who had managed to elude the attacking Germans and found their way into the swampy fields, were rescued by searching Americans. The total number of American casualties suffered by the several units involved in the battle for Hill 122 numbered more than 8,000. British historian Max Hastings later wrote, "Hill 122 joined a host of other Norman map references among the American army's battle honors."[2]

We later learned that Colonel Barth tried yet another attack on Beau Coudray reaching the edge of the town, and again he suffered heavy casualties. The battalion then withdrew long enough to bring in new replacements which, of course, meant they were less experienced as most of the new men were raw recruits, most of them teenagers. The new commander, Major Hamilton having replaced the failing Lieutenant Colonel Kilday, quickly reorganized and again attacked Beau

Coudray, this time capturing the town and going on through to Le Plessis. As of July 12 the 90th Division had lost 2,000 men in the fighting for Hill 122. As McManus wrote in his history of the engagement, "To be sure the division still had problems but it also...was dealing with the toughest enemy resistance (probably about 5,600 top-quality German troops). Weak commanders like Kilday were being weeded out. Slowly, but surely, the 90th was getting better."[3]

Looking back, I find it amazing that in that room in that small café in Beau Coudray filled with men whose wounds were sufficiently serious that none could walk away, there was hardly a sound throughout the night. Each man, alone with his thoughts and his pain, endured through 'til dawn. There was no medical care beyond tourniquets. The floor was awash with blood, the outpouring of some twenty-five men. I don't know how many died that night, silently. No one cried out (except for my own brief cries, thanks to my captor's generous gift of hard cider), no one complained. We waited to see what the day would bring.

Out on the street of Beau Coudray the next morning some of the dead remained where they had fallen. There were still several bodies there and I knew at least some of my other friends must be among them. I was surprised at the professionalism of our enemy who treated us all with civility. They could easily have been angry at the slaughter but probably were as unsure as we where the shells had come from. After a time a large bus with the seats removed pulled up in front of our shop and several of us were loaded into it, lying on the floor on straw-filled mattresses. By now my wounds were very painful and the unevenness of the mattress made them worse. I vowed not to show my pain, so grimly endured as the bus rumbled off, bumping over rutted country roads, heading to the city of Mortain. We all knew American planes strafed any vehicles on the road and we didn't know whether there was a red cross on top of our bus or not. Besides, some pilots assumed Red Cross vehicles were really carrying ammunition and blew them up anyway. It wasn't a pleasant ride but proved uneventful.

The bus finally pulled into the parking lot of the main hospital in Mortain. I was carried out, placed on a stretcher, then carried into the large parking lot which was nearly full of wounded men on stretchers. Most of them were German. They laid me beside a young German paratrooper whose arm was badly wounded. I assumed he was in the same battle, probably the same artillery barrage as I. We looked at each other for a time, then both of us smiled. It seemed very strange, two former enemies now reduced to the status of wounded patient and discovering we had something in common. We were fighting men who had served honorably, now were off the field. Though neither of us spoke the other's language, we spoke with our eyes the words of a strange kind of brotherhood. I thought how irrational that this young guy who could have been my classmate, my friend down the street, was lying there because I wanted to kill him and he had wanted to kill me. I wondered what kind of world we could ever construct as long as such mindless hatred divided nations. But we two, we were no longer enemies. It would be a long time before we'd live normal lives again, but maybe when we did we could become friends. How much better our world would have been if we'd found a way to become friends much earlier.

Maybe that sounds too easy. What about retribution? What about punishment for wrongs? Morality is a meaningless term if there are no consequences for doing wrong. The Hitlers and his kind must suffer the consequences of their crimes, but while the threat of punishment may stop the next evil man because he's afraid of the consequences of doing what he would otherwise do, that leaves him still evil. I could forgive that man next to me, but what's to keep it from happening again next time? Something has to change, something inside us. It was as though that man in that stretcher next to me and I were the nations in microcosm, both damaged, both so recently filled with animosity toward each other for reasons neither of us truly understood. What changes us? I think for me it was the realization of the other man's pain, and the awful pointlessness of our plight. But I have since wondered what he may really have felt as he looked at me. Did he feel the same? Did he forgive me?

I recall hearing German Admiral Martin Niemoeller speak at a church in Evanston, Illinois in 1959. He was one of Germany's World

War I heroes, a submarine commander in that war, who defied Hitler and was placed in Dachau concentration camp outside Munich from 1937 to 1945, in a cell from which he could see his countrymen die on a gallows for opposing Hitler. He said to us that since embracing the Christian faith he realized that to keep his heart filled with raging hatred offered no hope for anyone. Only forgiveness could do that. He became an honored hero of World War II, not as a fighting man but as an example of forgiving love, his country's only hope.

But we live in a world where many people don't forgive. We live by armed standoffs, finding our safety in our ability to inflict damage on the other. I think that day I only began to realize that without some power which can transcend our differences, we have little hope. I later recognized that remarkable feeling I sensed that day as I looked at the wounded man next to me as the gift of love. But where did it come from? It would take me years to give it a name, and the name was God. But as I matured, I further realized that the love that changes is not just something you feel. The love the Bible means when using the Greek word "agape" is something you do, not just something you feel. It's a verb. You act it out, then you begin to feel it. You do what love dictates, you treat with kindness and forbearance, with sacrifice for the good of the other even when you don't feel like it and, in time, you begin to feel love. Then, remarkably, the people around you begin to change. That's how it works. That's the only way it works. And one day, you forgive. That's the forgiveness which changes and overcomes evil. How insane a world it was, that more than 1,500 American boys and even more German boys died to exchange ownership of an obscure hill in a far country where none of us lived, a hill purchased at such a terrible price and to which we who survived would probably never return. All for no worthy purpose.

Dietrich Bonhoeffer, the German clergyman-theologian who returned to Germany from a comfortable position in Union Theological Seminary in New York to lead a Christian resistance to Hitler, was finally placed in the concentration camp at Flossenburg. It's said his jailers were constantly rotated because of his kindness to them, because he forgave them for what they had done to him. So they changed and could no longer abuse him. A German, no less, teaching his own people the one route to peace and happiness. When he was summoned to be hanged on April 9, 1945, he said to a fellow prisoner "When God calls a man he bids him come and die." He meant not only to die in the literal sense as he did a few minutes later, but to die in the sense of giving up our dislikes and hatreds, to die to driving self interests, replacing them with the same love that no one can resist just as those jailers could not resist Bonhoeffer. I would one day tumble to the fact that it's when we suffer and die to self in the practice of *those* things that people can be changed the way God wants. It's true for individuals. It's just as true for nations. But it must begin with one person who forgives the offender, an act which makes no sense apart from love, a person who grasps the irony in the words of Jesus who warned that when we forgive our enemies we find that God has forgiven us, a promise familiar to anyone who knows the Lord's Prayer.

I often hear people today pontificate about international relationships, and I remember that it's one thing to preach about acceptance and forgiveness, but when you're there, in the maelstrom of hatred and violence, "forgiveness" becomes more than a theological nicety. It is the one hope for all humanity, and to do it there, on the scene of battle, is the hardest thing of all. I doubt it can be done without being prompted and sustained by a power no person possesses within himself. To love someone who tried to kill you, personally, face to face, is a miracle and those only come from God.

Today our world is torn by nations whose guiding sentiment is hatred for their historical enemies. I look back to my many friends in the course of battle, captivity and hospitalization, and cannot recall a single instance of anyone spouting hatred for the Germans as individuals. We fought for the right, but we didn't carry hatred in our hearts, and so there was hope. The writer of the proverb in the tenth chapter of that book, the 12th verse, wrote: "Hatred stirs up strife, but love covers all offenses." Saint John wrote: "He who says he is in the light but hates his brother is in the darkness still." While Germany, Italy and Japan have become our friends, albeit like family, we have our differences. But love prevailed in 1945 when Americans chose to help rebuild those nations, to enter into trade with them, lend them money for reconstruction, encourage them to become our friends. The tragedy of the human spirit seems to be our inability to bring this harmony about until after one side or the other has been destroyed. One of my dearest friends, a man who suffered permanent damage to his leg while serving with the 90th Infantry Division in the Huertgen Forest, moved to Germany after the war and lived there for a year in order to understand the German spirit. He's a very devout Christian, and I asked him not long ago why he did that. He said, "So I could help the world find peace." He since has devoted his life to that cause. It's the only way, and it's the American way, the Judeo-Christian way. Jesus said it so clearly: "You have heard that it was said, 'You shall love your neighbor and hate your enemy.' But I say to you, love your enemies and pray for those who persecute you..." One wonders when our world's peoples will ever learn that eternal truth. Whether those of us who profess this noble ethic will finally, as a nation, live it out in our dealings with a Muslim world, so many of its adherents seeming to subscribe to an ethic of religiously-grounded hatred, we are yet to learn. I'm convinced that one day, if our hope for humanity is ever to reach fruition, it will be that somehow love finds a way to prevail. So long as we hate our enemies, whatever their faiths, we will continue to repeat the tragedy of World War II in new and ever-more devastating forms. And what hope is there for us?

Dr. Helmut Thielicke, also a German who endured and resisted the Nazis, said of Jesus as He looked out upon the people gathered at his crucifixion: "And even though he knows that the rich young ruler is going to turn on his heel in a moment and hurriedly leave his presence, that the young man may even join His enemies, or the despairing hosts of the indifferent, He still gazes upon him and loves him." And thus, He gazes upon us as well, loving us, and waits for us to look the same way upon our enemies.

After an hour or so two German orderlies picked up my stretcher - I couldn't and still don't understand why they took me and left their own man still untended - and carried me into a room along the side of the hospital. I have to say there were some moments during which I worried about what, exactly, was about to happen to me. I saw several scalpels on the table next to the cot on which I was placed. I was a bit scared, but decided to try not to show it. There really wasn't much I could do anyway but grit my teeth and see it through. I needn't have worried. A German medical man used some form of X-Ray machine to determine my wounds. There were several large pieces of shell fragment in my left leg, so they carefully injected some local anesthetic around the wounds, then swiftly, expertly, cut out several pieces of metal, then bandaged me without using stitches which I later learned was a not-uncommon medical practice with them. My treatment had been as gentle as I might have expected from our own people. I was carried outside again where we were briefly searched. I was wearing a hideaway money belt but it held nothing but a map of France, so when a German came by I declared it but he briefly checked the pocket, then moved on leaving the map. I wore a watch and a silver bracelet my parents had given me but they ignored those also, much to my surprise. Our treatment had been humane.

Looking back, I see kindness and humanity in the way I was treated. I wonder, however, how I would have been treated had I been Jewish, or had I been a Russian, or a gypsy. Still, I share the instinctive Christian tendency to look for the best in others, and I reflect on the German medic who stopped to care for Lieutenant Flowers, and the gunners who let his wounded comrade go for help, and the Sergeant who gave me the cider, and the doctors who cared for me even before caring for their own man lying next to me. Even those Germans who, doing battle with us, allowed Private Lutjen to live and be hospitalized. Later, I would hear other stories from men I'd meet in the hospital, of kindnesses by the Germans. Despite the unthinkable horrors perpetrated by Germans against the innocents, I have to believe there was still decency to be found among the Nazis. I have to believe that God was urgently seeking entrance to German hearts and was having some success. From German blood came Hitler and Goerring and all the criminals of the Naziism. But too from that same blood came Niemoeller, and Bonhoeffer, and Thielicke. For me it is a mystery still concealed in God's great plan for human destiny. I cannot explain the holocaust nor an Evil which prompted it in a loving creation. I can, however, perceive the evidence of His love moving within that destiny. That I can choose to trust.

We were carried into the hospital and put in a bed. Along came the dashing Sergeant Smith (which by the way was not his real name) who had learned that I had a map of France and grandly informed me that he planned to escape and asked if he could have the map since I wouldn't be going anywhere anytime soon. I gave it to him. I also wondered how he contrived to be in the hospital rather than a prisoner of war cage since he appeared to me to be uninjured.

I suppose I should be more charitable toward "Smith." There is no way to predict how a person will react under fire. No matter how well-trained, how macho, how enthusiastic a soldier may feel in preparation, when the bullets fly and the explosions begin to take their toll, all bets are off. Every man is suddenly tested in a way that is unique. I have no doubt Smith was sincerely anxious to prove himself in battle, had genuinely expected to lead his men heroically, but when it all happened, his fear overwhelmed all the rest and he was too disabled by that fear to function like he thought he would. Calling a man a coward is too easy. Those of us who have not been so overwhelmed cannot fairly judge. Smith should have been assigned to a training unit preparing others for combat. He was obviously good at that, having been promoted to sergeant, but some deep emotional reality simply prevented him from being quite what he had hoped to be as a warrior. I wish I knew what finally happened to him.

There are other forms of courage. Men who flinched in battle have gone on to become heroic men (and women) of moral courage and have led the way to fiery battles for human rights and justice. I have learned not to judge a person because he or she may not measure up to some particular standard without my knowing him far better than I knew those men. There are people who possess all the other highest qualities of personal character who simply are not equipped emotionally to succeed in wartime battle. There is physical courage. There is also moral courage.

An hour later we were carried out again and placed once more on our bus, which headed to the city of Rennes, the capital of Brittany. We arrived in the parking lot of a four-story former girl's school which had been converted to a makeshift hospital. It already held several hundred patients, mostly paratroopers who'd jumped on D Day, and soldiers who had landed on one of the British beaches, many of the patients being English. We were temporarily housed in a Quonset-type hut on the edge of the grounds. I was placed on a lumpy straw-filled mattress cover which hurt like hell now that my wounds had really become painful. We all received medical care but there were no pain killers to be had.

Across from me was a man who'd been blinded, another who'd been wounded in both legs by one bullet. To my right was a young Hispanic kid who had apparently received some surgery and was only just coming out of the anesthetic. He began a rambling speech in which he confessed to killing his girlfriend. He rambled sufficiently that we couldn't be absolutely sure without doubt that he said that so we passed it by. I recognized him as an L Company rifleman.

Later in the day I was placed back on a stretcher and carried up to the second floor of the main building and placed in a cot, one of some twenty in a ward. Mine was the first in line, nearest the door, which had the advantage of letting me have the risk of a snorer on one side only. Across the room from me was Sergeant Smith, Smitty to me, not the one from my outfit, a paratrooper. We soon became friends. He had a full beard and had jumped with the 82nd Airborne. These long years later I wonder at the fact that by some unspoken set of rules we did not discuss our experiences with each other. I became fairly good friends with Smitty, but know nothing else about him, not even his first name.

Another patient nearby was an Englishman, closer to thirty I'd say, who had one leg suspended in air and there was a hole in his foot you could see through. He had other injuries as well and never said a word within my hearing as long as we were there. Still another man nearby was a very officious English Sergeant Major who seemed mainly put-out at having to share space with mere Americans. Later in the day they carried in a man I recognized as being from my platoon but I couldn't remember his name. They put him in another room.

Medical care was provided by American medics who'd been captured, all of them enlisted men, not doctors, and by a medical team comprised of a young French doctor and his wife assistant. There were also some French nurses, the head of their group and the prettiest known to us as "Big Bertha." They all visited me, checked my wounds, did nothing, went on. I would only see them one other time during my imprisonment, but since I didn't develop any infection, and since I slowly began to heal, I assume the German doctor had done what was necessary. It later became apparent to me that the French medical people were pretending to play along with the Germans but were actually certifying everyone as requiring continuing treatment. There was a POW camp nearby and anyone who was obviously able to be up and around was soon sent there. Therefore, a growing number of men were pretending to be worse than they were, and the French went along. Apparently, as the front was moving, other medical facilities must have been receiving the more recent captive wounded as the flow into our hospital seemed to have almost stopped.

In recent years I have wondered at the memory of the man from my platoon whom I saw briefly as he was carried into another room in the hospital. I never went to talk to him. We had just shared the most traumatic experience of our lives and could have informed each other of some of the details, yet I never went to speak with him nor did he ever come to see me, though I could tell he recognized me as he passed. It was as though we really didn't want to talk about what had happened, maybe the very dynamic which characterized so many of us through the years. Let it go. I find that very strange.

Our room looked out on the main square of the city, and old timers pointed out a building cater-corner from ours and identified it as Gestapo headquarters for the district. This led to some interesting times watching Krauts go in and out. There was a small tree-lined park in the center of the square, flowers in tiny gardens, several benches for passing pedestrians, the outer perimeter of the square occupied by mostly three-storied, mansard-roofed homes. The peaceful ambiance belied our current inner turmoil as we talked among ourselves about our prospects for the future. Should the Normandy stalemate last much longer some of us would be shipped off to Germany to make room for newly-arrived casualties. I found it painful to walk but I also malingered shamelessly, hoping that whoever was in charge would continue to number me among the serious cases. I hadn't yet tumbled to the French medical people's collaboration.

It was a strange feeling to watch the street from our barbed-wire enclosed imprisonment, as civilians strolled by on their way to work, mothers pushed strollers. Children played on their ways home from school. We all discussed ways to escape, but I realized that with my legs damaged as they were escape was out of the question for me. We also realized our lot was surely better than that of the men who weren't wounded and now were languishing in prison camps. I wondered whether Huey and Duey and Mowrer and Paul Casteel had survived, and whether Jimmy Lynch was still alive.

The commander of the hospital was a Wehrmacht major, and a sergeant known to us as "Little Hitler" patrolled the building. He visited each ward every night and tried to require that patients lie at attention when he passed through but we all made fun of him behind his back. Despite wounds the men housed there were not easily intimidated by some self-important German whose only job seemed to be that of trying to scare injured men. We didn't scare and he never pressed the point with us. I understood that one or two of the paratroopers were hatching plans to disable German staff members if our troops got close, which boded ill for Little Hitler. German officers tended to treat us as they did their own people who were far more responsive to discipline than we. We must have been very frustrating for them.

The city of Rennes was not much. Located on the mouth of the Loire River in lower Brittany, one early description called it the "world's least attractive town." It is the capital of Brittany and was a strategically-located objective militarily as a hub for road and railroad communications. It was burned twice in previous wars and, as the article about the town concluded, it was "a straggling city that burned down twice and was rebuilt in worse taste each time."

Our main problem was hunger. After the last few days in which I'd had virtually nothing to eat but half a K Ration with Jimmy Lynch and one D bar I'd found in the deserted pack. I was ravenous. The food we received proved to be of little help. Captain Franklyn Johnson, a patient on the top floor reserved for officers, wrote a book about our hospital, Stalag 221 to the Germans, and described the food this way: "Most of what we eat is food for cattle at home. Breakfast is a cup of warm water with the smell of tea over it, or with luck even a few tea leaves floating in it. Unfortunately the attendants ladle this beverage out to us in small shallow receptacles of aluminum whose heat and unwieldy shape make us spill a great deal of our tiny breakfast... Dinner and supper are simple: black cabbage, rotten potatoes, and an occasional bit of horse meat made into a heavy stew. Every evening they issue each man a quarter loaf of hard black bread."[4]

Most of us decided that bread, which was only a couple inches square, was made of part sawdust. Many Germans were eating about as we were but we didn't know that then.

The Germans admitted there were many Red Cross parcels waiting in Paris but claimed there was no way they could be delivered here, and we never saw them. We whiled our time away concocting menus of the meals we would eat when we were freed, and I imagined all sorts of luscious hamburgers and pieces of apple pie. I dreamed of mother's wonderful meals and wondered if Mother and Dad knew where I was (they did not).

One night a newcomer was placed in the bed next to me which had been emptied by a man who had begun to recover. The new man was large, of foreign extraction though an American GI. His leg was terribly injured. I tried to get acquainted but he barely spoke and obviously he was only partially conscious. I think his leg was too badly damaged for the medical staff to repair. He had no appetite and the second evening he was there he offered me his meager supper and convinced me it would go to waste if I refused, so I ate it hungrily. That night the man died. I felt terrible.

A new friend, Ed Kochak, an Infantryman who was well enough to work in the kitchen, brought me two eggs one day. He'd swiped them and was now sharing with a couple of us. I was impressed as he was as hungry as I but he looked pleased at his generosity and had other eggs for himself. I decided I couldn't allow myself to eat both eggs while living among men who were starving. I had reached the point where I could limp short distances, so I made my way to the English soldier with the injured foot and gave him one of the eggs. He said nothing but his eyes said thanks. I was glad I'd done it.

We also had to live with the thought of German action if the fighting should pass our way. While our treatment had been in accord with the Geneva Convention so far, we also had begun to hear rumors of German atrocities. Would they allow us to be recaptured? Would they allow us to starve, which we were close to doing anyway? The German Commandant had warned that if the Allies got close we'd all be shipped back to Germany. We knew what happened to vehicles on the highways, and to trains on the rail lines, so the odds of surviving a journey to Germany were slim to none.

CHAPTER ELEVEN

RESCUE

A British Major named Marshall had a crystal radio set hidden in the attic above the fourth floor, so we had some news. He found a way to print a makeshift newsletter which was circulated among the wards. The Germans had withstood our attacks until late July, but on July 30 we learned that our troops had taken the high ground east of Avranches, just twenty-five miles from us. It was Operation COBRA, the breakout at Saint Lo. The next day our 4th Armored Division broke loose and was becoming known as "The Speed Demons of the Third Army" as they captured the dams of the Selune River and charged into Brittany. The 6th Armored Division was already on the way to Brest, an important port on the coast, while the 4th now began to move south toward Nantes, soon to be on the way to Paris. At last our armored forces were turned loose and the situation in Normandy was coming apart for the Germans.

All those terrible casualties had finally paid off, but the cost continued to be exorbitant. General Bradley estimated his casualties in just over two weeks at 40,000. One of his staff officers wrote "you become so dulled by fatigue that the names of the killed and wounded they checked off each night, the names of men who had been your best friends, might have come out of telephone books...all the old values were gone." General von Choltitz, German Corps commander, wrote "It was the most monstrous bloodbath, the likes of which I have not seen in eleven years of war." When we read this today it seems unthinkable that fine young men had to die by the thousands to thwart an insane maniac. But that's been true since the beginning of human history.

The next day we heard the shriek of fighter planes diving nearby. There was a train station a short distance from our hospital and Allied pilots were dive-bombing it as well as bombing a flak battery located just around the corner from us, the bombs and the 88 fire shaking our building. On August 1 I heard the sound of a machine gun in the distance and recognized its rate of fire as that of an American light 30. Suddenly, hope awakened. What we didn't know, however, was that our forces had totally destroyed the town of Saint Lo a few days earlier in order to break out of Normandy, and they had the same intentions for Rennes. Leaflets had been dropped on the city warning citizens to leave by 1500 (3 pm), and we watched as many of them carrying treasured possessions departed the city. Our hospital, which showed on maps as a girl's school, was in the path of the intended carpet artillery barrage. We watched this foot traffic for awhile and were pretty sure those French people knew something we didn't.

On the morning of August 3 the shells began to explode in the city, some landing in the town square outside our window, others bursting in our courtyard and several hitting our hospital. In his book written shortly after the event, Captain Franklyn Johnson includes this description: "Our guards have fled or surrendered to the Allied doctors, and Rennes' busy German defenders are oblivious to Stalag 221 and its inmates. The French civilians scuttle out of town with whatever possessions they can carry on their backs as the artillery and bombers set to work in earnest. We find ourselves in the middle of this; in fact, the 105 shelling from the west becomes so vicious that those of us who bunk on that side move into the center of the room. Direct hits begin to smash periodically into the hospital walls and blow large craters in the yard.

"Shouting and fighting in the streets divert our attention from the explosions. The jealous SS troops are quarreling with German regulars as well as trying to hold off the Americans! The three-way struggle goes on all day amid the bullets and mortar shells, but we cannot see enough to determine who is winning; we do, however, see a Wehrmacht soldier toss a grenade into the Gestapo building...bodies lie in the street and dust floats overhead. Our artillery, in spite of huge British flags flying there, pounds the hospital roof, and for the first time we understand what the hell of an American shelling is like. The 88 mm flakbatterie replies with a thunderous roar, but all we know or care is that Rennes is surrounded so that it is impossible to be carried captive to Germany."[1]

I felt sorry for the civilians. To have one's home and neighborhood bombarded by artillery fire, everything broken, probably without any insurance to cover losses, was awful. After all the people had suffered in their years of German occupation . . . how they must have prayed for the invaders to pass them by. Now to have to start over in life. Those of us who live in America and complain about shortages, about the inconvenience of higher taxes or high gas prices, have no concept of the tragedy of nations torn apart by war. I thought even then that if I should ever get back home I'd forever after appreciate the blessing of being an American. I knew, even as a nineteen-year-old boy, how fortunate Americans were to live as we do. Mercifully, the artillery fire on Rennes, while causing some destruction, wasn't the total destruction anticipated and suffered by many towns and cities. We'd later learn that little Saint Lo had virtually ceased to exist.

On August 4, some of us went to the basement after hearing machine-gun bullets rattling down the hallway. Fighting in the streets outside our building kept our heads down. The German garrison numbering some 2,000 men fought for awhile, then either surrendered or took off, headed west where they would then have been captured by Patton's armies on their way to the ports along the coast. Our guards had wisely fled earlier, but we remained there until quiet reigned. After a long silence I carefully climbed to the first floor, looked out the front door and saw a wonderful sight: down the road, heading in our direction came a line of marching men and a couple of jeeps. They were members of the 13th Regiment of the 8th Infantry Division. Something of a miracle occurred as men who had been bedridden suddenly scurried out to watch as our saviors walked by. As the GIs passed some threw K rations over the fence to us. A man in a jeep which had paused at the roadside radioed back the recapture of the first major prisoner of war stalag of the campaign. I found the numbers curious, that I was captured on Hill 122 and incarcerated in Stalag 221.

Eventually we would experience the full joy and excitement of rescue. For a time we stared in stunned amazement, trying to absorb the wonder of the hour. Men who smoked frantically tore open the rations for the cigarettes. Back then nearly everyone smoked and the cigarettes were almost as much in demand as the food. Many men were soon coughing happily. Others stifled tears. Most of us finally laughed in boisterous celebration. Suddenly, our darkened world was filled with light. My spirits soared. After two months of destruction and unending anxiety, I was free. I would make it home. Surely, it was a foretaste of salvation. I wasn't as smart as some of the more ambulatory patients who, seeing the exit of the hospital staff of Germans, broke into their offices and among other things found their liquor. A few men were soon extraordinarily happy it seemed, though their constitutions being what they were at the time, they soon regretted their lack of restraint.

Some of us began to stroll, or perhaps limp is a better word, around Rennes. The French people treated us like royalty, able to see by our disreputable condition who we were. I hadn't had a real shower or bath for two months. My torn clothes were the ones I wore in combat. Still, we couldn't resist a walking tour once we were assured the Germans were gone. While there had been some heavy damage to the city, the Germans had retreated before any carpet bombing became necessary.

There was, however, damage. The Germans had set time bombs for obscure reasons and had blown up the Post Office, the Palais du Commerce, and some university buildings. The August 14 issue of *Time* magazine described the shattered stained-glass windows of the Rennes Cathedral, and the feelings of the people as those jeeps drove down the street. "Nowhere in France had U.S. troops seen such wild jubilation," read the report, "such fierce passion," but it followed with this ominous conclusion, "such bloody retribution." The article went on to describe the arrests of collaborators by enraged citizens, and they included the mayor. Some were shot, many badly beaten. A new mayor was promptly chosen and he spoke from a balcony on the town square which was draped with the stars and stripes and the French tricolor. He announced that, "Up to now we have been slaves. Now we are Frenchmen," and the crowds went wild with jubilant applause.[2] We newly-released "Kriegies" weren't the only ones overcome with the joy of new found freedom that fine summer day in Rennes, France.

Cooks of the 8th Division who had been quickly summoned set up a makeshift buffet on the grounds of the 35th Evacuation Hospital. We could hardly wait and it was some hours before a meal was ready. Finally, I got in line with other ambulatory newly-released prisoners, and filled a plate with the only two items the cooks had been able to supply in large quantities: apricots and sausages. We were famished. I weighed 150 pounds, normally weighing 170 at a height of six feet, three inches. By sundown I was coming down off my high, felt suddenly exhausted, and dropped into a hospital cot where I slept for about two hours, then awoke with devastating nausea. I barely made it outside where I lost everything I had eaten, then retched until I thought I might die. It would be several days before I could eat solid food like that and it would be many years before I could eat apricots and sausage. Our stomachs had shrunk and the old cliché was actually true I guess, our eyes were bigger than our stomachs. I had plenty of company in my misery that night.

We looked like mountain men. I hadn't had a haircut for months and hadn't shaved for days. Surprisingly, I found Ed Kochak, my friend of the eggs, who turned out to be an amateur barber. He apparently realized he was going to need some money now so was charging twenty-five cents for a haircut. Where he managed to find barber's clippers I couldn't imagine. Of course most of us didn't have any money but Ed good-naturedly gave us credit, so I got a much-needed haircut. Everyone was in great spirit, nothing much mattered now beyond the fact that we were free, we were alive. The occasional bottle of wine or cognac appearing out of nowhere disappeared just as quickly. Once our shock at being freed had worn off it was one big party.

Despite our exhilaration, we were too young and inexperienced to fully realize how fortunate we were. We had survived battle and imprisonment, and a nasty two-day fire fight, and now were assured of VIP treatment and eventual safe journey home. The day would come when we'd fully appreciate the importance of that date, August 4, 1944, in our lives, but as it was we were still a little bit in shock, waiting to see what would happen next.

What happened next was crucial to the outcome of the Normandy campaign, and it was nerve wracking as we awaited evacuation to a safer clime. On August 6 the Germans launched a major counterattack against the area around the small village of Mortain located not far from Rennes, slamming into the just-arrived 30th Infantry Division. Fighting raged between fanatical SS troops with Panzer tank units and the surprised men of the 30th Division who, along with several other American units, suddenly had their hands full and more. Allied intelligence people had been convinced the Germans were in full retreat and, as so often happened, underestimated the Nazi fanatic refusal to be beaten. For several days the battle raged as Hitler had ordered a drive through to the coast with the intention of isolating American forces and stopping the breakout of COBRA. Masses of Panzer tanks and swarming infantry threatened American positions.

The focal point of the fighting was a hill identified on American maps as Hill 314. It commanded a view of the countryside and important road intersections where some 700 GIs stood between the enemy and their objectives. The men of the 30th Division fought with unbelievable heroism for several days, withstanding Panzer and infantry attacks over and over. They suffered terrible casualties as only 350 men walked off that hill, having expended nearly all their ammunition and having long since run out of medical supplies, especially mercifully sedating morphine so needed for the many wounded men, too many of whom died. But they held out for days against unrelenting German attacks. As I later compared their heroic stand to our debacle I reasoned that one crucial difference was their constant communication with their artillery battalion. Another was their commanders who knew what they were doing and had some sense of where the enemy was located. Still, theirs was a heroic stand which we could envy. The Germans retreated.

We had begun hearing disturbing rumors, erroneous as it turned out, about how we were in danger of losing the battle, in which case the American troops in Brittany would be isolated and, so the defeat-ists would have had us believe, we could be recaptured. There was a bit of truth to those rumors, but in fact they were wrong. Our men were outfighting the Nazis. We did, however, spend a nervous day or two waiting to see.

By this time American officers had begun to learn how to lead. One battalion commander, Lieutenant Colonel Robert Frankland, found himself surrounded with several of his command group in a farmhouse. A German Panther tank had pulled up outside his window and parked; German infantrymen were milling around outside. Frankland heard a commotion in the kitchen and, peeking between the door and the wall, found two German soldiers holding two of his men at gunpoint. He stepped back, drew his .45 pistol, then stepped into the kitchen and shot the German soldiers. He then went to the window, saw the tank commander standing in the turret of the Panther and, taking careful aim, shot the man. Frankland then dashed outside, jumped up on the tank and emptied his pistol into the tank through the open turret, hitting the occupants and putting the tank out of action. He then led his men to safety and resumed his command. Such inspiring leadership filled his men with confidence. Similar acts of bravery by other men drove the Germans back with heavy losses.

The men of the 30th Division are still memorialized by the people of Mortain to this day for their heroism in defeating the Germans, and for their heroic stand on Hill 314. A visitor there now would find a large plaque commemorating the battle. Recent histories have pointed out that the victory was a result of nothing less than the superior fight-ing ability of the American troops from August 6 to 12 in and around Mortain. The Germans retreated, and the fast-moving breakout from Normandy was once more underway. It was off to a place called Falaise for our forces.

A couple of euphoric days later several of us were loaded onto trucks and driven to a nearby airstrip. I'd had a glorious hot shower and been issued some new clothes. Some thirty of us boarded a C-47 transport airplane and we took off for England, landing near Swindon. One day shortly after arriving I passed a man who smiled and called me by name. He looked unfamiliar to me so I waved a courteous gesture and continued on. Ten minutes later I realized who the man was. It was Smitty, the paratrooper sergeant who had occupied the bed across from me for a month and had been my friend. I whirled around but he was gone. He'd shaved off his full beard, so I didn't recognize him. I never saw Smitty again.

Needless to say, we were all grateful to our comrades for our rescue. General Bradley, in leading the seventeen-day effort to break through at Saint Lo with twelve divisions, had progressed a total of seven miles and lost 40,000 men, seriously impairing the fighting capability of two-thirds of his army, and had broken through and out into the open country of Europe. Thousands of those men laid down their lives to set us free. That was a powerful thought.

There must have been a point at which the generals thought the whole Normandy experience was a gigantic exercise in futility. A small geographical area containing nearly a million American soldiers with many thousands killed and wounded, yet seemingly making no progress at all. General Eisenhower called it The Battle of the Beachhead, indicating that right up to the breakout he thought of us as contained in that tiny plot of ground called Normandy. But the price, exorbitant to be sure, was paying off. In our small battle, though we lost over 400 men in our part of the effort to take Hill 122, the hill was taken. The battle was won. As Eisenhower wrote, "The Battle of the Beachhead was a period of incessant and heavy fighting and one which, except for the capture of Cherbourg, showed few geographical gains. Yet it was during this period that the stage was set for the later spectacular liberation of France and Belgium."[3] Our companies may have lost our battle, but the casualties we inflicted on our enemies helped the rest of our division in the winning of Hill 122, without which the Allies might never have left Normandy. Soon the battle for Normandy would end, the most costly battle of World War II.

We can see how close to the edge the infantry units were when we note that General SLA Marshall, who made a study of World War II combat forces, reported that by August 5 "the entire reinforcement pool for infantry forces in Europe (men available to go into battle) consisted of one lone rifleman." Casualties had totally outrun ready reserves.

Much has been said about the motivation of fighting men during the war. How much was patriotism and how much loyalty to one's friends? I'd say mostly the latter, as each of us was vividly aware of our dependence on the others and how much each of the others counted on us never to fail them. That soon developed into a tightly-knit in-group, as close emotionally as any family could be. That's why it was difficult for newer replacements to break in. The relationships were already tight. You didn't just walk in and announce your presence. You had to prove yourself. You had to demonstrate your willingness to take orders, run whatever risks were asked of you, and keep your mouth shut if you didn't like something. After awhile, if you survived long enough, people forgot you were new and you became part of the family. Men didn't trust their lives to someone else until that person had been tested, and once tested, the comradeship became inviolable.

I'm not sure we nineteen- and twenty-year-olds were capable of patriotism in the best sense of the word. Certainly, we loved our country and were glad we lived here. But if true patriotism is to appreciate the values of our land, to embrace them and to abide by them, if it is to see our own country in comparison to other countries not denigrating the others but seeing how special America is and to be able to acknowledge that we are still far from perfect and to be willing to confront these realities and take responsibility for them as citizens of a great land . . . if patriotism is all of this, then I don't believe many of us had the maturity for that kind of patriotism. What we had was more akin to the sentiments one feels at an Old Oaken Bucket game between arch-rivals Indiana and Purdue Universities where everyone believes "my school is better than your school and by God, we're here to kick your butt and send you packing." We were proud of our team, of our country in that sense. But we were far from truly appreciating what we had. That would have to wait until we had seen more of life. It would have to wait for us to appreciate our responsibilities and accept them.

Winning medals on a battlefield is admirable to be sure, but it doesn't buy a free pass for the rest of your life. The occasional veteran one sees who, having fought, bravely perhaps, solicits charity and sympathy for the rest of his years is a long way from being a patriot.

We were still kids out for all the fun we could find, not yet men in the fullest sense of the word for all our willingness to fight our enemies. Millions of men would come home on ships that passed through New York Harbor and tell of their joy at seeing the Statue of Liberty, the symbol of our beloved land. But too few remembered having learned in school the words within that structure which declare what we believe ourselves to stand for, that invitation to outsiders who are poor, and scared, and heavy laden by life's inequities. We hadn't yet fully understood that we were preserving a country in which we are to host those searching souls and their descendants, to make them our brothers and sisters. That's what we fought for. Now we would go home and educate ourselves so we might understand the part we were to play, not just for our two or three years of military service, but for lifetimes as contributing men and women who understand and accept the additional costs we would have to bear if America is to continue on to become a great nation.

This was too profound for all but a very very few. The rest of us, we fought so those we fought alongside of would hold us in high regard. But we would learn. We would still become a great generation.

I notice the confusion today when people hear interviews of returned veterans of more recent wars, especially wounded vets, expecting them to express great relief at being home at last, only to hear them say they can hardly wait to get back to their "outfit." For all the horrors of war there are few if any relationships to compare with those one experiences in battle. There's an incomparable sense of self-knowledge that comes with having stood up to and stood firm against a common enemy. It bonds people together. The feeling dims with time but is never really gone. This may explain why veteran's organizations seem to flourish: so men can have moments of reunion with others who have known the feeling of belonging to that exclusive club, what one author has called the "Deadly Brotherhood." Somehow, discussing the experience with someone who hadn't been there was unsatisfying. You'd start sharing some terrible moment, then you'd begin to feel like you were bragging, or exaggerating, or trying to make yourself out a hero. It just didn't feel right. So the great majority of men, those who had been in heavy combat, would come home and perhaps share some stories with a fellow vet, but for the most part we chose to come home and put the memories away with the uniform and the medals. Once in awhile we'd hear someone holding forth at a gathering, spinning some harrowing tale of battle heroics and it was difficult not to suspect a bit (or perhaps more) of exaggeration, maybe even downright fiction. Obviously, this wasn't always true. There were men who were quite open and honest about their experiences, men who shared their true stories with their families and friends. But many were like the man featured in the movie *Flags of Our Fathers* whose family discovered among his effects after his death that he had won the Navy Cross on Iwo Jima. Only after we realized we were dying at a frantic rate did those who remained begin to open up. It was as though some cosmic permission was finally given us to tell the story, but that permission came far too late for most of us. Sadly, many great stories died with the men who never told even the people they loved.

We came home proud to have served but ready to put it all aside and get back to the work of living. No one I have ever known retained any negative feelings about his service. We felt it was an honor to have served. There was a familiar saying among combat veterans: "I wouldn't go through that again for a million dollars, but I wouldn't take a million dollars for the experience."

In the 1970s, when veterans of the Vietnam war returned, quite a number of them with what we believed to be whiny self pity, we just stared uncomprehendingly. On the one hand we felt kinship with them. They were now our brothers. But why all the complaining? We used to see photos of bewhiskered, tragic-faced men attired in used military garb, sitting on street corners begging, or leaning against the wall in Washington crying, many with the sign reading "veteran." The whole country seemingly grieved for them. All except World War II combat veterans who didn't buy it. Finally, careful investigation by men like B.G. Burkett uncovered the fact that the great majority of these men were frauds, most having never been to Vietnam. I myself was adamantly opposed to the war in Vietnam, but I honored the men who fought there and regret that their service remains largely tainted by the media insistence that those men were somehow permanently damaged even though the majority, as in World War II, were never in combat. Most of those who actually did the fighting came home and took their places as contributing citizens just as we did. One of their tragedies was the denial of pride and legitimate self-respect to which those men who actually fought were so clearly entitled.

Our hospital plane landed at an English airstrip and I was taken to the 186th General hospital located between Swindon and Cirencester, near the little town of Fairford, where I was sent to surgery for removal of some of the pieces of metal the German doctor missed. It proved to be more of a surgery than I expected, leaving twenty-eight small pieces still in my legs. The surgery was sufficiently serious that I remained hospitalized from August until December. I wasn't yet aware that men who had been prisoners of war were not allowed to serve in combat again according to The Geneva Convention, so I really didn't mind the extended stay. A warm bed and hot meals every day beat getting back in shape and returning to the front lines.

We only then began to learn why there had been some obvious disruption among the Germans while we were imprisoned. On July 20 a plot had been carried out to kill Hitler while he was convening a meeting of Generals in Rastenburg, Prussia. The meeting was in progress in Hitler's "Wolf's Lair" when Count Colonel von Stauffenberg who, along with many German generals, was convinced of Hitler's paranoia and incapacity to rule, placed a briefcase containing a bomb under the table where Hitler stood, then quietly slipped out. The plot failed. Hitler was partially deafened by the resulting explosion and his right arm was injured, but he continued his activities, even meeting with Benito Mussolini that afternoon. Far from seeing this as evidence of his own failing leadership, Hitler announced that his survival was evidence that God favored him, and he then devoted himself to revenge.

Von Stauffenberg was promptly shot. In the next few days several thousand people -- generals, family members, others -- were either executed or sent to concentration camps. Eight generals were hung on meat hooks, the executions filmed and shown to Hitler. He also decided that Field Marshall Rommel was implicated. Rommel was visiting his wife at the time, recovering from injuries suffered in a car crash, and received a visit from General Burgdorf, a man unanimously feared and hated by the other generals, along with some Gestapo men. Burgdorf informed Rommel that he could either be executed and his family dishonored, or he could drink poison in which case he'd receive a hero's funeral. He chose the latter and, after solemnly bidding his wife and son goodbye, accompanied the Gestapo men in their black car. When the car stopped some distance from the Rommel home, he drank the poison, and was buried as an honored general. Thus Germany lost the best officer in their army. In April 1945, a drunken General Burgdorf took his own life.

Clearly, Hitler's mind was badly warped. He began taking drugs which hastened that process until his mental illness would finally reach the point that he wished every German to die for the cause, that cause being Hitler's own grandiose dreams. Soon, of course, he would commit suicide.

Back home in America at the time of our recapture there was an outburst of enthusiastic optimism. The Allied advance, though temporarily held up by the ill-advised German counter-attack at Mortain, was rapidly exploding out of Normandy. *Time* magazine, comparing the breakout with an ascending rocket, reported that "even the most optimistic of the war correspondents had not anticipated the rocket's carrying power, the astonishing speed it had developed by this week. It had burst again and again, had shot out spectacular and stunning bolts in all directions. The rocket's red glare lit up these accomplishments in a historic victory of U.S. arms." Lloyds of London gave 5 to 8 odds on VE Day by October 31.

That poetic excess by some reporter would eventually prove premature in its optimism, though to be sure, the final breakout from Normandy called operation COBRA was indeed a very welcome if long-delayed victory. The "rocket" would continue for several days, by mid-August corralling 250,000 Germans in an area generally called the Falaise Pocket where, according to many latter-day military experts, the Montgomer-Bradley-Eisenhower team screwed up by adhering too much to their rule book and allowing 100,000 German troops to escape the trap. Still, after several days of one-sided battle with the Germans suffering horribly - some 10,000 Germans were killed - their commander acceded to the intervention of a Catholic priest, Abbe Launay, and surrendered the 150,000 men remaining in the trap, many of them wounded. They also lost most of the equipment and arms of the 7th German Army and the 5th Panzer Army. It was also significant that much of the transport for artillery of the Germans was horse drawn. Hundreds of horses died in the attack, a fact which underlined the relative poverty of the German army's transportation capabilities. Clearly, they were running short of fuel as well as transport vehicles. All in all, the battle of the Falaise Pocket was an Allied success, though not so successful as it might have been. It was, though, an overwhelming defeat for the Germans. General Eisenhower visited the scene of the carnage at Falaise and remarked that "it was a scene that only Dante could describe."

There was a flurry of premature optimism in America. The Federal Council of the Churches of Christ in America had prepared suggested worship services for the churches to use on VE Day, assuming that the day was near. Meanwhile, members of the C.I.O. Transport Workers Union in Philadelphia, presumably anticipating a return to business-as-usual and having contrived to avoid military service, went on a strike which was shortened by the arrival of the intervening U.S. Army on the third day. Still, we were all optimistic as we watched some fast-moving action after the seemingly endless crawling progress in Normandy.

On August 15 Hitler fired General von Kluge and replaced him with General Model, always a good sign we thought as we knew what it meant when generals got fired. Three days later General von Kluge took a dose of potassium chloride and a few seconds later was dead. The Allied armies were destined to continue their sweep for awhile, until General Patton's swift advances would outrun our fuel transport capabilities and things would again come to a crashing halt as winter was soon to set in. Those VE Day worship services would have to wait for quite awhile.

The next few months for those of us in hospital were more or less a round of reading novels, talking to other patients, and finally exchanging letters with loved ones. I hadn't heard from home for three months and was nervous in hoping that everyone was well. I learned that my dear Grandmother McGriff had quietly died but otherwise, everyone was well. My brother Stuart was now a Second Class Petty Officer in the Navy out in the Pacific.

On September 5 I celebrated my 20th birthday. We learned that a new movie had just arrived from the States and one evening many of us crowded into the tent set up for the occasion and watched Bing Crosby in *Going My Way*. A few mornings later a sergeant strolled through my ward and tossed me a blue box containing a Purple Heart Medal. It was my second, the little ankle problem causing the first one. I'd forgotten I had it coming and sent it home.

One day I saw a very short sergeant walking toward me and alongside him was a major with his arm around the man. That did not compute. Majors usually had little to do with mere sergeants, but this sergeant was one I knew I'd seen before. Then I recognized him. It was Mickey Rooney. He was visiting us and would give a performance that night in a nearby theater. Also with him was another, less-well known movie star, Freddie Bartholomew. The two of them had starred in a then-famous movie, *Captains Courageous*, with Spencer Tracy. We heard that there had been a controversy of some kind about the issue of how many jeeps *Sergeant* Rooney would be allowed to have when his group was in London. That left us with a rather dim view of movie stars who supposedly joined the armed forces. Anyway, we enjoyed the show. Incidentally, I thought that Major with his arm around Rooney was a perfect example of the word "obsequious."

As we began to recover, we were invited to do long marches in an effort to regain our fitness. I went one day and our small group passed a long column of infantry marching the other way. We talked back and forth and learned they were the just-arrived 106th Infantry Division which someone dubbed "The Hungry and Sick Division." Naturally, as was expected of us, we yelled all sorts of good-natured cat calls and insults, beginning with the then-popular "You'll be SAH-REE." Actually, though many of them were only a few months younger than I, they looked more to me like a Boy Scout troop marching by. How could we know that they would go into action on December 15 and days later they would be decimated by the sudden advance of the Wehrmacht in the opening stage of The Battle of the Bulge and would virtually cease to exist as a Division? All those young kids, and most were either dead or prisoners within a couple weeks. Thousands died. More thousands were wounded. Eight thousand were marched off into imprisonment.

I recall a conversation with several other hospital patients in which one man announced his undying hatred of the Germans. Another man whom I knew only as "Mike" quietly said he disagreed. He was in the hospital for a serious head wound, and went on to explain why he felt no such hatred. His unit, he said, had attacked a German position, been caught in an intense mortar barrage and been forced to move back. Mike had been wounded, was temporarily paralyzed, unable to move, and lay there exposed to the mortar shells exploding around him. Then he felt himself being dragged to a nearby slit trench and realized the man saving him was a German medic who not only pushed Mike into the slit trench, but climbed in on top of him, thereby protecting him from further injury. When the barrage ended, the Germans, realizing the seriousness of Mike's wound, allowed American medics to retrieve him.

I found Mike's story very disconcerting. My mind went back to the wounded German soldier who had pled with me for help and I had left him there as we retreated, probably to be killed. How could I make any sense out of all of this? We thought we were the good guys and the Germans the bad guys. Later, we'd know about the holocaust and nothing can ameliorate that, yet I couldn't quite convict all of them for the criminal acts of a few. We'd had our Ku Kux Klan. I could only wonder to what extent we Americans might respond to a concerted campaign of hatred as was practiced by Hitler. Would deranged people come out of the cellars and from under rotted limbs to do the same? I hoped not, yet it wasn't all that easy to make judgments. I would have to come to terms with that issue some day. We did discuss the fact that the SS and the Gestapo were special cases, and probably heavily peopled by men who, in an orderly society, would have been criminals. When the war was over, while many German atrocities would come to light, it proved to be the case that it was nearly always the SS and the Gestapo who were responsible.

I think most German soldiers were basically decent young men caught up in a damnable system which left them little choice. After all, if a society takes its finest children, presses them into militaristic organizations, persistently inculcates in them hatred for another ethnic group, harangues them constantly with assurances that they are superior, a master race, doing this while the children are still impressionable and are prevented from hearing opposing views, taught that even their parents, should they ever be heard to disagree with this psychological poison are only revealing their own imperfections, it's then not at all surprising that they become a generation of bigots. More the surprise that so many of them retained humane virtues. Thank God, we should reason, that men like Niemoeller and Bonhoeffer and millions of decent people in 1940s Germany had the courage to speak out against this moral atrocity. Many died because of this, but they preserved a spirit of Christian virtue among many people in Germany in the process. It's a lesson for any nation - or religion - which teaches hatred. If there is a God as so many of us believe, the end result will be no different from that suffered by the Nazis.

It wouldn't prove easy for Germany, though. While what I have written is true, it's also true that the average German soldier probably knew about atrocities, this was especially true on the Eastern or Russian front. Many Russian captives were summarily shot as were many Jewish captives. Doctor Wolfram Wette, Professor of Contemporary History at the University of Freiberg, Germany, has recently published a study of the German army, the Wehrmacht. He wrote that "within the Wehrmacht the principle reigned that individual soldiers should know only as much about the military situation as was necessary for them to perform their immediate assignments. Enlisted men were not to think about the bigger picture... the less they knew the better."[4] Wette then went on to explain that routine executions were carried out by specially-picked teams and always out of view of the other men. In theory, therefore, the other men were not to know, but of course there are no secrets in any army and everyone knew. The result was that former German soldiers went home carrying a shared sense of guilt as the world began to know of their deeds. Wette contends that for many years the people of Germany tried to ignore or deny their guilt, but deep down, the older ones knew and it has had a damaging effect on the German psyche. Part of that tragedy had to be the many young German boys who hated the insanity but dared not voice a protest, and could do nothing other than submerge their sense of complicity in rationalizations they knew, in their hearts, they could never really believe.

Shortly after the end of the war an English theologian paid a visit to a prison camp in which former German soldiers were being held. In a discussion with the prisoners one spoke disdainfully, insisting that there is no God. "If there is a God," he argued, "why doesn't he answer our prayers here for freedom and a chance to rebuild our lives." The theologian retorted "What is happening to you now is precisely evidence that there IS a God," he said. "The very fact that you have lost the war, that you are suffering punishment right now for what has happened is the best possible argument for the existence of God." The German had no answer.

In 1995 an exhibit of incriminating Nazi documents was held in Hamburg, Germany. Though an effort had been made by the Nazis at the end to destroy all records of their misdeeds, some had survived. Many of these were now placed on display: surviving documents, letters written home by soldiers, photos, and other surviving mementos. Wette wrote that "after fifty years, a few photographs eliminated at once the distance of time and place and of selective memory. Facsimiles of military documents as well as excerpts from the letters of Wehrmacht soldiers added to the powerful message that the organizers hoped to convey: the German army was complicit in the murders of Jews and other civilians."[5]

CHAPTER TWELVE
PAUSING TO MAKE SENSE

IN THE HOSPITAL WE SPENT MUCH OF OUR TIME IN SERIOUS conversation as we tried to make some sense out of our various experiences. Like killing people. The ultimate moral issue we all faced was to kill another person. Most of the men who became my friends were raised, like I, in Judeo-Christian tradition if not actual religious homes. "Thou shalt not kill." Yet we kids were charged to do just that. We had been confronted by men who, evil or not as individuals, represented an evil system aimed at killing us and were willing to kill the innocents whom we represented and were charged to protect. I know more than one American GI died because in that crucial instant of having one's sights on an enemy, he hesitated to kill, and the enemy was able. Of course I also knew of men who found the act of killing exhilarating, possessed of absolute power in an environment where the rules of humane morality were all but suspended. Some deep, primordial instinct genetically imbedded in our very being, I suppose, must have dictated how we'd react in an actual situation where to kill another man face to face was demanded. I think now of that instant of time in which young Paul Casteel made eye contact with the Nazi parachute trooper with the automatic rifle, then killed him. The German paused, probably hoping Casteel would surrender. Casteel fired from a distance of five feet, and today I wonder what images may have beset him in the years to follow, assuming he survived.

We faced a puzzling conundrum: how do you protect the innocent by stopping evil men when only by killing them can you stop them? And to do this, knowing that killing another is wrong, you must somehow become convinced that killing is morally right, yet the men you kill you have defined as evil because they kill. Few of us teenagers were ready to grapple with that perplexing issue.

Most killing was impersonal in Normandy. Machine guns and rifles were usually fired as covering fire, fire directed in the general direction of the enemy. Most casualties were caused by artillery or mortar fire, in which those firing the weapons couldn't see the enemy as individuals. But there were times when it all happened face to face, and it was that rare Audie Murphy, America's most decorated soldier, who could kill without compunction who often won the battles. Meanwhile, many a man who had exalted courage failed in the trial because of a morally sensitive heart. I recently heard a former combat infantryman say that if he had it all to do over he'd volunteer as a medic. In other words, he wasn't afraid to serve, but he just couldn't live with the thought of killing someone. I could only decide that in a perfect world, no one would be able to kill another person, and the very difficulty the armed services faced in getting men to kill was, strangely, a positive comment about our American culture. Good people, I decided, have difficulty winning wars.

A combat psychologist, Dr. David Grossman, conducted in-depth studies of the wartime killing of one man by another. He made some interesting discoveries, one of which was to confirm the earlier findings of General SLA Marshall, the man who was at one time considered to be the reigning expert on men in combat who claimed that in World War II, only fifteen to twenty percent of riflemen in Infantry combat actually fired their rifles with intent to kill. That claim was for a time rejected by later researchers. Grossman, however, contends that those figures are correct. He interviewed numerous combat veterans and those who commanded them. He investigated studies made in other wars including the Falkland War, the Napoleonic wars, our Civil War, World War I, British studies of several of their wars, and studies done by the FBI of law enforcement people who had been in gun battles, all in addition to World War II. All confirmed the thesis that men instinctively avoid killing another person, even in the heat of battle. Grossman concluded that "there is within most men an intense resistance to killing their fellow men, resistance so strong that in many circumstances, soldiers on the battlefield will die before they can over-come it." [1]

After the Civil War battle of Gettysburg 27,574 muskets were recovered from the battlefield. Of those single-shot muzzle-loading weapons, an incredible 24,000 were still loaded. Participants later admitted they pretended to fire, then went through the motions of reloading so their comrades would think they were actually firing. Some 6,000 of those muskets had been loaded several times without being fired. It's now evident that for every shot striking a man, hundreds of shots were fired by men who either purposely fired to miss or who fired without even aiming, indicating that the great majority of casualties in that war were inflicted by artillery. One participant in a battle at Vicksburg, Benjamin McIntyre, wrote "It seems strange that a company of men can fire volley after volley at a like number of men at not more than fifteen steps and not a single casualty. Yet such was the fact in this instance." Research reveals that long lines of men firing at each other with muskets scored an average of one or two hits per minute of firing rather than the dozens, or even hundreds depicted in movies. Grossman wrote, "The obvious conclusion is that most soldiers were not trying to kill the enemy."[2] Bill Mauldin said it well: "The surest way to become a pacifist is to join the infantry."

This was true as late as the Vietnam War, in which it is estimated that for every bullet striking an enemy soldier more than 50,000 rounds were fired. One combat medic in the First Marine Division, a man named Douglas Graham, later said "one of the things that amazed me is how many bullets can be fired during a fire fight without anyone getting hurt."[3]

If we do the math we see that if every combat infantryman in one army killed or wounded one man in the opposing army, that opposing army would cease to exist. In the battle of Beau Coudray and Hill 122, seventy-four Americans in our three companies died. An enemy Regiment had fired at us for two days, surely expending many thousands of rounds, yet most of those fatalities were caused by artillery fire. Apparently, German soldiers were no different from American soldiers in this regard. Grossman's contention that most men firing at other men tend to fire over the heads of the enemies intending to intimidate, confuse, and cause retreat rather than to kill brought back my own frustration during our final battle as a line of German Infantry moved toward our position and Huey McMillion fired our last machine-gun belt ten feet over their heads.

All of this and much additional research led Dr. Grossman to conclude, "There can be no doubt that this resistance to killing one's fellow man is there and it exists as a result of a powerful combination of instinctive, rational, environmental, hereditary, cultural, and social factors. It is there, it is strong, and it gives us cause to believe that there may be hope for mankind after all."[4] Of course there are enough exceptions to account for many casualties, men who feel no such restraint as compels the rest of us, but some very believable studies indicate these are a small minority of people. Two researchers, Swan and Marchand, estimated that two percent of men are predisposed to aggressive, psychopathic tendencies in battle. They discovered that these men tend to congregate in Special Forces, Rangers and paratroopers, and that the impression left by contemporary war movies that all men become like this in battle is erroneous. Interestingly, they also add that such men are more often than not high-achieving, contributing members of society when not in a war.

Grossman did say that more recent technology, coupled with training methods developed because of these very studies, have somewhat changed the equation. "Modern training and conditioning," he wrote, "can partially overcome the inclination to posture (the effort to intimidate rather than kill). Indeed, the history of warfare can be seen as a history of increasingly more effective mechanisms for enabling and conditioning men to overcome this innate resistance to killing their fellow human beings."[5] He concluded that as killing becomes less personal because of technological advances in weaponry, less face to face, men are less reluctant to pull the trigger. Still, that inner refusal to kill is a profound instinct in all but a few people.[6]

All of this raises the issue of the men native to places like Iraq and Iran who kill without remorse, who seem able to dispatch another person quite personally for no better reason than his religious difference of belief, not to mention the to us unthinkable act of suicide bombing. But then the Nazis were able to do this also. The rest of us are barely able to conceive of such conduct and can only trust that these people are members of a tiny minority of the human race whom the rest of us are charged with restraining. We're supposed to love our fellow man, but a loving mother doesn't let her kid break the neighbor's window, a loving society doesn't allow anyone to steal or do acts of violence, and a world struggling for peace and love must do whatever is necessary to restrain and, when there's no other way, eliminate those who commit such atrocities.

Quite a few men were wounded by friendly fire. It occasionally happened that an American GI would mistake another GI for an enemy soldier. This sometimes happened at night when a patrol was returning and somehow the exchange of passwords didn't go well. One of our companies lost two men this way. On a rare occasion a nervous man on guard would shoot before challenging someone approaching in the dark. One evening as we were quietly moving forward into Gourbesville a group of us were sneaking across a field when we were suddenly fired on and quickly dived into a ditch. When we located the source of the rifle fire, we began firing back. Someone yelled "cease fire" and we later learned our "enemies" were members of another of our companies. Mercifully, no one was hit. Also, misdirected artillery fire was common. It was not a perfect science. Short rounds happened often and when they did men were often wounded or killed.

On July 25 a flight of our bombers flew over the 30th Infantry Division and dropped their bomb load on our men of the 30th, killing 25 and wounding 131. The next day, that planned attack having therefore been postponed a day, General Leslie McNair, Commanding General of the First Army Group, went forward to personally oversee the attack. Unbelievably, the bombers proceeded to fly over and do the same stupid thing, drop their bomb loads on the men of the 30th. This time they killed 111 men and wounded 400. One of the men killed was General McNair. How incredibly idiotic that sounds today, but we weren't there and can't be the ones to judge.

Some casualties were caused by random bullets. A bullet from a rifle or machine gun could fly with deadly force for more than a mile, and with the frantic firing in many fire fights, thousands of bullets were fired high enough to carry great distances. Again, an example was our own Huey McMillion firing the remains of our last machine-gun belt over the heads of the advancing Germans. He was aiming in the direction of our own lines because we were surrounded, and thereby probably sprayed our own rear areas with flying unaimed bullets. More than a few men were hit in this random way, their wounds often mistaken for aimed fire by some presumably hidden sniper. I'm guessing that a large percentage of casualties attributed to sniper fire were, in fact, random shots from a great distance. Men in units a few hundred yards or so behind the front lines weren't entirely safe from this kind of accidental wounding. Major Richard Winters of the 101st Airborne, featured in *Band of Brothers,* was wounded by a spent bullet while walking along a street in a safe zone.

Being wounded was not necessarily bad. The government had made a serious mistake in requiring that combat troops must serve until one of three things: be killed, be wounded, the war ends. We did not have the luxury of thinking five more days, four more days, and so forth. We were there until death or, if fortunate, a wound. Paul Fussel quoted one infantryman as saying "Nobody gets out of a rifle company. It's a door that only opens one way. You leave when they carry you out, if you're unlucky, dead, if you're lucky, wounded. But nobody just walks away. That's the unwritten law."[7] Even the British periodically removed combat units from the front and gave them a week or so of quiet, restful time away from the dangers of front-line life. American infantrymen remained in action for extended periods of time.

Since we had no reason to think the war was going to end very soon, and being killed was an undesirable option, being wounded was the only way out. Of course no one wanted a serious wound, something like losing a leg or going blind. But a bullet in the arm or leg was welcome. It was generally called "a million dollar wound." When a friend was wounded like that we usually felt envy more than anything. The wounded man, assuming he reached medical care soon enough, spent time in a comfy hospital, had a more or less lengthy vacation, received a beautiful Purple Heart medal to wear the rest of the time, and had a significantly improved probability of getting home.

One potential problem we talked about a lot was that of our adjustment to the niceties of civilized conduct when we finally returned home. Our language was coarse, even among men who at home would be considered refined people. I knew one or two men who never swore, but that was extremely rare. It was just our language of human commerce to sprinkle expletives of various kinds in normal conversation. Worse, we had become inured to human suffering. To see men we knew killed, to have seen the ground littered with the dead and wounded, to see others in the hospitals where we spent a lot of time, men who were in varying degrees disabled, some mutilated, many with missing limbs, had required of us an inward subconscious adjustment that would protect us from constant revulsion and depression. Profanity, the native language of Hell I should imagine, somehow seemed to meet a need unmet otherwise. Also, we developed a hardness of spirit, a sense of life must go on, a lack of sympathy for anyone who felt sorry for himself. You face whatever it is, you tough it out, you go on as best you can. How much this would come through as insensitivity to the people back home we couldn't be sure. We would look pretty much like the same person when we returned home but we would be different within. Most of us went home and adjusted very well, but we retained the sentiments of the combat soldier. After sleeping night after night in rain-filled slit trenches with a soggy field jacket for a blanket, eating only packaged food, sometimes no food, drinking rain water out of a muddy helmet, sleeping four or five shivering hours a night with a two-hour guard tour in the middle, former combat soldiers don't have a lot of patience with people who complain about life's minor discomforts. We would be able to endure without complaint, and we'd remain unmoved when people, especially those the age we were then, complained of normal hardships of life. We were forever changed. We used an expression when anyone complained: "Go have the chaplain punch your TS slip." The T stood for "tough…" To borrow from psychotherapist Paul Tournier, I fear Andre Gide spoke for many of us with his anguished cry: "I have killed my youth, its innocent freshness."

Finally, in December, I was dismissed from the hospital and sent to London where I was temporarily stationed in central London at 63 Brook Street, near Grosvenor Square. It was a small, four-story Military Intelligence office still used today by an insurance company. The purpose was for me to be debriefed as a former POW, which seemed odd to me since, as a Pfc several months removed from battle, I couldn't be expected to know anything useful even if I had at one time, which I hadn't. The colonel in charge obviously thought the same thing since he ignored me, leaving me to enjoy a few weeks of unofficial vacation. That colonel must have had the easiest job in the ETO. None of the men I met knew anything still relevant by the time we arrived. The whole system seemed silly to me since the circumstances on a battle-field changed daily and the only intelligence of any use would be that which was obtained on the scene. I guess that's why I only laid eyes on the colonel once, briefly. He had other fish to fry, may have been one of those colonels relieved of a combat command somewhere and consigned to the sad fate of partying in London. It was fine with me. All of a sudden I was having a ball.

I made two new friends, one a technical sergeant who had been a waist gunner on a B-17 bomber and been shot down near the border with Switzerland, been interned for several months, then was repatri-ated back to England. The other man was a Pfc like me with a serious leg wound that would probably leave him with a permanent limp. He'd also been a prisoner of war. We three walked down the street in the blackout one night to Claridge's, the classiest hotel in London, and sat in the lobby, watching important people pass by as we sipped cognac and warmed to the realization that we were totally out of place. It was a grand, peaceful feeling sitting there with new friends. All three of us were exempt from further combat and, as I recall, that night we felt like kings.

In reflecting, I sometimes wonder why we didn't share more of our stories with each other, and the feelings that went with them, and why, for all our camaraderie and sense of brotherhood, we didn't really know each other very well. Many men continued to gather after the war in reunions, but it was more to relive old memories, to in some small way recapture the sense of bonding which probably tends to grow in memory. If you could sit and listen, you'd hear most sentences begin with "Do you remember when...?" or "I'll never forget..." Rarely is this an effort to reunite in some close relational way. Ask a World War II veteran what his friends wanted out of life, what they feared, how they loved, what were their dreams, what emotions they felt about the fighting, and the answer will almost surely be a look of mystification. Or maybe a look of wistfulness, of "I wish I'd taken time to ask." Back then we men didn't do much sharing of feelings. Maybe we still don't.

We were a generation of males raised to conceal feelings, especially any that we thought of as negative emotions. Only two emotions were permitted, hilarity and anger. No man dared reveal fear no matter how torn apart he might be within. Loneliness, anxiety, guilt, gentle sensitivity, all were verboten. Had some World War II vet hugged his buddies when parting from them, a gesture quite common among today's generation, he'd have been instantly tagged and avoided. I can't imagine any of us saying to another man "I love you" though in many cases we did. Those were relational no nos. If a man had cried over the death of a friend that would have been seen as manly, but to cry because of homesickness, or loneliness, certainly when in pain, that would have been perceived as weakness. It's just possible that today's generation of soldiery has healthier outlets for the stress of combat because they have a permission we did not have, to verbalize feelings. For us, we could die for a friend, but we couldn't tell him why. A gentle punch on the shoulder in parting was the most affection we ever permitted ourselves to show. I look back now and wonder how I could have known so little about the men who meant so much to me. Parents today who enable their children, particularly their sons, to verbalize and confront their feelings, give them a great, lifelong gift. One important requirement of a combat soldier was the ability to stifle feelings. I guess in some deep, primordial way, we feared for our manhood if we revealed the slightest hint of what, back then, we considered to be feminine traits.

Viewed today, some would say we were victims of a self-administered fraud which robbed us of an important part of our humanity. On the other hand, maybe we wouldn't have endured otherwise. I guess we were just part of the lumbering process of humanity's painfully slow process of self discovery, but it was a phenomenon from which most of us never fully recovered.

In a charming recent book about World War II vets entitled *The Girl Watcher's Club*, author Harry Stein, after spending time with a number of former GIs who have long since lived admirable civilian lives, writes about their attitudes which he finds typical of our generation. "If, indeed," he writes, "in most such conversations among the Girl Watchers, moments that seem emotionally fraught get stepped on, or hurried past, or played for laughs, that merely reflects an unspoken consensus, alien to the contemporary mind, that the deepest feelings are and should be a very private thing; and more, that the best way to make sure you never get anything done is to waste your time dwelling on them."[8] That says it pretty well for the men I know who fought in the war.

Surprisingly to many people today, most of my comrades in combat demonstrated very little anger toward the enemy. Of course we bought into the fact that we were there to kill each other. But I think nearly all of us would have been glad to call it a draw and all go home. Let the politicians and the generals have their victories. We were naive when it came to the economic-political aspects of the war. I think that's one reason we were so accommodating to the Germans we captured. In a strange way which doesn't make much sense to those who weren't there, and maybe not even a lot of sense to those of us who were, a certain bond extended to our enemy. I recall sitting outside in a group of recruits hearing a lecture at Fort Meade, Maryland, while waiting for shipment overseas. It was given by a young lieutenant wearing a Purple Heart and just returned from battle in North Africa. While he was speaking, a group of German prisoners, former members of Rommel's Afrika Korps, were marched by. One of our recruits made some sort of smart alec remark as they passed. The lieutenant paused, directed a steely glare of anger at all of us, and said "Keep your mouths shut. A year ago those men would have shot your eyes out." That was one man's respect for a formerly dangerous enemy, a brotherhood in which we were not members. The bond of mutual respect was stronger than any angry feelings from the fighting.

This doesn't mean we weren't angry while we were in Normandy, and we certainly are outraged to this day at the inhumanity of many German soldiers, but there was a certain kinship with those who fought with honor. As Historian John McManus wrote, "It takes time for the infantryman to realize that he is a breed apart and that, as such, he may have more in common with enemy infantry across the way than with the army in his rear."[9] I imagine aircrews and tankers felt the same way. No doubt Navy men in combat situations experienced similar emotions.

There were exceptions among us. There were men who fought with a fiery and growing hatred of our enemy and who never forgave, but they were a small minority. Most of us didn't harbor hatred. Of course we were unaware of the holocaust and the other inhumanities practiced by some of our enemies. Nothing can excuse the atrocity of the Nazi "Final Solution." But we have our own holocaust to expunge: our own treatment of the American Negro, treatment in some tragic instances no less outrageous than the camps, black men lynched without trial, dehumanizing social systems which lynched the spirits of millions. There was a black man in the bed next to me in my Army hospital. He was a wonderful fellow, big, friendly, kind. More than once he went out of his way to do small favors for me - with little in return. I liked him. But it never occurred to me to invite him to join me as the rest of us went to town. I never walked with him to the mess hall or ate with him. Come to think of it he ate in a different mess hall anyway. I was oblivious to the fact that a fine man was living a life of estranged loneliness because of people like me. No, for all their guilt, the Germans weren't the only ones. But we would go home and, with the leading of our children, try to change our mistakes. Millions of us would look inside ourselves, we would see what we had been, we would say "no more." We would honor that for which we had fought and for which so many of our friends had died.

It's deep within us all, part of the human condition, the very thing which underlies all wars. I saw it in myself when that Mexican man risked himself to save me, the very man whom I had rejected as unworthy of my friendship. Because we are an open society we Americans are perpetually called to account for our excesses – by our churches, our newspapers, our television commentary, our teachers – something the Germans of the Third Reich did not experience, so we haven't fallen as they did. But we can't know what we'd be like in a totalitarian environment, especially one with news media tightly controlled by a reigning authority. We may from time to time quarrel with our news media for seeming to take sides, to so often attack those leaders in government for whom we have high regard. But truth to tell, that's the point; it's one reason why we fought the war, so that freedom of the press was protected. The German Third Reich was a product of a nation's refusal to encourage the very dissent which sometimes makes us mad but keeps us free. No matter how upset one may get at one or another newspaper or television news program, we should celebrate their right to say what they want to say and print what they want to print. They help keep us free.

Hitler and his cronies were evil. Other evil men stepped forth to become part of his hell. Their counterparts are numerous among our own society today: criminals, drug dealers, pedophiles, wife beaters, rapists, sociopaths. Every society has them. I think it finally speaks well for us that we soon forgave and administered fair justice to those who were guilty of World War II but understood that in the end we were all part of a common humanity needing some power from beyond ourselves if we were ever to become anything other than what we were, sinful human beings.

It should be noted that for all our horrendous casualties, the Germans suffered many more than did the Allies in Normandy. General Erwin Rommel, commander of all German forces, was later quoted by his son as saying in mid-June of the Normandy fighting, "We had as many casualties on one day as during the whole of the summer fighting in 1942. My nerves are pretty good, but sometimes I was near collapse. It was casualty reports, wherever you went. I have never fought with such losses. If I hadn't gone to the front every day, I couldn't have stood it, having to write off literally one regiment every day."

In late July Rommel wrote a letter to Hitler stating that "the situation on the Normandy front is growing worse every day and is now approaching a grave crisis." Describing Allied forces, he wrote of "enormous" amounts of artillery and tanks and complained that he had lost 97,000 men and only received 6,000 replacements. "Even the bravest army," he wrote, "will be smashed." Rommel is also said to have turned to his staff and said of Hitler, "The man is mad." One German soldier of their 276th Infantry wrote, "The lack of any success at all affected the men badly. You could feel the sheer growing fear. We would throw ourselves to the ground at the slightest sound, and many men were saying that we should never leave Normandy alive."[10] British intelligence captured a letter from one Panzer division commander to his replacement, warning that "the enemy's incredibly heavy artillery bombardments is something new and terrible. The German air force is conspicuous by its absence. Only six German planes flew over our division area in four weeks - one and one-half planes per week." German Feldwebel Helmut Gunther's company was reduced from 120 men to twenty men, yet he was refused a request to draw back to a better position and was told, instead, to hold as long as he could. Yes, the senseless slaughter was ravaging both sides.

CHAPTER THIRTEEN

LONDON UNDER FIRE

IN A STRANGE WAY, LONDON WAS A WONDERFUL PLACE TO BE IN 1944. Later historians, looking back to the times, called London the crossroads of the world. It was also very dangerous. The 1940 blitz was probably London's greatest test because it was the very beginning of the people's exposure to the awesome might of the German Luftwaffe, their airforce. Literally hundreds of enemy bombers had arrived dropping thousands of bombs, mostly on the East End where the poorer people lived, the target being the dock areas. But before long the people adjusted. The Royal Air Force stepped up with unimaginable valor, and despite being badly outnumbered, defeated the German Luftwaffe in the Battle of Britain. One man told of going to the lounge of Claridge's Hotel and seeing a young Royal Air Force lieutenant having a drink and wearing a bandage on his face. The young man explained that he'd been shot down earlier that very day over the Channel and been rescued, having suffered a cut on his face. War was close and intimate for the British. One writer compared London to "a prehistoric animal wounded, burned, which would disregard its assailants to keep moving massively onward."[1] Bertrand Russell had predicted the worst, writing in a book that London would "become one vast bedlam, the hospitals will be stormed, traffic will cease, the homeless will shriek for peace, the city will be a pandemonium."[2] He couldn't have been more wrong. Of course the suffering and loss was immense and everyone was in constant and desperate danger, but they kept going.

The scene that greeted a first-time visitor to wartime London was one of drab, desolate neighborhoods intermixed with familiar sites basically untouched by the war. Many streets were little more than stacks of bricks, the remains of homes and apartment buildings, often scenes where women and children had died in their beds or at the dinner table, their bodies blown apart or crushed by falling debris. Yet most of the city was the way it had always been save for walls of sand bags stacked against the windows.

People on the streets all dressed in worn, dark, and long-since outmoded clothing styles, faces grimly determined as they waited in orderly fashion for the bus, or hurriying into the Underground, all headed for work as usual, nearly all defiant of anyone who had the temerity to threaten their land. It was considered unpatriotic for anyone to dress well. Mr. Oliver Littleton, president of the Board of Trade, bluntly told the people of London, "We must learn, as civilians, to be seen in clothes that are not so smart, because we are bearing yet another share in the war. When you are tired of your clothes remember that by making them do you are contributing to some part of an aeroplane, a gun or a tank." He went so far as to propose that men who did not look shabby were unpatriotic. It's easy to see how staunch the British character that they were able to maintain their morale in the face of that kind of privation.

Things got worse as the war progressed. Historian Philip Ziegler records that "the suffering of those made homeless, indeed, all of Londoners, was made worse by the harsh winter of 1944, the coldest for fifty years. Broken windows, cracked walls, missing roof tiles, combined with an acute shortage of fuel to produce a uniquely uncomfortable Christmas and New Year. Potatoes and other vegetables were in short supply, flowers virtually non-existent; at one school the ink froze in the pots and there was a delay of several hours while they thawed out in front of the only fire on the premises. There was even a shortage of shillings and sixpences to put in gas meters."[3] The shortage of wine and beer was so severe that in the combined areas of Kensington, Hammersmith, Fulham and Chelsea with a population of half a million people, only one person was arrested for drunkenness through the Christmas holiday.

There were, of course, the profiteers who always seemed to find a way to benefit from the sufferings of others. There was a healthy black market at work. Thieves tended to seek out damaged homes, and insensitive people were busily at work like the proprietors of one hurriedly-created establishment which displayed this sign: "Horrors of the Nazi concentration camps. Come inside and see real Nazi tortures, flogging, crucifixion, gas chambers, etc." They pleasantly added this helpful attraction: "Children's amusement section no extra cost."

Amazingly, the people carried on with the usual private grumbling but a heroic collective determination. Winston Churchill coined the term "business as usual" and it was repeated over and over. The people responded. Ziegler wrote, "The Londoners were not going to give in. Amazingly, few of those whose work kept them in London deserted their posts and only a handful used the raids as an excuse for non-attendance. They would leave homes damaged by the previous night's raid; find what transport they could; if necessary walk for miles through shattered streets, stepping around craters and over fire hoses, diverting to avoid UXB (unexploded bombs). In the end they would arrive."[4] Poet Stephen Spender said "I had the comforting sense of the sure dark immensity of London." Some even claimed a strange spiritual high as though some challenging fate had called them out for an ultimate test. Firemen told of having to disperse crowds from burning buildings as they gathered in a strange spirit of gaiety. While many people of course cringed, most of London held their collective head high and carried on, determined that no comic opera dictator was going to deny them their normal daily life.

The damage to London and its people was colossal. During a 57-day siege that began on September 7, 1940, there were two nights where 1,000 people were killed each night and 148,000 homes were destroyed. It was the year of the Battle of Britain, probably the most frightening, darkest year of the entire war for the people of England. Yet many years later when he was an elderly man Winston Churchill, after finishing dinner with Lord and Lady Moran, was asked by Lady Moran which year of his life he would most like to relive. Without hesitation he replied, "1940, every time, every time." That personified the unyielding spirit of the British people throughout the war.

Thousands of people slept in the Underground stations. While this must seem a terrible inconvenience today, it's said that many people continued to sleep there after the bombings had ceased because that's where they met their friends. One man reported the cessation of a raid by ten o'clock, but the entertainment in his Underground station home was so much fun no one went home until one in the morning.

Noting this fun dimension isn't to make the whole thing less than terrible. It is, however, to acknowledge the enormous element of determined courage on the part of a people who would not be defeated. Or as the above-mentioned historian put the matter, "Perhaps heroism is too strong a word, but the patience, the resourcefulness, the dogged determination of the working Londoner during the worst months of the blitz deserves profound admiration."[5]

By the time I arrived the V1 bombs which began puttering overhead like tiny planes on June 13, 1944 were still wreaking havoc. Looking like small airplanes, these forerunners to the cruise missile were twenty-five feet long, had a wing span of nearly eighteen feet and weighed 4,800 pounds. Their rudimentary yet ingenious guidance system carried them from the launching sites along the French and Dutch coasts to the larger London area where the engines would suddenly stop and the bombs would plummet into London. Some 10,000 V1s were launched at London, of which it's estimated that 4,200 were shot down by intercepting aircraft and anti-aircraft artillery fire. Still, in the course of nine months some nearly 2,500 V1s landed in greater London. They only ceased when the Allies finally overran their launch sites.

Time magazine in August of '44 described the effects of the V1 bombs: "London was eight million people obsessed. Their waking hours were haunted by one persistent, bedeviling fact; flying bombs." Comparing these bombs to the earlier blitz, the story went on to observe, "what had the Londoners on edge was that these things fell in no pattern at all," and they "made no military sense." It continued, "The bombs fell, haphazard, all about London's vast sweep. Seven hospitals were hit one day, three more the next day. In one, ten patients were killed. In one hut (next to a morgue that housed more dead) ten bomb-damage repairmen, just recruited in Scotland and Ireland, were killed." Everyone listened for the silence. One anti-aircraft crew coined the phrase, "If doodle dallies, don't dawdle, dive." General, later President Eisenhower stated in his memoirs that had the Germans begun the use of the flying bombs six months earlier, they would have prevented the invasion of Normandy. I spent the next few weeks living with the Londoners as we learned to go on with our lives and endure the flying bombs.

Much worse were the V2s which began to rain down on London on September 8, 1944. These monstrous rockets carried 2,000 pounds of high explosives and flew at 3,500 miles per hour making them impossible to see, much less intercept. Later records revealed that 1,000 were fired at London with about half reaching their target. This presented the British with a terrible moral decision. They had captured all the Nazi agents in England, having somehow spotted them as soon as they landed, a fascinating story in itself. The Germans counted on reports from those agents to know where their rockets were landing so they could adjust their aim.

A man named Eddie Chapman, a convicted burglar, had moved to the island of Jersey which was then captured by the Germans. Eddie, apparently a man devoted to his own best interests, quickly enlisted as a German agent and was dutifully parachuted back into England, which Eddie seems to have had in mind the whole time. He promptly informed British authorities of his upright standing with the Germans and was then enlisted to send back valuable - but false - intelligence information. He then became the German's primary source of information as to where their V2s were landing. Eddie sent erroneous reports which led the Germans to aim their devices to land in the least-populated portions of the London area, an arrangement which reduced the number of casualties but which later earned some authorities something less than appreciation from the residents of those areas once the ruse was disclosed. *C'est le guerre.* It has been estimated that some 5,500 people were killed by the V2 bombs and some 16,000 people were injured.

The British had a marvelous way of going on as though nothing was particularly wrong. Of course the city was blacked out at night, just in case Nazi air raids might resume, leaving London lighted only by whatever moonlight might show itself. You could stand on the middle of Westminster Bridge at midnight, stare down toward the Tower Bridge, see moonlight caress the Thames, and believe the war was gone, that there was peace on earth. Of course that was vain fantasy at the time. Still, it was a worthwhile dream to which I gave myself a time or two.

Wartime London was the essence of romance, celebrated in movies like *A Yank in The RAF* starring Betty Grable and Tyrone Power, filmed to the background music of "These Foolish Things." London after dark was featured in magazines, and in the mythical imagination of our own nation: darkness because of the blackout which banished all artificial light at night, young men far from home, constant danger in the air, the recorded sound of Big Ben's chimes, the voice of Edward R. Murrow assuring the world that the people of London were still going on, heads held high. Romantic relationships were brief, intense and too often tragic, as men in uniform passed through, quite a number falling in love with English women, then going on to their deaths on the continent, while men of England sometimes returned home to a beloved only to discover she had died in a bombing.

I walked with some friends to the dock district along the Thames River, to St. Paul's Cathedral. We had heard stories of the heroic actions of many church members on December 29, 1940, the night of what would be remembered as "the great fire raid." They climbed to perilous perches on the dome of the church the night of the bombing which destroyed virtually every other building in the vicinity. As a total of twenty-eight magnesium fire bombs landed on the roof, almost impossible to extinguish, the men would douse them in buckets of sand. St. Paul's Church survived almost unscathed. A photographer took an unforgettable picture of the dome surrounded by the smoke of the surrounding fire-bombed buildings.

On another occasion an 800-pound bomb landed on the steps of the cathedral - and didn't explode. Several days were required for fearless men to unearth and remove the bomb which, when exploded in a field, left a crater a hundred feet across and broke windows half a mile away. Those men received decorations for their bravery in extricating the bomb. It's hard to know whether God plays a hand in these things. I know it would have been an inestimable, tragic loss had St. Paul's been destroyed. But many grand churches were destroyed on both sides, so God must have let what happened happen. We climbed to the top of the dome and surveyed the area surrounding the cathedral. It was utter devastation as much of the destruction had been aimed at the dock areas and at warehouses along the Thames River.

I'll always remember my first visit to the interior of the Cathedral. It was beyond adequate words for me. I sat under the vast dome and felt myself overflow with some grandeur from beyond my world. I compare that in my mind with so many of today's churches which seem to pridefully display their heating pipes and their low ceilings, designed, I presume, to emphasize the everydayness of the Gospel and the relevance of their music. I have no quarrel with that if it inspires and changes its participants. Yet that vast and reaching beauty of St. Paul's captivated my twenty-year-old heart as nothing ever had. It was breathtaking, spirit-lifting, almost heart-breaking for me, as though something far more wonderful than my mind had ever conceived lay just beyond my imagining. To this day I am possessed, when I visit St. Paul's, by something indescribable, something of such beauty that I shall have to wait for a higher vision than I have known before I shall ever see its face. But it is there and it is here. It seemed to rise beyond all the denominational and spiritual distinctions of mankind to suggest a God whose love is boundless and able to greet and receive everyone who seeks him. Even German people. I, that winter day in 1944, surrounded by desolation and ruin, saw it there.

As one observer reported at the time, "the life of the city seemed to be going on just as usual. There was just as much traffic, and people were passing to and fro on their business...There is not the slightest feeling of defeat in the air or on the faces of the clerks and shopkeepers..." One night the Queen's Hall in Langham Place was destroyed along with all the musical instruments of the London Philharmonic Orchestra. Yet the orchestra played the following afternoon with borrowed instruments. The night on which the Café-de-Paris was destroyed with several people killed, a debutante ball was held nearby and one Charles Graves reported later that the only flaw in the evening was the absence of a member of royalty to cut the cake. When part of the Admiralty Building was blown away, Winston Churchill wryly observed that now he had a better view of Nelson's Column.[6] Terrible as those years may have been, the British character prevailed throughout.

Today we grieve for the nations of the Middle East, places like Iraq where violence seems to reign constantly and we wonder that residents can keep their sanity while living under such constant threat. We mustn't forget that the people of London lived like that for nearly six years. For example, on June 18, 1944 a V1 bomb hit the Guards Chapel on Birdcage Walk during Sunday worship at the very moment of the reading of the Te Deum, and the building exploded killing 119 people, seriously injuring 102. The Te Deum: "To Thee all angels cry aloud." What ironic prophecy.

A V2 hit Smithfield market while a crowd of housewives were queuing up for their ration of bread, killing 115. During the Christmas season of '44 happy crowds filled the Woolworth store at New Cross Road in Deptford. A V2 landed, killing 168 people, leaving 120 injured; eleven bodies never were found, including those of two tiny babies in their prams. One shocked Mrs. Robert Henrey, interviewed shortly after, said "The poor little trees with the ornaments torn from them, lay amongst the broken glass on the pavement."[7] What a description of all of London with all those bombs flying in from out of nowhere raining death down upon the innocents. Husbands and wives would leave for work each day, their children off to school, and each would have to worry all through the day whether they would reunite as a family in the evening. These terrible events occurred again and again.

One statistician computed the number of alerts during the years of the war and discovered that the people of London had endured a city-wide alert an average of once every 36 hours for five years. By July 1944, 200,000 children had been sent north to escape the danger. By

194 | E. CARVER MCGRIFF

the time the last of the V2 bombs hit the city they had destroyed some 30,000 homes and 250,000 were damaged. Some 10,000 people were killed by the flying bombs. Yet the people of London carried on.

CHAPTER FOURTEEN
LONDON UNDER THE AMERICANS

SOME NIGHTS I WOULD STROLL TO TRAFALGAR SQUARE, ITS WIDE venue especially beautiful late, after a light rain had turned the expansive walks into moonlit mirrors. It was pleasant, quieting, to just sit alone on a bench, the square all but deserted, and think about the future, wonder what life might be like in this great city when the people weren't at war, what the world would be like, as one popular song of the time promised, "when the lights go on again all over the world."

Piccadilly Circus was the magnet for GIs. There were many other places where people gathered, but the Circus was the favorite. The statue of Eros was removed to a hidden place, but Piccadilly otherwise looked much as it does today. Vere Hodgson wrote "Piccadilly is a thrilling place to be." Not only was it flooded with Americans, there were Free French, Canadians, many British, and there were "Girls, too, in their trim service uniforms by the hundreds," said Ernie Pyle, who once paid a visit and opined that there were way too many GIs staffing American headquarters. "Floods of American uniforms poured out of buildings" at lunch time, and "on some streets, an Englishman stood out as incongruously as he would in North Platte, Nebraska," wrote Pyle. Basically, we were too numerous for the British people, taking up space in the restaurants, crowding the streets at all hours, loud and raucous, able to spend what seemed to them to be too much money - a private in our army earned what a Flight Lieutenant in the British Air Force was paid - and they constantly complained that we were "arrogant, bumptious and cocksure." One survey revealed that only thirty-three percent of Londoners actually liked us. Still, most of us were oblivious to all of this and had to come home to read about it many years later. At the time, those men heading for combat had other things to think about while men stationed there were having the time of their lives, and those of us visiting from the outside felt some combination of envy and resentment that our brothers were fighting the war while by sheer luck of the draw those other dandies were living the good life in one of the world's great cities. The sense of being a "Great Generation" was a much later melting down of the differences which separated us all back then.

Everything focused on Rainbow Corner located at the corner of Piccadilly Circus and Shaftbury Avenue, the immense Red Cross facility which had the capacity to feed 2,000 men at a time, or, two evenings a week 2,000 men could dance with one of the 200 volunteer hostesses who joined with the same number of other employees to make the men feel at home. There young ladies, carefully sworn never to date any of the patrons, encouraged young men to write home, get something to eat and a cup of coffee, and feel welcome to just sit and visit with friends. It was good to hear the music we'd heard so many times played by Glenn Miller, Harry James, and the Dorsey Brother's bands, the music of a thousand senior proms, songs like "One O'Clock Jump," "Take the A Train," "Juke Box Saturday Night," "Paper Doll," "Chattanooga Choo Choo" and "Blues in the Night." Then the slow dances began with "I'll Be Seeing You," "Ghost of a Chance," "Someone to Watch Over Me," "I'll See You in My Dreams," "Making Believe," and then at the end of the evening the song that could bring tears to any homesick young man with a grilfriend, "Goodnight Sweetheart." You could hold some nice English girl in your arms, close your eyes, pretend she was someone else, and for just a few minutes you could be home again.

The truth is, while all of us went to London for a good time, there were many young men who were homesick, lonely, uninterested in drunken carousing, and actually welcoming a communal setting where they could read a good book, spend time with friends, and talk about home. I'd say the great majority of us, though perhaps fun-loving and maybe at times a bit carried away with the freedom of being far from home, were basically good people meaning no harm and oblivious to the irritating effect of the brash American personality on many British people. British writer Philip Ziegler wrote, "The American GI for his part experienced the disgruntled resentment of a knight who had disrupted his career and his family life to come to the rescue of a not particularly prepossessing maiden in distress, only to meet with carping comments about the quality of his armor and the ineptness of his swordsmanship."[1]

My friends and I spent our share of time at Piccadilly Circus. A visitor today during the tourist season, making one's way through the crowds trying to cross the street at rush hour, may have some idea what it looked like back then at night with the addition of the uniforms. Whatever our excesses, we certainly spurred the economy as prices steadily rose and I'm sure many an Englishman groused about the price of a pint as Americans swilled them by the billions. For a couple of years that was certainly the place to be for an American GI in the European Theater of Operations. I had the luxury, during my weeks there, of living at the heart of the action so to speak, just a brief stroll from Claridge's Hotel, and an easy walk to Piccadilly Circus. As I think about it, "Circus" was indeed the word.

The pubs were the center of London life. This has always been true in England, but during the war years this was especially true. The blackout was still in force and one could walk down a street in almost total darkness, the only light the moon's soft glow off the rain-washed streets, feeling one's way at times along a building wall, when suddenly you'd hear the sound of raucous laughter and slightly tuneless singing. Behold, right by your hand was a door handle, and when you turned it you stepped into a brightly lit and cheerful world where men and women were downing pints and having a great time. The pubs were required by law to close early by American standards, so the party started early. There might be a dozen GIs, some British servicemen, several women wearing uniforms, many office workers who stopped on the way home, the usual regular patrons, three or four young girls sitting together in a corner, the place full and cloudy with cigarette smoke. English custom allowed you to push in with any group you thought you'd like and you'd join in the fun. There was a unanimous "one for all and all for one" camaraderie that took you in whoever you might be.

Pubs were more than just bars. They were the center of community life. They were where people went to meet people, to remind themselves we're all in this together. The walls might resound with that most familiar of bawdy songs, "Roll Me Over In The Clover," which was sometimes corrupted to "Roll Me Over Yankee Soldier," or with a favorite, "It's The Same The Whole World Over" ("It's the poor wot gets the blame; it's the rich wot gets the gravy, ain't it all a bloody shame?"), or "Show Me The Way To Go Home," or "Roll Out The Barrel." The publicans who ran the places didn't encourage singing, but it happened anyway. On occasion, you might hear a distant explosion which was always followed by a moment of quiet, but soon, the talk would continue in a "there's nothing we can do about it, so let's go on with life" spirit. Sometimes, though, toward the end of the evening things would quiet, almost as if everyone knew it was time, and as the publican rang a bell and said, loudly, "last call, mates, last call," the people might sing "There'll Be Bluebirds Over The White Cliffs Of Dover" ("Tomorrow, Just You Wait And See"). They rarely got teary eyed, but they would now. British people were stiff upper lip and never seemed to me to feel sorry for themselves. But sometimes, if you're human and they were surely that, you have to express your emotions, and as the people stood to leave someone would often lead them out singing "There'll Always Be An England, And England Shall Be Free." When we considered the tiny isle so close to the mainland where the Nazis had reigned for five years, and when we considered the doughty people, their old men armed with pitchforks sometimes, or ancient World War I Enfield rifles, ready to fight them over the moors and down the city streets if they must, you were glad those Brits were on our side.

Though the British didn't particularly care much for Americans for awhile, they eventually, especially the girls, seemed to become increasingly crazy about us. That is, the girls one met in pubs. And these weren't all bad girls. Some were of course, and Ladies of the Evening were numerous to be sure, but most of the girls we'd meet were shop girls, office girls, people who were just tired of the dull sameness of wartime. Their own young men were away and after years of loneliness we GIs apparently looked pretty good. As time went on the British people seemed to get more and more used to our more outspoken ways, and by the time the great majority of us left England for the continent they seemed to genuinely grieve at our departure. To "go out on the town" where all of us GIs gathered was, to the English girls, to be where the action was.

British soldiers weren't so happy about our presence. Their well-worn complaint was that the problem with Americans is that we were "overpaid, oversexed, and over here." To that we would accuse the British soldiers of being "underpaid, undersexed, and under Eisenhower." British historian Max Hastings reported, "Already many British servicemen were irked by the extraordinary social dominance the Americans had achieved within Britain, with their staff sergeants receiving the pay of British captains, their vast reservoirs of equipment for themselves, and candy for the British children...Impeccable tailored American officers - and NCOs - crammed the London hotels and restaurants."[2] It was the old exchange rate situation and we were the beneficiaries.

When the pubs closed the streets were soon crowded with weaving, singing, laughing GIs, heading for some Red Cross hostel where they'd fall in bed, be asleep a few minutes later, then be up, either headed back to duty somewhere else, or headed to the nearest pub when it opened if they had time left on their passes, or off to duty in London.

The British were way ahead of us in their attitude toward black soldiers, complaining about the way they saw blacks being treated by some American white GIs, and generally finding them more charming and well mannered than white soldiers. White English girls dated black GIs and to the end of the war refused to countenance the prejudice of many whites. One popular song of the times, "Chocolate Soldier from the USA," bespoke the English acceptance of black soldiers as equals. Sadly, there were several riots as black and white GIs clashed in pubs, most of these quickly hushed up by the authorities. I can attest that the men who were my friends displayed no prejudice toward the blacks, but we did hear from some men (mainly from the southern states) some bitter attitudes. Segregation, still acceptable at the time, kept us all apart; and the only black GI I had occasion to know was my friend next to me in the hospital.

One night I was walking late in Piccadilly Circus, just leaving the Rainbow Corner Red Cross. I was in blackout darkness when a young girl no more than fourteen or fifteen stepped out of the shadows and asked if I'd be interested in her services. I asked her how much and she replied "is a pound too much?" I don't know why I asked the question. I had no intention of going with a prostitute. I guess I was just curious. But when I heard her tiny, timorous voice I felt a sudden sadness. Something in me wanted to tell her to go home, help her mother, stay off the streets, that one day she'd be so glad she kept herself pure. I wondered if this was her first night on the streets. She was only a child. But I was only just turned twenty and didn't have the wisdom to do anything other than just say no and walk on. I hoped everyone would say no but she probably found someone before long. There was no way to know the difference between the hardened professionals and the young girls either trying to survive or looking for some way out of intolerable boredom, or perhaps a tragic search for love. God knows there were many wartime casualties not measured by the statistics in the newspapers.

The English had their own sense of humor. They told of a Sea Lord walking into the Admiralty war room with its large wall map showing the locations of the various vessels at sea. A WREN, one of the female service members, was standing on a high ladder reaching up to mark a location. The Sea Lord looked up and remarked with classic English reserve that "either those ladies need to wear trousers or we'll have to move the convoy down to the south Atlantic."[3]

They were always amused at our comparative wealth combined with a more or less devil-may-care manner as compared to the sober British. *Time* magazine reported a joke being told at the time about a GI and a British soldier standing side by side in Piccadilly Circus as a dilapidated old car pulled up. The GI pompously asked "Do you know what we'd do if a car like that showed up in Times Square?" The Brit replied, "If you treated it as you treat everything else over here you'd probably either drink it or kiss it."[4]

Wartime humor was salty. A Baptist Chaplain named Randolph Gregory swore the story was true: one Chaplain accompanied a bomber on a raid over Germany, and was heard giving this prayer during an attack by some Focke Wulf 190s: "Our Father which art in heaven... Get that bastard coming in at 2 o'clock...Hallowed be thy name...Blast that SOB at 12 o'clock."[5]

One great story concerned General Eisenhower. It also made *Time* magazine. He was visiting a military camp and chose to go through the mess line with the troops. A directive had been issued with his permission, ordering that men be careful not to take more food in their mess lines than they could eat. There was an imminent food shortage and they must empty their plates. However, Eisenhower on this occasion, was full long before his plate was empty. But he had issued an order and would now have to live by it. Somehow, he managed to cram the rest of his food down and later, an aide reported talking to the lady in the mess line who said 'Blimey, I gave the General a double helping of everything, and he ate it all. He eats like a paratrooper lieutenant."[6]

GIs had our own communal humor. Two expressions were universal, remaining part of the common American language for many years. One, SNAFU, was an abbreviation for "situation normal, all fouled up," (that being a nearly accurate translation, usually moderated as done here for refined company). It was used generally in regard to mistakes made in situations where any well-adjusted, reasonably bright person should have gotten it right. Since combat was more or less a continuing process of mistakes by generals and lesser ranks, the issues being determined by which sides' generals made the fewest mistakes, the term originated in that province and was employed constantly by men of the armed forces throughout Europe, eventually universalized to apply to any mixup.

The other bit of humor was begun by some witty GI, name forever lost to history, and consisted of a drawing of a nose and eyes looking over a fence, two sets of three fingers, one on each side, with the motto "Kilroy was here." The face was optional when the words appeared. It began as a 1944 counterpart to the current "in your face" and originally meant "you may think you're something special because you made it this far, but I've already been here and gone." It was a challenge to any combat unit entering a town which someone else had already captured. The expression eventually degenerated into ordinary graffiti and appeared widely wherever American soldiers were to be found. It appeared on walls, latrines, sidewalks, revealing a general lack of imagination, and was soon purged from the American culture. Not, however, before it became emblazoned in every GI's memory.

London was our first exposure to the real United States Army, the Army that has served and protected through the centuries with its tight hierarchical structure, its books of rules by which each member lives, its strict dress code, its written-down solutions to every problem, its system of rewards and punishments, its *esprit de corps* by which each arm is believed by its members to be the most important reason for an army in the first place. Most of us were young kids, temporary employees you might say, who were drafted because of the war, were thrown into hurriedly-built training camps, taught the rudiments of the structured, highly-organized life of the armed services, then were shown how to shoot rifles and machine guns, given some familiarity with things like bazookas and mortars, then shipped out to some area of combat as replacements for men who were casualties. Most of us were only dimly aware of the Army's plan for us throughout our training, ready to do the bidding of almost anyone wearing stripes. We had virtually no contact with officers beyond the fact that when we met them we were supposed to salute them. Being an officer wasn't easy, and in combat was extremely dangerous. I can't see any possible way for a man to prepare for what it proved to involve. Not all officers had what it took, but most of the ones I saw tried their best, many of them to die in the effort. We really had no way to evaluate them until we saw them perform in combat.

Historian Robin Neillands, after careful study of the new Infantry divisions entering combat for the first time in Normandy, wrote "Many Americans, British, and Canadian officers of all ranks, would be found inadequate for the task before them, and replaced in the coming weeks. The fallout among senior officers was a notable feature of the Normandy campaign in all the Allied armies."[7] Clearly, success in a peacetime army does not guarantee that an officer is fit to lead in wartime. Lieutenant Elliott Johnson told of landing on D-Day with the 4th Division and encountering the colonel whom he had most admired as a training officer, only the man was roaring drunk, leaning against his command car and had to be helped to his seat. Johnson said the man never did sober up and was worthless as a combat officer. On the other hand, we also heard stories of over-aged Captains and Majors ready to retire for having been passed over for promotion, who suddenly became colonels because they might not have been good at details and management, but they could sure lead men in battle.

General Patton was the worst showoff of all with his pearl-handled six shooters and his non-official regalia. Normally we'd have seen him as some sort of a clown, but we all admired him because we knew he'd won a Distinguished Service Cross in the first World War and unlike nearly all the other generals, had actually spent time on the front lines getting shot at for many days long before he became a general. Grand entrances notwithstanding he'd been where we were, knew what it was like to sleep in the mud and face imminent death daily, and that gave him the moral right to send the rest of us to our deaths if it should turn out that way.

Being a successful general was not a personality contest nor a beauty contest. Generals were an assortment of men with widely different social personalities, but who shared certain indispensable traits, the most important one being able to say "Yes, let's move that battalion around to the right. If we can take that town and have no more than fifty men killed, we'll have done a good day's work," then sleep well that night. Otherwise, men of more sensitive natures would go nuts in a hurry. This, of course, refers to combat generals. I suppose the more removed a general was from the actual fighting, the less sanguinary he needed to be. The ones who functioned more as corporate VPs, many remaining in the United States while others were somewhat comfortably situated in England until Paris became available, may very well have been businessman types whose eyes were primarily on the military equivalent of the bottom line. After all the logistics of supply were monumental, and it was all overseen by a vast army within the Army of men, and some women, who made sure the whole thing worked efficiently without having to worry whether the town is taken or not. But sending men to their deaths and living with the knowledge was a quality without which combat generals could not win wars.

The squabbles between generals Eisenhower, Patton, Bradley, and British Field Marshall Montgomery are legend. Montgomery wanted Ike's job and never got over the slight; Patton nagged Bradley as being timid, while Ike's frequent scoldings of Patton for his unrestrainable big mouth almost cost us our best general. Patton was a constant fly in the ointment to Ike and publicly called Ike a "poor fool." Never able to shut up once he got started, he elaborated that "Ike is bound hand and foot by the British and does not know it. We actually have no Supreme Commander..."[9] Patton, of course, was an unmitigated glory hound which thankfully didn't prevent him from knocking the daylights out of the Germans. He was partly right, actually. Eisenhower was a politician and knew little about actual combat. Bradley, meanwhile, appears to have disliked Patton for any of a number of reasons, including, one suspects, envy of all of his fame and adulation. Former Colonel Carlo D'Este wrote later that "Theirs was a relationship based in no small part on Bradley's jealousy, cloaked in the contempt of one rival for another." To this he added "The real Omar Bradley was rather narrow-minded and utterly intolerant of failure."[10]

A new player arrived when, on the first of August Patton was turned loose with his Third Army, Bradley was promoted to command of the newly activated Twelfth Army Group, and Lieutenant General Courtney Hodges joined the pack as replacement for Bradley in command of First Army. Hodges didn't score many accolades either as several of his associates, in the words of one, "thought him the reverse of a strong military commander, but instead the model of a rumpled assertive, small-town banker." Meanwhile, back at the ranch so to speak, General Tooey Spaatz, head of the Air Corps who hung out in a comfy office in England, loftily bragged that we could win the war with his airplanes if the ground troops just had more guts. One might get the impression that in the armed forces, as I suppose is true of every organization, there is a lot of politics and no small amount of jealousy.

There's every evidence that some good, loud donnybrooks took place behind the scenes among these and some other, less-renowned generals. Quite a few were sent home, including two commanders of the division I served. In short, history suggests that Ike knew little about battle tactics, Bradley had trouble accepting responsibility for his mistakes and was sometimes shortsighted and timid, Montgomery was malicious, jealous, and self-important, Patton was arrogant and devoid of people skills, Hodges was an "officer of limited imagination and self-effacing personality" and General Spaatz had no idea how hard fighting a war on the ground could be.[11.] They all, of course, were absolutely sure they were right. Ike, who never actually led combat troops, had to win the war with a gang like this. Which he did. It seems a wonder that the Allies were able to defeat the most formidable war machine in history with nothing to work with but generals, a few good men, and a bunch of kids. Somehow, that quirky assortment of generals managed to win.

The gap between officers and enlisted men was a yawning chasm. The greenest Second Lieutenant just out of Officer Candidate School, newly arrived, outranked the toughest, battle-hardened top sergeant wearing a Silver Star, and could, if he wasn't very bright, require that "Top Kick" to stand at attention and say "Sir" at every turn. This was necessary, because out on a battlefield when an officer of any rank tells an enlisted man of any rank to get up and go across that field, the enlisted man must, without hesitation, without protest, get up and go even if there's a German machine gun team with their MG-42 loaded and aimed, waiting for that fellow to just try it. We all had to be completely conditioned to the wonderfulness of every officer so we wouldn't refuse the order when it counted.

Good combat officers, of course, were very respectful and careful about that. A true leader never abused his authority and always understood that his job was not just to order that man across the field, his job was to *lead* that man across the field, or at least to have in some way demonstrated his own courage under fire. We soon got the measure of our officers and had great respect for those who measured up. It was back there in places like London and Paris that we didn't feel quite the same. There, we had little to go by and we measured them by their respectfulness toward us. We didn't mind saluting and sir-ring so long as we were convinced the officers were good men doing their duty, which was true of the majority of officers. We did not have much respect for those officers who we could tell looked down on us, saw us as merely nameless functionaries there to carry out their orders.

Sergeant Bill Mauldin, who won a Pulitzer Prize for his editorial cartoons and had recently been the subject of a cover page article in *Time* magazine, distinguished himself throughout the war in being where the action was, even winning a Purple Heart in Italy. Mauldin went on to receive the Legion of Merit medal, an almost unheard honor for an enlisted man. A gathering of generals assembled and a full colonel, the-lowest ranking officer present, read the citation and pinned the medal on Mauldin. The generals applauded politely, then recessed to head for the bar. The colonel, name lost to history, called Mauldin over, said "congratulations," then told him to go find the company sergeant who would take him to the enlisted men's mess. So much for democracy in the Army. I'd have to guess that none of those generals had ever commanded in combat.

One place where everyone learned true democracy was in front line combat. The newly-arrived starched-back rookie "shavetail" Second Lieutenant, even if he was just out of West Point, learned very quickly that on the front lines the true hierarchy was not rank or where you went to school. It was how well you knew how to fight the enemy, and how scared you were while doing so. Wise company commanders often assigned new officer platoon commanders to battle-hardened sergeants with orders to follow the sergeant around and do what he says "until you know what the hell you're doing." Even the rare hotshot lieutenant-just-arrived got suddenly very egalitarian when he figured out that men follow those leaders whom they respect, and find endless ways to circumvent the orders of men whom they don't. Get someone killed unnecessarily, and you may find yourself suddenly out there all by yourself.

There was always inter-service rivalry. Deep down we realized it took all of us to win the war. But we were all sensitive to varying ideas of who had done the most. The Air Corps came in for a lot of razzing from the infantry men, partly because they had the spiffy uniforms and a lot more rank. Air crew enlisted men were always made sergeant or above so if they were shot down and captured they'd at least receive the fairly good treatment of a non-commissioned officer, not that of mere privates. I still vividly recall seeing a chubby kid in the men's room of a hotel where I was washing up for lunch. He'd removed his shirt and we chatted for a moment, then he slipped his shirt back on which bore an Air Medal and the stripes of a Master Sergeant. I could only gulp.

They were also paid a lot more than ground troops of the same rank. We infantry guys understood this with our heads, but felt it unfair since they went though a little bit of hell to be sure -- maybe a couple hours times however many missions they made, say 60 hours of hell for 30 missions -- about the same amount as an Infantryman experienced his first three days, if he lived so long. The Air Corps guys then went home, had a tasty meal, went to town, got drunk, went back to their warm beds and prayed for overcast weather. The infantry guy was sleeping in mud. In June *Time* magazine reported that the United States Army had awarded 89,500 medals in Europe so far, of which 83,000 had gone to the Air Corps. That's how infantrymen saw things. We used to say that most of those medals were awarded to airmen for preventing a rape; they changed their minds.

Bill Mauldin told of visiting a First Armored Division company which was dug in on a hill in Italy. The rest of the battalion was trying to drive a company of Germans out into the open where the entrenched company could shoot them. Apparently, Mauldin reported, the Germans had somehow escaped the trap. However, two P-51 Mustangs came screaming down firing their 50-caliber machine guns, their fire slamming into the division position. Frantic GIs were scrambling for cover as the ground erupted in clouds of dirt, rocks and vegetation. Obviously, the American pilots had intended to strafe the missing Germans and had overshot their mark.

Mauldin, a sergeant, gathered up a handful of spent bullets and visited the fighter squadron's mess that evening. He informed the pilots of what had happened and tossed the bullets on the table. On behalf of GIs everywhere, he felt some accountability was necessary for all the times Americans had mistakenly been killed or wounded by the 8th Air Force. A man who'd been standing in the corner listening strode over to Mauldin, who belatedly noticed the star of a brigadier general on the man's shoulder. While *Sergeant* Mauldin gulped, the general, fixing Mauldin with a steely glare, invited him to come along on a flight in a P-51 which was especially fitted with an extra seat, to see how hard it is to identify the front lines from the air at several hundred miles per hour.

The next day, bright and early, Mauldin arrived and was strapped into the rear seat of the Mustang. They took off and the general proceeded to treat his passenger to the most frightening series of aerial acrobatics known to man. Mauldin said that despite having skipped breakfast to be safe, he felt like he lost everything he'd eaten for the past three days. After a strafing flight on a deserted enemy village where they fired at a bicyclist and missed, the general then flew over the area of the position mistakenly strafed the day before and ordered Mauldin to try to point out the exact location of the American lines, which Mauldin was able to do. Probably disgusted at this tactical failure, the general landed and a miserably sick but triumphant Bill Mauldin headed back to his headquarters still convinced that the airmen, for all their heroics and good intentions, could be a lot more careful where they dropped their bombs and fired their guns. Mauldin, always on the side of the mud-covered GIs who did the fighting on the ground, wrote that "My opinions about the air force remained about the same. My lesson was to be careful who's listening when you tell a story."[12]

Naturally, the Air Corps men were unable to see the logic of our reasoning, arguing that they had to ride in a freezing plane for hours on end, never knowing when an ME-109 might jump them, or when a wing might be blown off by ack ack in which case, unlike the infantry men who could walk away from a broken truck, or hide in a hole in the ground, they all went down with the plane. Truthfully, each service suffered terrible losses. To keep the record honest, after the war it was estimated that a fighter pilot had only a sixty-percent chance of completing his tour of missions, air crew in medium bombers had a fifty-fifty chance, and air crew of heavy bombers only a thirty-percent chance of completing thirty missions unscathed. End-of-the-war statistics revealed that while for every man killed on the ground three or four were wounded, the ratio was the opposite in the air: for every airman wounded six were killed.

In later years, after learning what combat air crews went through I'm forced to admit that to me the thought of doing what they did is terrifying. It's only fair to acknowledge that between April with the planning of Overlord through the end of the Normandy campaign in August, the Allied airmen suffered 28,000 air crew casualties over France. Truth to tell, they were all heroes. I always remembered that P-51 pilot who died before my eyes, and the fact that the reason the Germans didn't strafe the hell out of us was because those flyboys had courageously tackled them one on one and beaten them to death. All told, in World War II more than a 100,000 Allied airmen were killed in action. So, long years after, here's a very sincere salute to the men of the United States Army Air Corps.

Bottom of the heap in the minds of those combat men was anyone working in London in a job sheltered from the fighting, partly because we envied them. They all wore a blue-star insignia and were lumped together in our culture as "Blue Star Rangers." We used to sing "Oh Mother don't you fear, your son will never die; he's a blue star Ranger in the service of supply." This was all unfair, of course. Everyone went where they were sent. Combat forces would have been immobilized without all the support services. Many of those blue-star men were former combat men as I would soon learn. I guess from their side there was the illusion that the more intelligent men were assigned to skill positions, like non-combat jobs, and the dummies were sent directly to the infantry. As I have earlier acknowledged, the war would have been lost but for the many rear echelon men and women who did their jobs just as well as we did ours. Nonetheless, there was plenty of rivalry among us all.

In late December I was transferred to the 10th Replacement Depot, known not very affectionately as a "repple depple" near Birmingham. It had an outlying area called Pheasy (or Feezy) Farms which housed those men not being assigned to a unit immediately. There I was thrown together with new friends as we were billeted in what had been low income housing units. The camp was notorious for its inhospitable treatment of soldiers awaiting transfer to regular units. One graduate, a paratrooper with the 101st Airborne, later wrote that "Feezy Farms was a nightmare. The place was surrounded by barbed wire and cantankerous MPs, the food was terrible, the mess hall was on a hill over a half-mile away..."[13] The commander, one Colonel Killian, was later court-martialed for his incompetence.

Eight of us lived in a room the size of my family room. Lou Silvermintz, Jimmy Haigh, Ed Hansen, George Schickler, and Bruce Weigel became my friends. We were the gang that headed to town every Saturday, returning somewhat the worse for wear on Sundays. All had been wounded and seemed pretty lively to me but for various reasons were never returned to combat. Again, as tradition demanded, we became close friends but said little or nothing about our combat experiences, though I did learn that Jimmy Haigh had landed on Omaha Beach with the 29th Division on D-Day.

Our room was heated by a small coal stove. There were four double-decker bunks, and while we slept there we spent little time there otherwise. Too cold or too hot depending on what part of the room you were in. It was a historically record-setting cold winter and we had to scrounge for our own coal for the stove. It was a rather dreary place and when that was added to the bleak winter landscape of that part of

England it wasn't always easy to remain cheerful. Usually, though, the camaraderie held it all together.

It was here that I celebrated Christmas 1944, if "celebrate" is the word. The difference between our fantasies of remembered Christmases as children and the reality of bleak Pheasy Farms made the contrast quite painful. We did little to mark the event save take long, private walks and indulge ourselves in rather sad reverie. I thought about home and hoped Mother and Dad were well. Unlike today with email and cell phones enabling instant contact, a letter from home could take two weeks or more to reach us and a reply a week or more in return. Letters could take a month to reach us if we'd been moved

Nothing was done by the Army to lift our spirits except, I presume without recalling for sure, that we had a better than average dinner that Christmas day, an accomplishment easily achieved. Many GIs stationed in permanent settings who had become acquainted with English families were invited in for Christmas celebrations. There again, we replacement types were always in transit somewhere with no opportunity to make friends with English families. It was mainly men who were more or less permanently stationed in non-combat jobs who managed to become friends with English families, friendly enough to rate invitations to their homes. But we also knew that many of our comrades were spending the holidays sleeping in frozen mud in open fields, so we counted our blessings and I don't think any of us complained among my friends.

We began to hear that a large number of new casualties were arriving in the hospitals which, therefore, were necessarily emptying out their wards of men who were able to return to some kind of duty, so our depot began to fill up. Stories came through of a sudden German onslaught just when we thought they were finished. German Field Marshall von Runstedt, prior to being relieved of command, had proclaimed to his troops "Your great hour has struck. Strong attacking armies are advancing today against the Anglo-Americans. I do not need to say more to you. You all feel it. Everything is at stake. You bear the holy duty to achieve the superhuman for our Fatherland and our Fuhrer." Following that, on December 16, just after dawn, a major portion of the German army had stormed into the almost impenetrable woods of the Ardennes Forest on a sixty-mile front reaching from the Huertgen Forest to Luxembourg. Supported by a 250,000 troops German troops, 1,900 pieces of heavy artillery, and 970 Panther and Tiger tanks, they rampaged on smashing everything in sight. Sadly, this included those young guys we'd met that day near our hospital, the 106th Infantry Division. Even the long-dormant Luftwaffe showed up with bombers and fighters in support of the Nazi ground attack. They were headed for Antwerp, and for awhile it looked like they might get there. They slammed into the forest east of Malmedy decimating our forward positions, American generals having mistakenly assumed the Germans were not able to launch such an attack.

It could have been fatal. General Sepp Dietrich's 6th Panzers steam rolled over Middleton's VIII Corps, the 5th Panzer Division heading south to intercept Patton's fast moving 3rd Army units. Field Marshall von Runstedt's aim was to cross the Meuse River and drive through to Antwerp, cutting off Allied troops in Holland and Belgium which could have resulted in their destruction. Rear areas were torn by confusion; no one at first able to make sense of the situation. It was, after all, a known fact that the Germans lacked sufficient forces to mount a major attack. Wasn't the war almost over? Or so everyone believed. One Intelligence officer on General Bradley's staff, Colonel "Monk" Dickson, had repeatedly insisted that the Germans were planning a major attack in the area of the Ardennes. He was alone. Everyone else, including all the generals, scoffed at this, one general even suggesting that Dickson be sent on a long leave to get over whatever ailment could have caused him to think such a thing at all possible. Everyone was settled down for a pleasant, quiet Christmas. It was another example of a failing from which the American leaders never fully recovered, to underestimate the fierce determination of the Wehrmacht to prevent the occupation of Germany.

Entire battalions surrendered. GIs separated from their units clogged the road. High-ranking officers stared at suddenly outdated maps. Communication lines were cut. English-speaking German commandos roamed among the Americans, changing road signs, reporting troop formations back to their units. Pockets of heroic resistance were quickly overrun by exultant German infantrymen, supported by charging Panther and Tiger tanks. Long columns of captured American infantrymen, many thousands of men, streamed to the rear of the German lines to prisoner cages. Ice and snow rendered American tank traffic nearly impossible, limiting them to heavily mined roads. Powerful German columns thundered toward the gateway to victory, the crossroads village of Bastogne. They were finally stopped by the heroic stand of the 101st Airborne Division at Bastogne. Fifteen thousand GIs were surrounded there for days. Low on ammunition, food and medical supplies, the skies sodden with heavy, low-lying clouds which prohibited our planes from helping, they fought on against fanatic Nazi attacks until the skies finally cleared just before Christmas and supplies were dropped while fighter planes were finally able to start blowing up German tanks. So much for Christmas 1944. We were saved by those "Battling Bastards of Bastogne."

I thought how cold the winter was, and I couldn't imagine sleeping out in foxholes and slit trenches in that weather. No battle is good, but I knew that if I had to be in one, I'd take Normandy over the Bulge. Despite the constant rain, cold nights, and broiling hot days of Normandy, it had to beat what the guys were going through up there. I prayed for them. It all proved to be one of those bad things which became a good thing. People who believed that God was helping us have a great example in The Battle of the Bulge. The Generals had been wishing the Germans would attack, "come up out of their holes" as General Bradley put the matter, allowing the Allies to be the defenders for a change. That's what happened. The Germans were so badly beaten, finally, that they never again were able to mount a significant offensive. According to many historians, The Battle of the Bulge became one of our great victories.

Our lives in England went on while living on Easy Street. Many of our memorable adventures in this stage of our Army life were of the social variety. We loved to get together around a table on Saturday nights at the Gunmaker's Arms pub in Birmingham, order pints of bitters or half and half, and sing and laugh the night away. Great hilarity prevailed and laughter was the order of the day, much of the humor consisting of smart aleck insulting remarks to each other, all of which were taken in good spirit. Girls began to join us, Lily and Violet being two of my friends. We had great times together. Lou Silvermintz was the genuinely witty member of our circle. He and an occasional member, Murray whose last name I have forgotten and who also had a great sense of humor, kept us entertained with their constant repartee. Murray fell in love finally, and spent his time with Evangeline, so dropped out of our little company. The two of them were madly in love and had long discussions about where they'd finally settle when the war was over. We didn't get to know Evangeline very well but decided that if Murray loves her she must be Miss Right.

I have to confess there are times today when I wish I could walk back into the original Gunmaker's Arms again, just for a day, be twenty again for a few hours, sit at a large table with George, and Jim, and Bruce, and Ed, and Johnny, and Lou. We'd take the biggest table in the place and we'd guzzle half and half, and we'd sing "Don't Fence Me In," and "Birmingham Jail," and "Roll Out The Barrel," and we'd laugh until our sides hurt, and we'd be together again. The noise would be loud and raucous and we'd love it. It would be like it was, and I'd be happy, and my dreams of adventure, and new friendship, and camaraderie would all be coming true again. We were all kids then. Ironically, given our reason for being there, it was a time of youthful, exuberant innocence beginning its inevitable transition to the sometimes harsh realities of the real world. Those times in our lives can never be recaptured, but they remain as treasured memories. I'd bet every surviving man who was there shares these feelings today.

Also on Snow Hill in Birmingham was a Red Cross center, a large establishment which appeared on Sunday mornings to be one of the world's largest detox centers. A dozen sleeping GIs could be seen sprawled on the floor of the main sitting room, men only just recovering from a night of carousing, most of them kids whose friends had failed to slow them down on the local beer. In the dining area were long lines of semi-paralyzed men who had struggled out of bed in one of the nearby Red Cross-run hostelries, staring with bleery eyes as they waited their turn to receive a cup of life-giving coffee and a couple of utterly tasteless doughnuts by means of which a slow return of blood flow would enable them to resume their individual personalities in time to return to duty. The old maxim "never buy a car made on Monday" applied in many an Army installation throughout Britain as men of all ranks slowly regained their strength.

Parents today decry the drinking habits of their college-aged kids, and well they should. But the Greatest Generation were at least their equals in that department, only with the luxury of acting out their adventures where the folks back home were none the wiser. It was a crowded mix of hospital patients, former combat men from the repple depples, and Blue Star Rangers from various Army units stationed nearby, with the latter group predominating. Mercifully, nearly all of us would go home and straighten up, lead responsible lives. A few, a very few, would never recover. Also mercifully, while drinking was a favorite vocation while on pass, few men had access to alcohol during the week and most of us lived sober lives otherwise. When we were in transition or in training or on duty the quickest way for a man to get in serious trouble was to be found under the influence of alcohol. Also, there was very little access to hard liquor except for the alcoholics who managed to discover where the British kept it hidden. Drinking was draft beer in its several varieties and I sometimes suspected it had quite a bit less alcoholic content than does today's American beer. However, it would be to rewrite history to pretend this wasn't the All-American past time when on a pass.

Regarding passes there were basically two kinds, Class A and Class B. Class A passes were issued to enlisted men for a stated period of time, usually somewhere between 24 hours and a weekend. Each week a man had to hope for a pass for the coming weekend and they weren't, by any means, always forthcoming. Men in permanent billets in places like London and Paris, however, normally had the luxury of a Class B pass which permitted off-duty men to go where they pleased. Therein lay one of life's little inequities: combat men were usually limited to Class A passes, non-combat men usually having Class B passes.

My guess is that the grand total amount of alcohol consumed by the average GI in situations like ours was not nearly so much as what's written here may seem to portray. The problem was it was usually concentrated in short time frames, such events widely separated by hard work and healthy recreation on base. Still, on weekends for most GIs it was Katie-bar-the-door.

This all pretty much characterized life in major English cities for American GIs. Life was good for nearly everyone not involved in the fighting. Officer's clubs thrived. Dining rooms and bars of the finer hotels were usually filled with Americans. Officers were highly paid by English standards and had access to all the social amenities. The authorities were permissive of Americans, and there were so many of us we must surely have been a great boon to an economy that was sadly depleted. Only the poor GIs doing the fighting were to be pitied. It really was a class system with the fighting men at the bottom until they managed to get themselves wounded.

Someone wrote a nonsense song that we sang over and over. It was sung to the tune of "Humoresque" and went like this:

(first verse)
"Gentlemen will please refrain
From passing water while the train
    Is standing in the station, I love you.
But if you must pass your water
If you will just call the porter,
    He'll place a vessel in the vestibule.

(second verse)
We believe in constipation
While the train is in the station,
    Moonlight always makes me think of you.
Drunken soldiers on a lark
While kissing statues in the park,
    If Sherman's horse can take it so can you.

(third verse)
Now that we have reached our station
We are at our destination,
   Still, there's one thing we have yet to do.
You have all been simply grand,
And we can quickly understand,
   Now all of you are free to use the loo.

That was it. There were other verses which I mercifully don't recall. It was sung often in the pubs of London and Birmingham and clearly deserves to be lost to history. It does, however, depict the intellectual level at which most of us functioned much of the time.

We were assigned to the 1st Base Post Office near Birmingham and employed sorting mail, not exactly the kind of work one wanted to come home and tell friends we'd done for the war. It did, however, free many of those Blue Star Rangers for real service, one of whom we later heard won the Medal of Honor. We were transferred to hurriedly-constructed barracks near the little town of Minworth and placed on the night shift, which meant we went to work when everyone else was headed home, and vice versa. Half a mile from our quarters was an airfield specializing in repair of combat damaged planes. It took awhile to get used to hearing a limping B-17 rumble in at 200 feet over our roof for service while we were trying to sleep, but we eventually did. That schedule hampered our social life at times. On the other hand, we were off duty on weekends and, being night people, lasted well beyond pub closing, which necessitated locating private clubs which could remain open until early morning.

I suppose it's only fair to note that there were a fairly small number of men who were more mature and more serious than the rest of us. They often skipped the pub-related adventures and spent time in libraries, museums, and even churches. Most seemed rather humorless to my gang but I suspect many of them were the ones who most quickly began to succeed in civilian life when we all went home. Somehow, these admirable young men never seemed to gravitate to my crowd.

A mile from our barrack was another pub, The Hare and The Hounds, especially loved because of its proximity to our billet by short walks. The reader needs to be reminded again that visiting a pub in England wasn't quite the same as hanging out in a bar at home. It could be that, of course, but it was also a community center, a place where people gathered to be with friends. Families gathered in one side of the pub, frequently bringing their children. We often went there to meet English people or just to sit around and talk. It was about the only place where we could get together outside our living quarters. Sometimes men didn't want to go all the way to Birmingham, or they snuck off from the work bus loading and weren't noticed, or claimed to be too ill to work until the work bus had departed, so they could all head over there for the evening's entertainment. Most of us felt a mild sense of guilt, realizing how many men were still fighting. However, now that the so-called Battle of the Bulge was resolved and the Siegfried line had been breached we knew it couldn't last much longer.

Getting into Germany, incidentally, could have been more costly than it was. Hitler had ordered the destruction of every bridge crossing the Rhine River. This was done except for one bridge near the town of Remagen. The Ludendorf Bridge had remained standing. To cross the river without a bridge would have required paratroop drops and boat crossings, both of which would have entailed numerous casualties. But on March 7 a lieutenant of the 9th Armored Division led some men across the Bridge at Remagen which the Germans had tried but failed to destroy, which led General Eisenhower to write that "the traditional defensive barrier to the heart of Germany was pierced."

Of course the Germans immediately set about trying to blow the bridge. They ordered a bombing mission which missed. Meanwhile, Allied forces were moving across the bridge, and in desperation the Germans found seven volunteers whose job was to tow bundles of high explosives down the river in the dark and try to blow the bridge. Someone saw them, opened fire, and three of those bundles exploded, killing their German frogmen.

Hitler, probably insane by this time, ordered that the officers responsible for failing in the destruction of the bridge be shot. Four of them were marched into the Westerwald Forest and put to death, men who did their best executed for not performing the impossible. Those frogmen, brave men called on to perform a suicidal mission in an unjust and clearly lost cause, dead. Hundreds of decent young German soldiers were being executed for failing to fight to the death, a common practice by German officers, done on the spot in the waning days of the Third Reich. There were no trials, no burden of proof, no hint of compassion, just death. Several thousand German soldiers are said to have died this way. Fourteen- and fifteen-year-old boys were fighting as infantry without the foggiest idea what they were supposed to do, hundreds dying without ever having even lived. The entire German army seemed to have descended into madness. Nothing better exemplified the difference in spirit between the Germans and the Americans.

Terror camps throughout the region were filled with the wasted bodies of innocent Jewish men and women who had done no wrong. When a Russian Army company marched into Budapest they found an estimated 10,000 dead unburied bodies. Millions of young German boys were now dead, all dedicated to a cause with no redeeming purpose, their nation in ruins. The entire story exemplifies the depravity of the Nazi's approaching demise. For a German it was a time of reaping the whirlwind of death, the inevitable outcome for a nation so acquiescent of totalitarian leadership, a nation willing to be denied the ability to call its leadership to account, a nation devoid of the courage to speak out against and otherwise defy such demonic evil. It has seemed to the rest of the civilized world that such a travesty of human conduct got what it deserved. People who witnessed first hand the final days saw the fires of Hell, and for the architects of this madness Milton's words come to mind: "Hurled headlong flaming from the eternal sky with hideous ruin and combustion down to bottomless perdition, there to dwell in adamantine chains and penal fire..." The Germans had their own word for their fate: "Gotterdammerung," a disastrous conclusion, from Wagner's "Twilight of the Gods," a nation whose children were raised devoid of any sense of the divine spirit in their midst.

For ten days Allied forces streamed across the bridge at Remagen. On March 17, finally hit by German artillery fire, it collapsed killing twenty-eight American GIs. But the Allies were across.

On April 12 I was sitting in a restaurant in the town of Sutton-Colfield when a GI came in and announced that President Roosevelt had died. The British reaction amazed us. The people of London mourned. He had been their savior. Author C.P. Snow wrote, "I don't think I have ever seen London quite so devastated by an event. Even my old landlady was crying. The underground was full of tearful faces far more than if Winston had died I'm sure."[14] A service was convened in St. Paul's Cathedral on April 17 and was attended by the King and Queen. Another writer reported that American ambassador Joseph Winant then escorted Winston Churchill to the door, Churchill in tears.

By May we began hearing that the war was about to end. On May 7, 1945, at 2:41 a.m., German General Alfred Jodl, Hitler's Chief of Staff, signed an unconditional surrender document committing all German forces to lay down their arms. Co-signers were American General Walter Bedell Smith and Russian General Ivan Susloparov, Eisenhower having very pointedly arranged not to be present. Incidentally, General Susloparov unwittingly sealed not only the fate of the German Third Reich but his own as well. When he returned to Mother Russia he promptly disappeared; later efforts to learn his fate were unsuccessful.

The ceremony took place in Supreme Headquarters Allied Expeditionary Force (SHAEF) headquarters war room in Rheims, France, a room which had been used frequently as a recreation room for staff members. However, the agreement wasn't to become effective until late on the 8th. This produced some confusion as the agreement was immediately leaked to the world at which point the celebrations began, only to be quelled when the announcement was rescinded, then reissued. Of course the people of London were most affected because this meant the bombing would cease, then no it wouldn't, then yes it would. Officially on May 8 it did, which did not mean we were going home. There was still a war in the Pacific to worry about, and while I didn't have to worry about combat anymore, I did wonder if they were going to need mail clerks in the Pacific. Instead, however, we were transferred to Paris, an arrangement we thought just fine.

I was able to be in London from time to time after moving away, and was interested to see how the British celebrated VE Day. Or not. Of course they still had to give thought to the war in the Pacific. But either way London would now have peace. The reaction was pretty much English understatement. Considering the terrible suffering the people of the country, and most especially of London had suffered, the celebration was, at best, muted. There was dancing in the streets, and it was a great excuse for many people to get drunk, but all in all, it was pretty tame compared to the celebrations in New York and San Francisco. Comedian Robb Wilton captured the essence of British elation when he said "There's nothing to look forward to now. There was always the All Clear before."

The traditional celebration for English people was bonfires and London was soon alight with flames. The tepid celebration to follow is best exemplified by the event in Chelsea where the mayor lit the fire, then danced around it singing "Knees up Mother Brown." Over in Enfield it was reported that there was "a very pleasant victory party." That was England for you.

Of course everyone was happy. Literary critic Desmond MacCarthy, noting that after nearly six years of blacked-out streets the lights were on again, wrote that "The dome and cross of Saint Paul's were picked out by searchlight, looking like a marvelous piece of jewelry invented by a magician." The streets were filled with revelers, but one newspaper described it as more or less one great family outing. It was generally early to bed. The crowds outside Saint Paul's began to melt away and as yet another observer wrote: "Slightly dejected revelers joined hands to sing "Auld Lang Syne" outside the deserted church...the crowds... drifted aimlessly away, until at last the streets were empty."[15]

CHAPTER FIFTEEN

HELLO PARIS

ON THE 19TH OF AUGUST 1944, THE LEADING ELEMENTS OF THE 79th Infantry Division had crossed the Seine River at night, and the liberation of Paris had begun. Some 20,000 French resistance members began to mobilize in the city, most of them without weapons and with little idea how to go about the business of resisting the German occupation forces. Fortunately, most of the Germans they would see were either second-class troops used for the occupation, or combat troops on leave and thus disorganized and only lightly armed. On the 25th the French Second Armored Division arrived led by General Leclerc, paving the way for the arrival later in the day of General Charles de Gaulle, the international symbol of French resistance. The City of Light was free at last. It would be awhile, however, before there would be much light.

General de Gaulle's arrival officially began at the Arc de Triomph at 3 p.m. on Saturday, August 26, 1944, and was nothing less than a tour de force. First he relighted the torch of the unknown soldier which the Germans had snuffed out in 1940. Then he began his majestic trek down the Champs Elysees preceded by several police cars and four Sherman tanks. Accompanying him and strung out behind, pushing as much as decently possible so as to get in any photos, were crowds of self-appointed freedom fighters, what one observer called the "late-arriving heroes," as well as assorted politicians hoping, no doubt, for a life-altering photo op. Simone de Beauvoir wrote, "Mixed in the immense crowd, we acclaimed not a military parade but a popular carnival." The carnival proceeded down the Rue de Rivoli to the Notre

Dame Cathedral, the Bishop of Paris notably absent since that gentleman had been inordinately chummy with the Krauts.

There was work to be done. The city was still infested with pockets of Nazi soldiers, but the cat was clearly out of the bag. Thousands thronged the street, hundreds of American troops marched along the Champs Elysees and nearby thoroughfares. Ernie Pyle was there, riding in a jeep and later wrote "I felt totally incapable of reporting it. It was so big I felt inadequate to touch it. I didn't know where to start or what to say. The words you put down about it sounded feeble to the point of asininity...a great many of us feel we have failed to present adequately what was the loveliest, brightest story of our time. The sky was pure blue, the sun was bright and warm."[1] He saw one very short lady carrying a step ladder which she would occasionally climb in order to see the General. Frenchmen, long stifled and restrained, now swaggered along the sidewalks, young girls found carefully-preserved dresses from bureau drawers. Sergeant Richard Tewksbury, riding in a jeep, was showered with flowers and told of seeing some of those pretty young girls dancing in the fountains of Place de La Concorde later that night. I wish I'd been there, what a splendid day. But I too knew what liberation felt like. (Incidentally, rumor has it that some of those cavorting ladies did so dishabille, as they say in Paris though Sergeant Tewksbury says he is unable to confirm this).

There was some shooting, initiated it's believed by some wild-eyed FFI (French Forces of the Interior) members, many attired in bullet-filled bandoliers, eyes alight with the fire of demon rum as they also used to say. Amazingly, nearly everyone hit the deck except the General who stood in heroic confidence to be described by Malcolm Muggeridge this way: "With all eyes fixed upon de Gaulle; he alone appeared majestic, fearless and untouchable." It was the General's day to be sure. It was also the end of the FFI as soon as de Gaulle could get that done. By the way, shooting was more or less rampant throughout Paris thanks to the combined participation of the Germans, the FFI, many independent partisans, and who knows how many young people who managed to obtain firearms. It has been determined that

2,873 Parisians, plus a bunch of Germans, died in the liberation of Paris. It took awhile for all the Germans to depart.

German General Dietrich von Choltitz had governed Paris during the occupation and in early August was ordered by Hitler to destroy the city by whatever means possible, by bombing if nothing else. Probably seeing how things were going and not wanting that on his resume, Choltitz ignored the order. Instead, he surrendered to General LeClerc who was accompanied by a leader of the Resistance, a Communist who had fought in Spain. This somewhat scotched Allied plans to place Paris under control of an Allied governmental team. General de Gaulle was having none of that, and upon learning that the Allies had issued special currency for the country threw such a fit that the Allies backed off and de Gaulle then declared a French provisional government at the Hotel de Ville on August 30. General Eisenhower decided he could live with that. General Marshall, Eisenhower's boss back in America, had insisted on an American-led provisional government but Ike, who also had five stars on his shoulder, seems to have paid little attention to Marshall. He and de Gaulle had an understanding. They were both game to battle verbally in working out the details, but de Gaulle, who didn't ordinarily care much for American generals, took a liking to Ike and vice versa. They were both military men, generals, and found in that brotherhood a basis for mutual respect. It didn't take long for an amicably agreeable government, French led, to take effect. de Gaulle soon oversaw the appointment of appropriate leaders throughout the country and obviously set the stage for his eventual election as president of France.

Back in America there was unrestrained rejoicing that Paris was free. *Time* magazine reported that when the news arrived, "A blizzard of confetti, ticker tape and torn newspapers fell dizzily through the afternoon sun into Manhattan's Rockefeller Plaza. The crowd wept happily." People who'd never been there somehow viewed Paris as the symbol of the good life in Europe, something long missing from the collective American consciousness. Those celebrities who had been to Paris acted as though the important part of the war was at last accomplished. *Time* reported that the news "made the whole free world catch its breath...it was one of the great events of all time." The writer went on to elaborate that "Paris is the city of all free mankind, and its liberation last week was one of the great events of all time." *Time*'s Chief War Correspondent Charles Christian Wertenbaker, the first newsman to enter the liberated city, effusively reported, "I have seen the faces of young people in love and the faces of old people at peace with their God. I have never seen in any face such joy as radiated from the faces of the people of Paris this morning. Your correspondent drove into Paris with eyes that would not stay dry."

Everyone at home needed some good news, and the liberation of Paris somehow became a symbol of eventual victory. Even untravelled people were delighted, as though some sacred city of the mind was now safe. As one 19th Century traveler wrote: "A man can die never having seen Paris, and yet he will have been there, he will have seen it in his dreams and in his imagination." Opera Star Lily Pons, attired in her USO uniform, sang the "Marseillaise" as people waved the Tricolor and the Cross of Lorraine. Hildegarde, a popular singer of the time, sang the tearful "I'll Be Seeing You," and Tallulah Bankhead, who had taken a vow of abstinence from alcohol until final victory, is said to have promptly fallen off the wagon.

There was a downside. In one suburb of Paris a cemetery was found in which lay the bodies of 75,000 people who had been executed during the occupation of France. In the Surete Generale on Rue des Saussaies it was discovered that the Gestapo had tortured prisoners where final messages were found scratched on the walls of cells. In the old Jewish quarter only 10,000 of the original 100,000 residents remained, most probably having fled but many having been carted off to the camps.

There was a bit of sweet revenge as a group of partisans rounded up twenty-four Gestapo men, took them to a nearby rifle range where patriots had been executed, and without further adieu, shot them. The terror would now cease.

Paris had suffered terribly during the occupation, mainly by neglect. The buildings were dirty, the people underfed and docile and more than half the produce of French farms had been sent to Germany. It is estimated that the diet of the average Parisian was 850 calories per day. Diseases were rampant, mostly those resulting from dietary deficiencies. The death rate doubled from that of prewar Paris. The gardens of the Tuilleries, Luxembourg, and Invalides were torn up and turned into vegetable gardens. Clothing was in short supply, sometimes made with paper and cardboard. Photographer Jacques-Henri Lartique wrote, "Paris looks as if it has fainted. You can hardly hear it breathe." Hot water was in short supply because of the shortage of heating materials leading one writer, Colette, to give this advice to Parisians: "Economy and hygiene unite to sum up my message: go to bed."

Transportation had come almost to a standstill. At the beginning of the war there were some 350,000 operable cars in Paris. During the occupation it's estimated the number was no more than 4,500. The number of buses was reduced from 3,500 to 500. Fortunately, the Metro still operated. Bicycles were the primary mode of transport. In the first three months of the occupation 20,000 bikes were stolen, though after awhile the manufacture of bikes was permitted and by the end there were an estimated two million bikes in Paris.

Famous writers, Simone de Beauvoir and Jean Paul Sartre among them, had begun gathering in cafés to do their writing, mainly because cafés were heated and there was conviviality, a rare commodity at the time. They favored the Left Bank cafés of Sainte-Germain-des-Pres, the Café Flore a favorite. It was here that Existentialism began.

While the law-abiding people of Paris were not directly mistreated by the Nazis so long as they stayed out of trouble, this fact was not true for the Jews. On July 16 and 17, 1942 the Nazis rounded up 12,000 Jews and sent them off to Auschwitz. Collaboration was a major problem as many Parisians, encouraged by the Vichy government which had entered into a devil's compact with the Nazis, actively supported the occupation. The local police, glad to deflect Nazi antagonism to someone else, were sometimes much too cooperative in running down Jewish residents. Others, while not by any means favoring the occupation, played along with the Nazis for their own good, guaranteeing a lot of name calling and lifelong bad blood among the citizens when the Germans were gone.

In the opinion of most outsiders, and probably many Parisians who deemed it better to keep their mouths shut, the recriminations got out of hand once the Germans were gone. The most common punishment of women who were accused of having consorted with the enemy was the shaving of their heads. Their clothing was often torn, they were beaten, all were humiliated in front of their countrymen. Hundreds of women, many innocent, were treated this way.

Malcolm Muggeridge who served in British Intelligence at the time wrote that he "was struck by the horrifying callousness of the young members of the FFI." He also observed that he was amused to note how many Frenchmen, suddenly wishing to appear to have been patriots throughout the occupation, told of helping downed British and American airmen escape the Germans. Muggeridge, unconvinced, wrote "I often reflected our Air Force would have been so huge that we should have won the war before it began."[2]

Many of the people who resisted the Germans at the end were Communists, though a large number were Nationalists, the FFI. Some 600 barricades were created by tearing up asphalt from the streets and adding in furniture from nearby stores. Weapons appeared, and quite a number of solitary German soldiers caught unaware were shot to death. Some were beaten, then interned. All this was intended to make continued occupation more difficult for the Germans who, in most cases, were quite anxious to depart the city anyway. Ultimately, though there was some shooting and shelling, the damage was minimal, certainly so as compared to the major cities of Germany. The one widely-mourned casualty was the major wine-making facility and warehouse which went up in flames and lit up the night sky all over Paris. However, one contemporary citizen recorded that grieving was brief as the shortage was quickly corrected. Mercifully, because the General whom Hitler had ordered to destroy Paris ignored the order, the sights of Paris survived intact.

Obviously, once the liberation had taken place there was joyous celebration, but a lot of work to be done. It would take time. There would be intense squabbling and name calling and bribery. While de Gaulle was not a very friendly sort of man when it came to international cooperation, he was the strong rallying symbol which finally held everything together. Meanwhile, the entrepreneurs quickly began to provide the city with the amenities which would attract the money-laden Americans and others who would be arriving. Theaters, restaurants, night clubs and stores would thrive. And so, too, would the black market. For the American service troops who would now begin arriving in Paris it was Let The Fun Begin.

On the 8th of June 1945, almost a year to the day from my first landing, we sailed aboard the Empire Rapier from Southampton, England, to the French Port of Le Havre. There we boarded trucks which headed north to the Channel-side village of Etretat, a resort of less than 2,000 population. We all immediately fell in love with the charm of the place with its winding streets and tall, antique-looking buildings, with wine shops, inns, little stores. Our truck pulled up in front of one of the most charming-looking inns and we climbed out and discovered we were in for what for a Frenchman in peacetime would have been a very expensive vacation.

Into the inn we piled, two to a room. The length of our stay there was never defined to us but we had no duties and were free to explore the village. A horse-drawn wine cart with iron-clad wheels rattled by as we hit the street, and one of our more daring members ran along behind and committed what the locals would probably have considered an unforgivable atrocity: he swiped a bottle of red wine. Our introduction to Etretat was, thus, incomparably pleasant.

Etretat is locally known for the remarkable rock formations along its coast, made famous by the drawings of the French landscape painter Claude Monet. High, gently sloping hills rise from each end of the village, and a walk in either direction gave a splendid view of the distant scene and the rock formations below, which were repeatedly bombarded by a crashing surf. In the days to follow we spent much of our time on one or another of those hills, looking down on the village or out in the direction of the English coast where we convinced ourselves we could see the white cliffs of Dover.

Nights involved gatherings in the local inns, or sitting out at side-walk cafés sampling the local food and, on occasion, wine, this time paid for. It wasn't very good. Apparently the French people in Etretat had not heard about their reputation for French cuisine. More likely, the war only just over, they didn't have much food or good wine and were wise enough not to waste it on passing vandals like us. No matter, we had a great time.

Near the train station was a secret tunnel which ran underground, exiting under one of the steep cliffs which fronted the high hill. That is it was supposed to be secret, but we found it and traversed its some 200-yard length to the Channel. As we stepped out onto the narrow beach at the foot of a sheer, high cliff, we found the remains of a German gunboat beached there. Locals had beaten us to any souvenirs, but we considered any man with very many souvenirs to have bought them or else to have served well behind the lines anyway.

Any souvenirs we might have had were routinely stolen from us by certain of the medical people who, while having loving hearts when it came to human suffering, seemed to have no compunction when it came to blatant thievery. I suppose that indictment only applies to a small minority, but I never met any man who, having passed through the aid station hospital process, made it out with any worthwhile souvenirs, certainly not if he'd had surgery and been anesthetized. It's probable that any man making it home with a Luger or a P38 pistol bought it at a heavy price or was an officer who was never wounded. Thievery was also common in the various postal units, excluding ours because we knew how it hurt to lose a treasure.

One infantryman named Harry Arnold told how he and a friend managed to acquire some German helmets, daggers and rifles, and following all the rules had them packed, addressed and shipped home. He said "not one of them reached my home. All was swallowed up by the heroic minions to the rear." Disgustedly, Arnold wrote "Non-combat personnel are the most successful collectors of war trophies."

I'm sure it was only a few dishonest service people who did this, but the problem was serious enough to cause most men who served on the front lines to come home empty. Maybe the actual medical people were innocent. It's not fair to blame any class of individuals. Certainly there were no more honored men in an Infantry company than the medical men. However, the U.S. Army seems to have had a rather significant number of crooks in the ranks and many were officers. I'm guessing no combat medic ever stole. They were one of us. However, to anyone who came home with some German weapon or equipment and who did not serve in a combat outfit, my advice is to never mention that souvenir to a combat veteran, certainly not to someone who was wounded and came home empty. John McManus, in a very blunt assessment of the souvenir situation, wrote "A man with a house full of war souvenirs is not any infantryman - he can lug only so much. Non-combat personnel are the most successful collectors of war trophies other than death, dismemberment, and injury."

Doctors, by the way, were by no means safe from enemy action. Most were, of course, well behind the lines for the sake of the wounded. On the other hand men like Dr. Murray Franklin, a Major in the Medical Corps, were fearless in caring for their men. Franklin learned back on June 14 while we were attacking Gourbesville that some of our men were isolated beyond our lines, and their small medical unit was lacking supplies to care for several wounded men. He gathered up all the medical supplies he could carry and dashed through enemy lines to reach the unit, being wounded in the process. He remained with the men, giving aid to the wounded, until they were relieved eight hours later. He was later awarded a Silver Star for gallantry.

All good things must end and our stay in Etretat ended after seven memorable days. We were finally loaded back on trucks and driven we knew not where - no one ever seemed to think mere enlisted men should have any idea where they were going - and we finally, after an hour's drive, saw departing behind us from the back of the truck the suburbs of a city. Several miles of this and it dawned on us that we were in the environs of Paris. I felt like a man in a dream as I looked out of the back of the truck and saw the Eiffel Tower. The war was only just over, the lights were on again. Paris, the City of Lights, of life, was becoming light and lively once again. A light rain had just quit and the streets were wet, reflecting the light, and we could see images of tall buildings in their mirrored surface. It was a grand almost unearthly feeling in me to be in the heart of one of the world's greatest, most storied cities and to know I was now to be a resident.

The truck finally pulled up in front of Magasin Dufayel on Rue de Clignancourt, a large, upscale department store which the Germans had commandeered as housing for German occupation troops. Now it was our turn. When I entered, I saw an enormous stairway, and on its landing was a magnificent mirror some twenty feet high. The building was in excellent condition. We went to the next floor which was filled with cots, and that became my home. It was mid-June. We were issued Class B passes, which meant instead of needing to get a pass to go somewhere we could go anywhere we wanted within reason when not at work. I felt like a wealthy tourist. Through the window near my bed I could see the Church of the Sacre Couer atop the Montmartre, its glorious pearl-white dome glistening in the sun. It was close enough for an easy walk. We were, it seemed, in the artsy section of Paris.

It's probably fair to say that by the time we arrived the novelty of seeing all us well-dressed Yankee saviors had all but worn off for the French people. It hadn't taken them long to discover that we had access to all sorts of merchandise which they had not seen for years. Men were frantically writing home for nylon stockings, and many a man quit smoking when he realized the price his five-cent pack of cigarettes could command on the black market. Prices didn't take long to rise when one of us came into view. However, we thought we were in, well, if not paradise, then at least a very fun place to spend a war. We didn't complain.

Our bosses were a few non-coms who had been with the post office since the beginning, and while they tried to appear self confident and commanding it was easily apparent that they were somewhat ill-at-ease trying to contain more than a hundred men who had survived battle and were, for a variety of reasons, exempt from going back. Someone passed the word that several of the men were battle fatigue cases which suggested, of course, that they weren't exactly mentally competent and might be subject to impulsive and, conceivably, violent behavior. This wasn't true, but it had the effect of causing some of the mail people to look with apprehension at two or three men who definitely appeared unusual and acted suspiciously, not to mention the possibility that any one of us could be unhinged. That, of course, was the reason for the rumor in the first place.

Our first morning my friends and I went exploring. We strolled the Montmartre, climbed to the Sacre Couer, made our way by Metro - there was a station two blocks from us - to the Champs Elysees and walked to their grave of the unknown soldier. I bought a cigarette case just so I'd have something from a store which a few months earlier had been selling them to the Germans. We discovered that our billet was on the very edge of an area known as Place Pigalle, a bohemian-type area where a large percentage of the evening residents were what, in elegant terms, might be called ladies of the night. Some of the men thought just possibly they had been transferred to heaven. The area had become known to GIs as "Pig Alley" by the time we arrived. Each night Pigalle came alive with lights and music and laughter, the streets crowded with people who apparently slept all day. Using a word which has long since assumed a different meaning, late night Pigalle was the essence of "Gay Paree." To be blunt about it, Pigalle was the Red Light district of Paris.

We had arrived only after the people of Paris had had a few months to adjust to freedom again. It seemed to me that the people had made a remarkable recovery. Maybe it was my imagination but the men seemed to swagger down the Champs Elysees and the girls, well, suffice it to say the clothing stores were already in full swing. I learned to love the phrase *savoir faire* as I watched the French people going about their daily lives. They weren't exactly friendly with us but neither did we feel unwanted. The atmosphere was strongly one of what today would be called "doing your own thing." Definitely, Paris was the place to be at that time in history.

We learned that the bad news was that we were all on the night shift. We would go to work at 10 p.m. and work until 6 a.m. which, though I have to believe the head of the post office hadn't thought of this, meant we had to walk down Place Pigalle at night, in the dark, past dozens of painted ladies, to get to the Post Office. Talk about casualty rate, he was lucky if eighty percent of the men arrived on time or even at all. On second thought, though, I had the impression the boss was pretty busy himself in Paris. As far as I could tell he was a Captain, seemed to be a nice guy, was rarely around, and once when I walked past him with several friends as we arrived later than the rules required -- some of my friends reeling dangerously -- the Captain smiled and looked the other way. I don't recall ever seeing him again. The highest-ranking man we had to deal with was a skinny little Tech Sergeant who always looked desperately outraged at this incursion by completely unskilled mail people like us. However, he never bothered us, and probably went home with plenty of war stories of a different kind himself.

Most of us realized that our friends and fellow GIs wanted mail desperately and we'd be skunks not to get it to them. We decided, not by discussing it but because it was obvious to each of us, that we would dutifully see that the mail went through as efficiently as possible. Most of the non-coms who ran the place were bureaucratic types who stuck to business, so despite anything else said here, the mail went to the troops.

This did not seriously hamper our social life. We had weekends off and as long as most of us showed up there wasn't any trouble. Some of the more athletic members seemed somehow able to make their way through Pigalle, pause for an hour or so if you know what I mean, then arrive only somewhat slower at work than usual.

CHAPTER SIXTEEN

AN AMERICAN IN PARIS

BEING IN PARIS WAS HEADY STUFF FOR EVERYONE IN 1945. HENRY Van Dyke once wrote that "London is a man's town, there's power in the air; and Paris is a woman's town, with flowers in her hair." After spending time in London, we quickly understood what Van Dyke meant. Compared to drab old London, Paris already had a liveliness that was totally new to us kids from the American heartland. In the months since its liberation Paris had begun to regain its health. Celebrities and the wealthy began flocking there. Famous newsmen and women headquartered in Paris along with writers like George Orwell and Ernest Hemingway who hung out at The Ritz. The painter Picasso complained that too many old friends had arrived for him to entertain them all. "Paris was liberated," he wrote, "but I am besieged." Simone de Beauvoir and Jean Paul Sartre visited Hemingway, and Sartre admitted he woke up the next morning with a hangover to see Hemingway hiding bottles so the hotel workers wouldn't know how much they drank. Marlene Dietrich arrived to stay at The Ritz which was rapidly filling up with the famous and would-be famous leading one observer to term the process "Ritzkrieg," a play on the word Blitzkrieg, the German juggernaut which invaded Europe at the beginning of the war. Maurice Chevalier returned, singing the sentimental song "Fleur de Paris" to an initially cool reception by some who considered him to have been a possible collaborator. Edith Piaf came to sing at Ciro's which the French officers, after General de Gaulle's triumphant return, had commandeered as their officer's club. Everyone who was anyone in France wanted in on the fun. This included some well-connected English ladies who, once assured there was no danger, arrived from

London "wangling a joyride" as one reporter put the matter, to share in the exquisite new wave of night life. "Almost everyone in London with a good excuse made sure of a trip to Paris as soon as possible after the liberation."[1]

The British decided their higher-ranking officers needed a proper officer's club too so they commandeered Maxim's, the famous restaurant on Rue Royale. The Americans, discovering how important morale is for generals, laid claim to Place de la Madeleine whose wine cellars had been concealed throughout the German occupation and were now open. They were also welcomed at another well-known hangout, Tour d'Argent, which offered free admission to officers of a certain rank. The famous Jockey Club also welcomed officers to free membership.

This was all for the upper classes, of course. But anyone familiar with American GIs would not be surprised to learn that we had just as much fun. We did have access to the well-known dance revues which, in America, would have been called burlesque shows. Follies Bergere was filled the night we all tried to go so we settled for The Casino de Paris and the audience, including many GIs, had more officers per enlisted men than I had ever seen. It was there we learned the exact meaning of *savoir faire* when we used the gentleman's room, a very large area surrounded by three full walls of urinals, the entire area presided over by pleasant-faced ladies who sat in our midst and collected a tariff upon our departure.

Generals found themselves attracted to Paris, no surprise. General JCH Lee, the Commander of the Services of Supply and described by Stephen Ambrose as "the biggest jerk" in the ETO,[2] never in his life heard a shot fired in anger. During the period of critical gas shortages when General Patton's attack was held up for lack of fuel, and in direct disobedience to General Eisenhower's specific orders, Lee moved his entire staff to Paris, bringing 8,000 officers and 21,000 enlisted men with him. From then on they spent a good part of their time enjoying Paris and, to again quote Ambrose, "getting all the girls." Lee also commandeered so many Paris hotels which General Eisenhower had ordered to be made available to combat veterans on leave, that those veterans were left to stay in Red Cross hostels. Eisenhower was enraged, but the only consequence Lee seems to have suffered is the present one in which his name is remembered by those who were there for what he was.

What I didn't know at the time was that quite a number of American soldiers had deserted and made their way to Paris, many having been listed as Missing in Action and presumed to be prisoners. Many airmen were among them, some just waiting for their units to arrive. Back in 1945 Andy Rooney told of one remarkable case, that of "Joe Doyle," a Flying Fortress pilot in the 305th Bomb Group. That wasn't his real name but the reporter who recorded the story kept that part a secret. Joe, when preparing for a mission, always carried an overnight bag with toothbrush, spare underwear, most of the things we carry today when flying on long trips in case our luggage is lost. He told his crew mates that if he were to be shot down he planned to make for Paris.

On Joe's twenty-second mission his plane was badly damaged over Lille. He made sure that all of his men had safely bailed out, then Joe gathered up his overnight bag and followed them out. Three crewmen landed safely, avoided capture, and were finally led back to American lines by members of the Underground. To their officials they reported Joe as missing. Then, to trusted friends, they told of meeting Joe at a crossroads, Joe jauntily swaggering down the road with his trusty overnight bag swung over his shoulder. His men, of course, had welcomed him and assumed he'd join their French guides in heading home. But Joe laughed, told them he'd see them in Paris, said "I got three addresses in Paris and that's where I'm going. Been wanting to go there all my life," waved goodbye and headed on down the country road in the direction of Paris. When the troops arrived a year and a half later it is rumored that Joe was standing on the curb, waving, and welcoming the American army.[3] Rooney insisted that was a true story.

Dance halls and night clubs began to spring up all over Paris. One night we all went to a GI night club we'd heard about which was some distance from our billet, so we made our way there by taxis. It was a genuine night club, reminding me of the Indiana Roof Ballroom in Indianapolis. We found a table on a balcony, and ordered champagne.

None of us had ever tasted champagne and decided that if you're going to hang out in Paris you had to know how to drink champagne. It wasn't very good and, we thought, tasted a lot like Seven-Up. We decided a bottle apiece ought to be about right and placed our order.

A band was playing and the leader invited anyone who could sing to have a try. An enormous African American GI climbed up on the stage and, as the music began, sang a song with a great booming voice without having any idea what the words were. He made it through the entire song and I presume what with all the champagne flowing that night, everyone thought he was great. The man finished to a round of enthusiastic if tipsy applause, and the night went on.

I received an unexpected language lesson from an attractive young French girl seated at the table next to us in the company of a young American corporal. He was intently delivering his romantic come-on line, (what we generally referred to as a "snow job"), while she gazed glowingly into his eyes. My friends and I couldn't resist tuning in to the fellow's routine. The girl replied a couple of times in her native French, which the corporal clearly didn't understand and finally, assuming what I thought to be the obvious, I remarked to my friends that "she doesn't understand a word he's saying." The girl, overhearing me, turned, smiled, and said in perfect English, "Oh, but I do." Thus, for me one of life's embarrassing moments. Only then I discovered that the French people were a lot better with English than we were with French. Speaking of which, we all learned a rudimentary French vocabulary which proved, upon our return home, to be useless. Any surviving veteran of that era will recall that about all we learned of the French language began with the phrase "Voulez-vous...?"

Dancing was, of course, the main purpose of a night club but we had two problems. George, who came from a high-society family, was the only one who knew how to dance very well, and since we were not exactly socially in demand we hadn't met any nice French girls. One or two of my friends seemed not to require that they be nice, but the rest of us decided the hour was late and we were getting sleepy for some reason, so, at some advanced hour lost to history, four of us headed home and decided we'd just walk. There still was very little traffic back then so we walked side by side down the middle of the boulevard singing a variety of songs we'd prefer Mother not hear and, to our surprise, were unable to walk a straight line. As the euphoria gave way to exhausted yawns, we found a cruising taxi and went home to bed.

One highly memorable event for us took place on July 14, Bastille Day, the French version of Independence Day. It was, there's no other word for it, wild. It was their first national holiday since the end of the war and everyone wanted to celebrate. It was no holds barred. The streets were filled with celebrants, including every GI in Paris. It started early and by midnight Paris was a maelstrom of celebration. Most GIs were somewhere between tipsy and plastered. American GIs did not know how to drink despite extensive practice. French people seemed more expert at drinking while GIs in staggering numbers were, well, staggering. Military Police were present on every corner, most of them probably steamed at having to miss the fun. I always wondered why anyone would have wanted to be an MP.

The atmosphere was one of giddy hilarity, an almost explosive common bursting forth of freedom, as though, after five years of fear and privation, of the constant threat of enslavement or death, it was possible now to believe that, "Yes, we are really free, we can run and jump and yell and laugh, we can swear and defy, we can say 'yes' and 'no,' we can snicker at funny clothes, cheer for whom we choose, sing our songs of love, we can go where we please, eat what we want, travel to a distant planet if we can find a way." The freedom had begun ten months earlier. But this was Bastille Day, this was freedom day and all the pent-up relief and jubilation was expelled in completely uninhibited celebration. It was the first everyone-is-free, riotous outpouring of national welcome-back-to-life-day since the departure of the hated Hun. It was a night of rebirth and it lasted 'til dawn.

George, Bruce, Jimmy, Johnny, Lou and I along with several other members of our gang spent the night into the early morning hours helping the Parisians celebrate their recent liberation. Being on the night shift we easily went full tilt until dawn. The streets were filled with circus rides, clowns and acrobats, a million colorful balloons, lots of dancing, music everywhere. Girls were hugging strangers, it was the Mardi Gras of France. It was one memorable night.

This entire line of thought brings to mind the one article of equipment used constantly by every GI: condoms. Now before the reader makes any assumptions, that comment needs to be explained. The style leaders of the ETO (European Theater of Operations) were the paratroopers. This was because of their boots. Those boots were what kids used to call high tops, and were worn rather jauntily, highly polished, with the trousers bloused over them. It became common practice for the rest of us to take our ordinary GI shoes to a local shoe store and have a six- or so inch strip of leather sewn to the regular GI shoes, thus converting them to makeshift boots. This enabled us to wear our trousers bloused like the paratroopers. It reached the point that any GI wearing straight trousers was looked upon as whatever the 1945 word was for today's "nerd." But to blouse the trousers required an elastic band of some sort to place around one's boot, under which the end of the trousers could then be tucked. The answer was condoms. Every office, every company orderly room, maintained a large container of individually wrapped condoms, and must have dispensed literally millions of them - so we could wear our trousers bloused and be in style in 1945 Paris.

There were other uses for condoms. In training and again in combat infantrymen used them to place over the bore of a rifle to protect from rain or snow. Still another use, frequently employed while we were in Paris, was to fill a condom with water like a balloon, tie it off at the end and, when an unsuspecting friend was to be seen strolling down the boulevard on his way back to Magasin Dufayel, especially if he swaggered a bit as though having achieved some proud conquest, the condom was lofted from an upper window in the man's direction, everyone quickly disappearing, as the projectile struck on or near the recipient. Veteran Dufayel men instinctively walked out near the curb when arriving back to barrack in the evening. There were still other uses for condoms, and they were clearly essential equipment for the American Army in World War II.

Back to the French people, I'm somewhat understanding of their apparent dislike for Americans today. In 1944 we tore up their land, demolished their cities, destroyed their bridges and rail lines, killed thousands of their citizens, massacred their livestock. Not only that, we weren't always civil in the way we treated them during our occupation of their country in the late-going of the war. From an American point of view we had no choice. We tried to be as humane as we could. We did, after all, chase the Germans out of France. But from the French point of view, we decimated their country.

To us it was just a pretty country filled with foreigners who didn't even speak English for gosh sakes. It was also a chance to cut loose and live without the social strictures which confined most of us at home. Little wonder we didn't leave a very good impression of Americans. It's not surprising that their elder generation remembers and has probably passed along a somewhat revised and biased interpretation of those years of American occupation to their succeeding generations. Most of us must have appeared not to have a serious bone in our bodies. Whatever we may have accomplished behind the scenes, all most of them saw was a crowd of adolescents making rude remarks to the pretty girls - they didn't seem to mind terribly by the way - and heading in noisy groups toward the nearest bar. It would have been inconceivable to them that we would one day be called our nation's Greatest Generation. We were, however, in varying degrees, growing up.

Today our differing cultures seem to cause us to inherently dislike each other. I suspect my generation can take some of the credit for that. On the other hand some of us have dear friends there, find the country beautiful, and can dare to hope the day will come when we can sincerely declare as we once did before the war: "viva la France."

Perhaps this is as good a point as any to take note of the anticlimactic end to the sad life of Adolf Hitler. On April 16, 1945, he moved into his bunker, grandly known as the Fuhrerbunker and lived a life of unreality. On April 29 he signed his last will and testament for his secretary Trudi Junge, shortly after midnight that day married Eva Braun, then ate lunch. There's no better example of his total departure from reality than the fact that according to secretaries who shared his last lunch – spaghetti -- he discussed dog breeding and explained how lipstick could be made from grease. At 3:30 p.m., he and Eva went to his study. A shot was heard. His valet, Heinze Linge, accompanied by Martin Borman, entered the study and found them both dead. They noticed the smell of burnt almonds, a sign of cyanide. Hitler also had been shot in the head, his pistol by his side. The two bodies were carried out to a small garden, doused with gasoline and set on fire.

The Russian Red Army by this time had pretty well captured the heart of Berlin, shot the daylights out of the Reichschancellery, and raised their banner over the Reichstag. A few days later they found the only partially-burned remains of Hitler and Braun which were carted off to be buried and otherwise used in ways still controversial. The latest word is they were finally burned completely and the ashes dumped in the Elbe River. I enter this here as it was about this time we learned what had happened and were, all, of course, disgusted that the man didn't at least take up a rifle and die like millions of his deceived followers. The great military genius, it turned out, was a coward.

One morning a rather sleazy-looking Frenchman stopped me on the street and asked if I had any cigarettes to sell. The black market was big business in Paris at that time. Things like soap and cigarettes were in constant demand and short supply. We could buy a bar of soap at the PX, take it along with a large bag of clothes to any local laundry, and for the price of half of that bar of soap get our laundry done. I assume they used different soap and kept the good one but we didn't care. Cigarettes cost us five cents a pack and went for a dollar on the black market (This was a time when, as I remember, I was paid under $80 a month).

Now it so happens that when I was back in England in the hospital I stumbled across a quartermaster tent loaded with all the clothing needed by a GI and there was no one on duty. I therefore helped myself, which was only expected of any self-respecting Pfc at that time. I'd carried off an extra field jacket, several shirts, some extra trousers, stuff like that. I'd hauled it all over England and France and I saw immediately that here was my chance to unload everything I didn't really need. Army clothing commanded a very high price on the Paris black market, so I made arrangements to meet the man – he with his barely passable English, me with my ten words of French – and I went back to my billet and told Moye Featherston about my appointment. I knew he had a few excess items as well and Moye decided to come with me.

I was very fortunate not to encounter friends as I left Dufayel since trafficking with the black market was very illegal. I was wearing two field jackets, two pairs of pants, three shirts, and had a bag under my arm. Moye was pretty much the same, both of us looking like we'd suddenly gained thirty pounds, and we went to the corner where we were to meet our criminal. I only half expected him to be there but, on the other hand, that was his full-time job so I wasn't too surprised when the man showed up with a friend. A very big friend.

We followed their lead down the main street, down several unfamiliar little streets, down an alley, back out to a small, dark building where we were met by two more men. All appeared middle European, wore scarfs or handkerchiefs on their heads and dressed exactly like Warner Brothers would have dressed them. I almost wondered if this was some sort of gag, except our new acquaintances did not smile. We showed them what we had to sell and for some time we negotiated by writing our offers with a rock on the sidewalk. Finally, we reached an agreement and then the deal took an ominous turn. They told us we must follow them to another location, because making the deal in public could expose them and maybe even us to police observation. I didn't see any policemen around, but we'd gone this far.

We were led down an alley to the side of the building and into a darkened hallway, up a dingy flight of stairs, then into a large room which was occupied by several other men. Moye and I hurriedly divested ourselves of our trade goods, handed over a bag of cigarette packages, and accepted payment in cash. There was only about half as much money as we had agreed to. Not a good start. I protested and the leader of the group, who suddenly didn't understand any English, shrugged his shoulders.

This was one of the life's memorable times of decision for me. Two thoughts ran through my mind. On the one hand, no one had any idea where Moye and I had gone and these guys might not like the idea of us knowing where their hideout was located anyway. I could imagine our bodies dumped in the Seine, and what with the army folks being accustomed to dead people in great numbers, I thought it probable there'd be very little effort to find out what happened.

On the other hand, I reasoned that these were businessmen of a sort. They couldn't know that none of our friends knew where we were. If they wanted other sources of supply, they needed us to report back the ease with which we had done business and the integrity of our customers (I realized that word "integrity" was probably not big in their lexicon). Also, if two early adventurers into the Paris black market failed to return, no one else would give it a try.

This latter reasoning made more sense to me. I decided that on behalf of black-market-dealing GIs everywhere I'd show staunch courage. Hoping the throbbing in my throat wasn't noticed, I demanded the full price as agreed. The leader shook his head. I made a gesture as though to retrieve our goods, which suddenly didn't seem all that valuable to me at the moment. Their leader held up a hand, I desisted, and he handed over the rest of the money. Moye (who hadn't uttered a word) and I breathed a very quiet but deep sigh of relief. The head criminal then opened a pack of cigarettes, took one for himself, then offered one to us with a smile. I thanked him with two of my ten words, "merci beaucoup," and Moye and I peacefully departed, walking down the alley, swiftly, as I recall. It was my one and only transaction with the black marketers. In looking back, I realize how impoverished many of the people were at that time, and the acquisition of high-quality clothing one way or another was an understandable desire. We felt we had just made life a little easier for the people of Paris.

We all continued to do some touristy sight seeing, including Napoleon's tomb, and a visit to the Louvre which was opened very briefly, then closed to everyone. I was there in time to see the Winged Victory and the Venus De Milo. We visited the Eiffel Tower which the Army had requisitioned for some reason, strolled up and down the Champs Elysees, wandered the Ile St-Louis, and were deeply impressed at the majesty of the Notre Dame Cathedral. We spent a lot of time on the Metro which was up and running as though nothing had happened. But life in and around Place Pigalle, the Montmartre, and the neighborhood surrounding Magasin Dufayel occupied most of our free time. The sidewalk cafés were open and numerous, and though lunch was free at home we sometimes gathered at some popular sidewalk bistro and ate lunch there. The Montmartre, home to Pigalle and the area where one would find the Moulin Rouge, for instance, was a sight of particular interest to visiting GIs, and I could tell I was something of a celebrity merely by the fact of being a resident. Having to report to work at 10 o'clock at night, we were filled with energy in the evening which, for us, was like early morning to the rest of the world, so before we were done many of our number became fairly well known denizens of the Pigalle night.

One custom quickly revived by the Parisians which we enjoyed was sidewalk carnivals. With Ferris wheels, clowns, and mimes, these were as much a part of Paris life as her cabarets, sidewalk cafés, and street artists. Because the powers who ruled such things had ordained that GIs generally were not allowed to visit Paris, the given reason being shortages of food and other necessities, those of us stationed there had the run of the place without the teeming uniformed crowds which otherwise would have surged around us. The absence of automobiles, except a small number which had evaded requisition by the Nazis, and the limited availability of bus transportation, also a result of gas shortages, required that for us walking be the preferred mode of transportation. Being infantrymen, this was fine with us. My wounds were healed and by walking we were able to mix with the people and sightsee extensively. Most Parisians either walked or biked.

It was great fun, and a bit dangerous I might add, to wander rather late at night in the Isle de-la-Cite, what we thought of as the Greenwich Village of Paris, though I don't think most of us had actually ever heard of Greenwich Village. Small cafés, dimly-lit bars, shady characters standing in the shadows, swarthy men with welcoming smiles, girls with painted faces - we were starting to become world-traveled sophisticates, or so we liked to think. Finally, while most of us could still function, we'd make our ways back to billets, struggle up the grand stairway, and gratefully tumble into bed.

We had all stayed apprised of the progress of the war. While in the hospital I had seen a regular flow of casualties from Falaise, the race to Paris, Patton's tanks running out of gas just as he was set to burst into Germany, the Huertgen Forest and the early portions of the Bulge battles, so we had some idea of the conditions faced by those men. We'd had access to English newspapers which seemed to be convinced that but for Sir Bernard Montgomery, their beloved general, all would be lost, and the *Stars and Stripes*, our own newspaper which balanced that nicely by implying that Montgomery was a nuisance. I had certainly felt genuine guilt at times as I snuggled under the covers of my cot knowing men like my friends and me were going through hell in frozen foxholes in Germany. We were properly grateful the war had finally ended.

One evening, a half-open package of photographs came through the mail and as I tried to put it back together some photos spilled out. I couldn't believe what I saw. They showed stacks of skeletal bodies. This was our first hint of the revelations soon to follow of the Nazi death camps. Some GI had taken photos and sent them home. We had seen our share of horrible scenes, but these photos turned our stomachs. We'd soon know the terrible truth depicted there. The note scribbled on the back of one photo was a single word, one I'd never heard: Auschwitz.

Our work was boring, bottom-of-the-vocational heap, even in the Army. We had a lot of fun though. We had a sergeant named Bader. He was one of us, wore the Silver Star for gallantry, was movie-star leading-man good looking, did dips between two metal mail bag holders until his arms bulged, and he stood around all evening doing nothing. Perhaps he did one thing: he waited impatiently to get out of there so he could go out on the town. I liked Bader well enough. He did, though, have one strange habit. When a friend would accompany him on his many romantic escapades, the friend was required to wear a Silver Star ribbon which Bader carried as an extra so he wouldn't have to be seen with non-heroes. A friend of mine, Luis Goldsmith, a sophisticated New Yorker, liked to go with Bader so he could wear that Silver Star.

Speaking of undeserved insignia, it was said that an occasional file clerk with a cushy office would tack a division patch on his uniform and pin on a purloined Purple Heart, the better to attract the ladies. The MPs were alert to such deception. If a man wanted serious trouble all around, let him be caught wearing insignia he didn't deserve. In recent years it has been revealed that a great many of the publicly celebrated, one might say professional, heroes of the Vietnam War are fakes, a man by the name of Roy Burkett having devoted his life to exposing many fake Navy Cross, Distinguished Service Cross, and Medal of Honor "winners."[4] Burkett also wrote that even today, "More than fifty years after the end of World War II, veterans of that war continue to peddle sham tales of heroism to the public."[5] Unfortunately, that sort of thing is true during and after every war. Anyone can manufacture a heroic past. It has recently been estimated that in our country today there are more fake medal of honor "winners" than real ones still living.

One mecca for GIs in Paris was the Grand Hotel which was turned into a Red Cross club by the authorities. It was a great place to socialize. The large, high-ceilinged lobby with its glassed-in sunlit meeting rooms off to the sides made room for crowds of us. My friends and I went there often in the daytime. On one occasion ten or so of us were sitting around a large circular table when some men with movie cameras approached us and asked if they might take our pictures. They were from Movietone News and explained that we would in due time appear in newsreels back home. This sounded great to us.

We were instructed to sit and talk to each other and just seem to enjoy ourselves. Now that last was probably not the best thing for the photographer to request. We were already enjoying ourselves. In fact we were feeling quite energetic. That man, seeing those Combat Infantryman Badges, and those Purple Hearts and a Bronze Star or two, must have thought "I've got me some real live fighting men here." There were two or three pretty girls at the table which always caused men like my friends to show off a bit. Bottom line, we were acting like kids who'd just made it to our seats after drawing the teacher's picture on the blackboard. Everyone was giggling, joking, roughhousing, not at all the image of serious men serving their country that the photographer had envisioned. He filmed for awhile, thanked us, departed.

I didn't give us much chance to make the Uptown Theater back home but I couldn't take the chance I was wrong. I wrote Mom and Dad and told them that just in case they went to a movie, they might keep an eye open for their son in the Grand Hotel. My parents probably saw more movies in the next month than they'd seen during the war. We were never seen on the screen.

One day I ran into a friend from our Pheasy Farm days who asked if I remembered Murray who used to party with us back in Birmingham. Of course I did. He then told me that he'd recently learned that Murray had been sent back to his combat unit in Germany and near the end of the war had been hit by an artillery shell which blew his leg off above the knee. I was horrified. Murray with the great sense of humor. Murray, madly in love with his dear Evangeline. I asked my friend if he knew anything about her and was told that he'd heard that Murray was being sent back home and apparently had lost touch with her. His letters to her weren't answered. I hoped Murray had somehow retained his sense of humor. He'd certainly need it now.

CHAPTER SEVENTEEN
HOMECOMING

IT WAS A SPLENDID TWO MONTHS BUT IT HAD TO END. WORD CAME down that former prisoners of war were now eligible to go home immediately ahead of everyone else, the normal evacuation determined by a very unfair point system. I debated going for awhile, weighing my natural desire to get home, see my family and start a real life, against my regret at leaving my friends and a very satisfying life in Paris. Besides, long-awaited promotions had begun. I realized I'd come home as a Staff Sergeant if I'd stay a month longer. As sergeants with high points were sent home, men with fewer points were suddenly promoted for the two or three months they had remaining in the service, mainly so the work could get done and the officers would not have to work too hard. The authorities realized these men would all be out soon so it cost little to do a lot of last-minute promotions. Many men served through the war as Pfcs and then were promoted to Staff Sergeant for a couple months at the end of things. Just days after I arrived home I heard from Bruce Wiegel that he'd just been promoted from Pfc to Staff Sergeant. But I decided we'd all be going home anyway soon and really didn't want to remain longer than necessary, so I agreed to go. Only a great many years later did I realize I probably could have enjoyed a great educational year had I chosen to remain to serve in Germany for awhile.

The war in the Pacific came to an explosive end. On August 6 the atomic bomb was dropped on Hiroshima, Japan. When the Japanese refused to surrender, another was dropped on Nagasaki three days later. The consequences were stupefying. Hundreds of thousands of Japanese civilians were killed. The atomic bomb introduced a new era in international relations, revealing humanity's capability of destroying the entire world. The Japanese emperor Hirohito announced their willingness to surrender, a decision which probably saved many thousands of American and Japanese lives, as it headed off a land invasion of the Japanese homeland. On September 2, 1945, aboard the Battleship Missouri, the surrender document was signed by Japanese officials and by General Douglas MacArthur. World War II was over and America enjoyed a nationwide celebration on "VJ Day."

My orders dated August 9, 1945, directed me to make my way to Camp Wings, and there to wait for transportation to the ZI which was the Zone of the Interior, Army talk for the U.S. A week later a jeep pulled up outside Magasin Dufayel. I carried my duffel bag down and turned, looked at the place I'd never see again and still the home of men who'd been my friends whom I'd also probably never see again. I experienced a spasm of grief. I was leaving my other family. In a somewhat hard-to-explain way I felt an emptiness at the realization that the men who had been closer to me than any former friends in my life, men with whom I had laughed and argued and disagreed and with whom I had enjoyed an implicit mutual understanding of a kind which today we'd call intimacy, were fading from my life. Yesterday we were trusted companions who took for granted that we would go on living our great adventure together. Now they would go on, but I would henceforth be alone. I could easily have gone back. But in the Army, when you receive official written orders, you go, so I hopped in the jeep and a corporal drove me to the train. Later in the day I arrived at Camp Wings, the debarkation camp. There were several such camps, each named after a brand of cigarettes, Lucky Strike, Camel, Wings, and so forth.

I was assigned to a canvas tent and told it would take a couple days, then we'd be on our way home. As I walked down the company street to my tent I was met by an interesting man whose actual name I never heard because he was known to everyone as "Phoney." He was obviously of Italian descent, squat, muscular, mustachioed, a bragging guy you couldn't help but like. At my first meeting he greeted me, shirtless, telling me he was "Phoney, and not only that," he said, "I'm a hero."

Sure enough, Phoney wore the Silver Star. Everyone seemed to like Phoney who held forth wherever he went, bragging about himself all the way.

A few days later several of us were shuttled to a port where we boarded the Pachaug Victory, which we of course called the PayHog. The next day we headed out into the North Atlantic. It was just as it was on the way over, too many men for the space, crowded into a hold, sleeping in a bunk edged in metal with canvas on ropes and some guy sleeping above you whose bunk squeaked whenever he rolled over. But at least it would all soon be over. Although the Army called it a troop ship, it was really the world's largest floating crap game.

A couple days out I saw Phoney sitting in a chair on deck, expansively informing some avid companions of his great adventures. I heard him boast that he had a cabin to himself since he was a Staff Sergeant. He seemed to be quite pleased with himself, being a self-described hero and all, so three or four of us got together and asked Phoney if he ever got seasick. He scoffed and said "never." As pre-planned, we then stood side by side, merely conversing with Phoney, but gently swaying back and forth, back and forth, while talking about feeling a bit seasick. It actually worked. Phoney began to look uncomfortable. He finally admitted he wasn't feeling all that great himself. He excused himself and went to his private cabin and I never saw Phoney again. Pleased with a job well done, we went our separate ways.

We encountered what the Boston newspaper called the worst storm in the north Atlantic in many years. For three days it was horrendous, the prow of the ship reaching into the air one moment with water pouring back into the Atlantic, then plunging to disappear into the depths until it was nearly impossible to stand up on deck. Everyone went to his bunk and the heads were filled with men jammed side by side throwing up. I thought how ironic, to survive one of the fiercest battles of the war, then die of seasickness. The joke went around about the man leaning over the rail, vomiting, and a friend consoled the man by saying "No one ever died from seasickness," to which the poor man replied, "that's what I'm afraid of."

After awhile it became necessary to eat something. We couldn't go for days without food, and we did to some extent master the art of moving about on the flailing vessel. As long as I lay on my bunk I felt fine. It was when standing up I'd feel a little nauseated. They told us – "they" being Navy men who were having a great time watching us - we'd do better if we ate. So I made my way at last to the food line which some genius had located in the bottom of the ship requiring us to fill our mess kits with food, fill our metal canteen cups with boiling hot coffee, then climb the stairs (which had a totally different name on a ship, and I couldn't care less about that by then). That entailed, one moment, lifting a leg only by gigantic effort as the ship rose out of the water, then flying up two steps, coffee splashing, food slopping, while the ship plunged once more into the deep. It was almost impossible to get more than half of everything to the top, the rest strewn down the front of one's fatigues. I began eating a lot of apples which I could put in my pocket, eating whatever else I had as I walked to the stairs, then concentrating solely on getting my coffee up safely (being only some-what successful). Navy men, of course, seemed to take the steps two at a time and not lose a drop, a display which they enjoyed, showing how expert they were. It was their territory.

When we finally arrived in Boston Harbor, we disembarked to an impressive absence of brass bands despite the expectations raised by newsreels we had seen, and were transported to Camp Miles Standish, Massachusetts. I only retain one memory of the two days we spent there. Three or four of my newest acquaintances and I were sitting in the Post Exchange drinking coffee. At a nearby table were several GIs. One was a man I had only noticed at a distance. He was a short, stocky man, probably a year or two older than I and my friends. He wore the ribbon of the Distinguished Service Cross, the second highest award for bravery given by our nation. The others were clearly impressed by the man who, judging by his demeanor, was impressed with himself. Into the PX walked a teenaged soldier, a private, wearing his uniform the way new recruits do. He was an ordinary looking young man and still had long hair. I remembered how proud I had felt my first few days in the service, wearing my newly issued khakis, and I think I understood how he felt.

The man with the DSC saw the young fellow, was obviously offended at his long hair, this being an era in which "real men" wore crew cuts. He called the boy over and tossed him a half dollar coin. It rolled across a table and clattered to the floor. The hero called so all of us could hear, "go get a haircut." The young fellow blushed, turned and walked out. I could feel his humiliation, his helplessness there among all those men, the unimportance he felt. I hated that hero, hated the very self-importance which a few, very few, returning men would display. I think I realized then that there is something I don't ever want to be. The warrior mentality, when it fights oppression and evil, is admirable, and even necessary if a world is to have peace. But the moment it becomes proud and insensitive to the young, and the weak, and the innocent, it becomes ugly. Whether in an individual or a nation, the willingness to fight heroically is only worthy when it protects, cares for and respects those whom it presumes to represent. That man, that ugly hero, was a man I never wanted to know. I hoped, when I reached home, I could represent something better.

Two days later it was off to Camp Atterbury, Indiana, then home. The train ride of course was tiresome, but my spirits were high. I would still have a sixty-day furlough, a week in Fort Oglethorpe, Georgia, then back home and out, a civilian once more.

In looking back to the Normandy experience, I realize that expert judgments found much Allied command incompetent. Some historians deemed nearly all Allied leadership as, at best, barely competent. "Few American infantry units arrived in Normandy with a grasp of basic tactics - a failure for which many men paid with their lives,"[1] Max Hastings wrote. In his widely-read book about the Normandy campaign, Hastings elaborately insisted that the American and British armies were not, man for man, equal to the Germans, that our superiority in materiel made the difference. He argued that had German generals not had to contend with Hitler who continually prevented them from doing what they knew was the right thing in battle, we probably would not have won.

John Mosier did research on the German army in World War II and in his book *Cross of Iron* wrote that towards the end, "although it was no longer capable of maintaining the kinds of offensive operations it had executed in the first part of the war, the traditional excellence of the (German) Army in defense ensured that the Germans would be tough opponents, and this advantage was increased by two factors. On the one hand, the Allies kept dispersing their forces, mounting offensives in areas where the result was to pit new raw recruits against seasoned veterans defending a terrain that was perfect for defensive operations, and a nightmare for the attackers, and their technical superiority in airpower and mechanization counted for little and, as a corollary, the Allies had to keep throwing fresh and therefore inexperienced troops into battle."[2]

Perhaps they are right. Perhaps. But Germany in the 1930s and '40s was a predatory, warlike nation, one which forcibly trained young men, brainwashed them into a zealous hatred of their enemies, all at a time when American kids were hanging out at the drugstore, training for sports, learning to date, and getting ready for worthy vocations, or the peaceful pursuits to be learned in college. It may, from a military point of view, seem a compliment to the Germans that their men were superior on the battlefield if, indeed, they were. But to me it's a compliment to our nation that we meant no one harm, that we desired to be a peaceful nation of people living useful, contributing lives, that we did not extol as virtuous the ability to outmaneuver and kill people. The very fact that kids like us could find in ourselves the courage to go, to take up arms, leave family and all our youthful dreams for our futures in order to fight such people is a testament to our nation's heroic spirit. It's worth remembering, after all, that we were required to do our fighting far from home on land which meant little to us while the Germans were desperately fighting to protect their homeland. Every one of us would have preferred to be back home once we realized what we were facing. But we all, with a few sorry exceptions, did our duty. We did, after all, win the war with men who were not warlike and that, so far as I am concerned, speaks for itself. The Germans had their own battle fatigue cases just as we did. The difference was that in all too many cases they were shot on the spot by their own officers while we nurtured our men back to health.

Starting in late 1945 The Boys Came Marching Home, along with several thousand women, nearly sixteen million of us in all, less 406,000 who would never return alive. Nearly every one of us who returned wanted a place to live, a car, a job and for the great majority, a spouse and an education. Veterans were honored when we appeared on the streets. Flags were flying, bands were playing, uniforms were in fashion. A lady even offered me her seat on a bus when she saw my Purple Heart ribbon, and a uniformed friend and I, when standing in a long line to see a movie, were promptly ushered to the front. It was all just one great period of celebration. Everyone was excited to see us return from the war safely. We were delighted to be home.

In the movie *Summer of '42* the main character, a teenaged boy named Hermie, many years after the events of that memorable summer, muses: "In the summer of '42 we raided the Coast Guard station four times. We saw five movies and had nine days of rain. Benjie broke his watch; Osey gave up his harmonica. And in a very special way, I lost Hermie, forever." That's what happened. We all lost something we had been before, lost it forever. Nothing could ever again be like it was. The generation which won World War II, whether in the armed forces or as civilians keeping the economy going and the supplies we needed flowing, and as mothers, fathers, sisters, and younger brothers praying for their loved one's safety would now go on to face the challenge of a rapidly-changing world.

As for me, I married a wonderful woman, Ruthanne, and returned to the life God seems to have planned for me from the beginning. I would, for the rest of my life, wrestle with the theological question of whether God protected me through my ordeal because of plans for me to serve Him many years later. I have long felt a profound sense that God called me out for a particular mission in life, to tell the Jesus story in my own way so that others would hear and respond. I look back to the Normandy experience and see countless times when I narrowly escaped death. I'm troubled at the thought that other young men, most far more able to contribute to God's world than I, were not spared, almost as though God gave me some special protection. I am unable to believe that. Yet through the years I've had a deep sense of being guided, all too often when I wasn't really paying attention. God seems to use these horrifying scenes of war to bless us if we let Him despite His outrage at the fact of war. As of now I am only able to trust that God is always with each of us, has a plan for us which, if we try to be faithful, will be carried out, and that somehow, somewhere, answers to these questions which perplex us all will be answered. When they are, we'll be amazed and happy.

The boys who marched away came home as men, ready to find our places in that new postwar world. It wouldn't be easy. Housing, education, employment, finding a new car, all would be major problems for each of us to solve. The world was turned upside down and it wouldn't be easy for all the other people who served on the Home Front either, as they absorbed sixteen million veterans back into a peacetime society which had adjusted to our absence. Exciting, challenging days lay ahead. Millions of us would begin enrolling in colleges, thanks to the GI Bill which gave free educations. Romance was the order of the day as most of us got married and started families - thirty million babies were born in the 1950s - and soon we descended on the job market. America would never be the same.

In one sense each of us had a unique experience in the war. Not everyone was able to end on a high note. Many men came home to recuperate from wounds. Others remained in active combat units into Germany. Still others served in one of the myriad of supply, maintenance, communication, transportation, and other service jobs which continued to maintain the complex organization of the United States Army as it defeated a powerful enemy, as it learned to live among foreign people, and finally, as it began to administer the oversight of captured territory while transferring the millions of us back to the United States and into civilian life.

There was, however, a commonality of experience which would unite us all. We had grown up. We had been removed, whether we liked it or not, from what would have been for most a humdrum world, most of us hometown people destined to live out lives of routine continuation of the lives of our parents, few of us ever to see much beyond our front yards. Not now. We'd seen the world, been to faraway places, come into contact with different cultures, been thrown together with comrades from other parts of our nation, from differing socio-economic levels of our society, and we'd learned to live together in brotherhood. We'd been forced to learn to accept authority, take responsibility, prize loyalty, work together and, for so many, to accept risk as part of everyday life. Our horizons now were endless, our possibilities unlimited. We'd come home with bold dreams for tomorrow. An old World War I song comes to mind: "How you gonna keep 'em down on the farm now that they've seen Paree?" Yes. God would now reach down into the awful tragedy of war and create a great nation of men and women who would make those daring dreams come true. We people of the 1940s, we were ready to go out and do things we'd never otherwise have dreamed of doing. And once again, as a nation, we would win.

We would instill in our children the values of honor, respect for others, generosity, and openness to diversity which would make us a home for troubled souls who come to our shores for mercy. We would found our values on Judeo-Christian principals but we would welcome those who understand God in a different way. We would argue, disagree, struggle over a seemingly endless stream of social, moral, political and international issues, but we would preserve at any cost the rights of those who disagree with us to speak and write as they believe. We would care for our homeless, our sick and frightened children, our hungry outcasts and those who dwell in poverty. As a people, we would believe in the power of love.

CONCLUDING POSTSCRIPT

I'VE WRITTEN WITH THE LUXURY OF SEEING HOW IT ALL TURNED out. Most of them are gone now, those men and women who saw America safely through her darkest days. Other dangerous times have beset us, perhaps they always will, and so far we've made our way successfully. I think it's not so much because of a Greatest Generation but because of the great members of every generation. Still, those men who fought the battles of the Second World War have come to epitomize the essence of the courage which has thus far kept our nation safe and strong. If those traits are preserved in our youngest generation, they too will see us safely and proudly through, proud not in the sense of self-importance, but in the sense of having stood tall in the sight of God and our fellow countrymen during times of testing. The great Presbyterian minister of that era, Peter Marshall, called them "sun-crowned men," men who were willing to pay whatever price was required in order to remain faithful to every fine and worthy cause in which they believed. It was a terrible time in many ways, a time of privation, fear, and sacrifice. But it was also a grand time to be alive, a time when all of us felt in every fiber of our being the pulsing thrill of living for something eminently and ultimately worth living for - and dying for.

I recently watched members of The Service Club of Indianapolis, a couple hundred men who served their country in wartime -- a gathering of old men mostly -- as they walked to their cars following lunch. They're mostly men of World War II, and really, some of them only barely walked. They're known to the community as former successful business and professional men - insurance men, doctors, attorneys, salesmen, media people, politicians, businessmen, educators, even some professional military men - but they're also known to each other as men who once were boys, teenagers, men who stood up and stepped up when their country needed them. Here they came, some on canes, on walkers, one with an oxygen device, some breathing hard from the walk to the parking lot. Many have replacement hips and hearing aids and lots of remedial things of one kind or another. Listen carefully, though. No one ever complains. They're laughing, several heading off to a bowling alley, others to the golf course. Give up? I don't think so.

Young people sometimes thoughtlessly make fun of old people. They should sit through a meeting of that gang of men, hear the camaraderie, the flying insults, the total seeming disrespect, the ribald humor, the utter lack of any intimidation because of someone's local fame and then witness their solemn respect as one by one they slip away to be with the God they believe themselves to serve, or hear the brakes immediately applied to anything off color if a lady should happen to attend – old-fashioned men I guess. They love each other. They were boys together, kids like Tom standing on the corner as I watched. He's 82 now and walks with a decided limp. When he was 17 he starred on the Shortridge High School track team. When he was 19 his foot was blown off in the Huertgen Forest while he was saving lives as a combat medic, and winning a Bronze Star. Standing off to the side is Jim, still tall and straight. Jim and I were kids together on Carrollton Avenue. He's also 82 and somewhere in a dresser drawer has a Silver Star for gallantry while fighting his way up from the south of France with a sniper-scoped rifle. He spent many months in Army hospitals in 1945 slowly recovering from life-endangering disabilities suffered from several months in a German prison camp. Marshall, 83, heads for his car, a former bomber pilot who spent several months as a prisoner of war when his plane was shot down over Romania. Bob, also 83, soon comes out. He flew 175 missions in B-24s out in the Pacific. Both men received Distinguished Flying Crosses. On they come, dozens of them, the men who won the war. People who make fun of old people, let them look around, think for a bit of the wonders of the land in which they live. Then let them look again at those old guys and reflect that but for them, and millions more like them, it couldn't be like this,

this freedom to grow up and be whatever we want to be, say what we want to say, think as we want to think.

What about the women? They made it all possible, they who raised those boys to be the fine young men they turned out to be, who filled the roles of the factory workers and helped to make the tanks and guns and planes which made victory possible, who silently, tearfully, watched their loved ones march away. They raised their younger children alone, grieved in the lonely nights, did the work of both parents keeping the social fabric of America intact while sixteen million young men were gone from home. They were the girls who worked for the Red Cross, who kept their baby sisters and brothers while mother worked, who wrote their letters and prayed for the boys they knew. They were the ones who waited. And when we all returned, they were the ones who had to adjust every bit as much as the men. They were the ones who put up with us until we tamed down, got our feet back on solid ground. And some of them were the mothers and the wives and the girlfriends who grieved when their sons and lovers did not come home.

What made us like this? Were we somehow an especially great generation in our youth? I think not. I look at my teenaged grandsons, and my twenty-something step-daughters. I see in them and their friends a great generation; ours was no greater. We went as they would go, served as they would serve. We, though, were summoned by a great and righteous cause, something in which we each could believe, something worth sacrificing for. It called out in us all the inner qualities which seem always to lie buried until some extraordinary demand is made to which a man or woman is willing to give himself. I firmly believe the rich blood of heroes flows in our children's and our grandchildren's veins no less than in our own. And if another cause so great should arise, I believe without doubt they would step forth as did the boys and girls of 1941. But we're the ones who did.

When we arrived at the scenes of battle we soon cried out for God as we were horrified at the evil which awaited. I discussed religion earlier and agreed that most of us came with little in the way of religious faith. But I believe that every one of us turned to God in the secrecy of our frightened hearts, often with no sense that God was there. But now I know. God was there. We came to him as Jews, as Catholics, as Protestants, as Evangelical Christians. We came to him as new believers, as doubters, as cynics, as agnostics; even, I suspect, a few as atheists. And each of us was greeted by the God who waits, who accepts us in all our differing faiths, the God who made and loves each of us and celebrates our diversity. And even as we laughed and cried and swore and turned away, he remained with us, breathing into us the needed qualities by which we prevailed. From him we gathered courage, the will to go on when fear urged otherwise. It was God who enabled us to sleep at night, to accept unthinkable hardship without complaint, to do the hateful things which victory required, to stand fast when death approached. And when we failed and ran it was God who forgave and renewed our courage.

In the Old Testament book of Daniel there's a splendid story about three men who are thrown into a fiery furnace by evil men. But the fire consumes those evil men, and the three innocents are seen walking safely through the fires, accompanied by yet another figure no one had seen before. So it was for all of us as we served according to the work we were called to do. And as most of us would only realize in later years, God was always there just as he was with those three men. But what about the many who died some will ask? I reply that they know this truth best of all.

Once, in a dark night of my own soul, long years after the events described here, I cried out to God in the name of Jesus Christ, and when he appeared I wanted to say that "it was you all along, wasn't it, you who have been the one I notice from time to time walking nearby, you who strengthened me, and loved me, and stayed with me in all those times when I turned from you, and most of all, in my darkest night of all?" That's the God we knew, the loving Father who looks deep within our hearts, sees every fear and pain, every stumbling misunderstanding, every hopeless misery of despair, who never leaves our presence. He, the pursuing God, the Hound of Heaven, the Lover of our souls who knows us perfectly, who hopes for great things from us, but loves us just the way we are.

BIBLIOGRAPHY

Ackroyd, Peter *London - The Biography,* New York, Doubleday, 2000

Ambrose, Stephen E. *Citizen Soldiers* New York: Simon & Schuster 1997

Ambrose, Stephen E. *The Victors* - 1998

Ambrose, Eisenhower, *Soldier and President,* New York, N.Y.,Simon & Schuster 1980

Balkoski, Jos. *Utah Beach* 2005

Bowen, Robert *Fighting With The Screaming Eagles,* London: Greenhill Books, 2004

Bradley, Omar N. *A Soldier's Story* New York: Henry Holt & Co. 1951

Brown, Anthony Cave. *Bodyguard of Lies,* Globe-Pequot Press, Guilford, Ct., 1975

Burkett,B.G, and Whitley, Glenna *Stolen Valor* Dallas,TX: Verity Press 1998

Cooper, Belton, Y. *Death Traps,* New York, Random House, 1998

Daugherty, Leo *The Battle of the Hedgerows,* MBI Publishing Co.,St Paul, MN 2001

Deever, Anthony and Cooper, Artemus *Paris After The Liberation,* New York: Penguin Books 2004

D'Este, Carlos *Decision In Normandy,* New York: Harper & Collins 1963

D'Este, Carlos Eisenhower, *A Soldier's Life,* New York, N.Y.,Henry Holt, 2002

Deux, Pierre *Normandy,* Clarkson N. Potter, Publ., 1988

Eisenhower, Dwight *Crusade in Europe,* Doubleday Dell Publ. Gp., 1997

Evans, Richard, *The Coming of The Third Reich,* New York, Penguin Books, 2003

Fussell, Paul *The Boy's Crusade,* New York: Modern Library 2003

Graham, Don *No Name On The Bullet,* New York, Viking-Penguin, 1989

Grossman, David *On Killing,* NY, Boston, Little Brown & Co 1995,1996

Hackworth, David H., *About Face,* New York, Simon & Schuster, 1989

Halberstam, David *The Fifties,* New York, Random House, 1993

Hargreave, Eichard, *The Germans in Normandy,* S.Yorkshire, Pen and Sword Military, Ltd, 2006

Hastings, Max *Armageddon* New York: Vintage Books 2005

Hastings, Max *Overlord D-Day and The Battle For Normandy,* New York Simon & Schuster 1984

Henry, Mark *The US Army in World War II* Illinois: Osprey Publ. Ltd. 2001

Herman, Judith *Trauma and Recovery, 1992*

Higonnet, *Paris - Capital of the World,* 402, 423

Horney, Karen, *Neurosis and Human Growth,* New York, W.W. Norton and Co., 1950

Humes, Edward *Over Here ,* New York, Harcourt, 2006

Hutton, Bud, and Rooney, Andy, *The Story of the Stars and Stripes,* Farrar & Rinehart, Inc. 1946

Isby, David C, ed., *The German Army at D-Day,* London, Greenhill Books, 2004

Johnson, Franklyn *One More Hill,* New York: Funk & Wagnall Co. 1949

Jones, Colin *Paris - A Biography ,* New York, NY, Penguin Group, 2004

Mauldin, Bill, *The Brass Ring,* W.W. Norton Co., Inc., New York, 1971

Mauldin, Bill *Up Front,* New York: Henry Holt & Co. 1944

Mauldin, Bill *Back Home,* Wm. Sloane Assoc., 1947

McManus, John C. *The Americans At Normandy,* Tom Doherty Assoc., LLC,2004

McManus, John C. *The Deadly Brotherhood,* New York: Ballantine Books 1998

Miller, Donald L. *The Story of World War II,* New York, Simon & Schuster, 2001

Morning Report of the 357th Regiment, France 1944

Mosier, John, *Cross of Iron,* New Yor, Henry Holt, 2006

Neillands, Robin *The Battle Of Normandy 1944*, London: Wellington House 2002

Niebuhr, Reinhold *Beyond Tragedy*, New York, Chas. Scribner's and Sons, 1937

90 Infantry Division History, Nashville: The Battery Press 1999

Perrett, Geoffrey *There's A War To Be Won*, New York, Random House, 1991

Robinson, Derek *Invasion, 1940*, N.Y., Carroll & Graf, Publ. 2005

Stein, Harry, *The Girl Watcher's Club*, New York, Harper and Row, 2004

Stern, Fritz, *Five Germanys I Have Known*, New York, Farrar & Strauss, 2006

Time Capsule 1944, New York: Time-Life Books 1967

Tournier, Paul *Guilt and Grace*, New York, Harper and Row, 1962

Turkel, Studs *The Good War*, New York, The New Press, 1984

Wette, Wolfram The Wehrmacht: History, Myth and Reality, NY, Harvard Press, 2006

Ziegler, Philip *London At War* New York: Alfred A. Knopf 1995

END NOTES

Heading

1. D'Este, Decision In Normandy, 507

Chapter One - Darkness Falls

1. Eisenhower, Crusade In Europe, 250
2. Hastings, Overlord, 248

Chapter Two - Marching Off To War

1. Hastings, Overlord, 51
2. bid, 50

Chapter Three - On To The Field

1. McManus, The Deadly Brotherhood, 4
2. Fussell, The Boy's Crusade, 45
3. McManus, Deadly Brotherhood, 282
4. Cooper, Death Trap, 22
5. Ambrose, Citizen Soldiers, 37
6. Burkett & Whitely, Stolen Valor, 143
7. Herman, Trauma and Recovery, 44.
8. Ibid, 165
9. Ibid, 26
10. McManus, The Americans at Normandy, 23
11. Herman, Trauma and Recovery, 26
12. Horney, Neurosis and Human Growth, 74
13. Ibid, 114
14. Hastings, Overlord, 246
15. Ibid, 247
16. Bradley, A Soldier's Story, 296

17. Ambrose, The Victors, 195
18. Eisehower, Crusade in Europe, 268
19. McManus, The Americans at Normandy, 103
20. Ibid, 104
21. Ibid, 47

Chapter Four - Then The Fire

1. Stern, Five Germanys I Have Known, 4
2. Ibid, 50
3. Evans, The Coming of The Third Reich, 233
4. Horney, Neurosis and Human Growth, 27
5. Niebuhr, Beyond Tragedy, 201
6. Miller, The Story of World War Two, 309
7. McManus, The Americans at Normandy, 133
8. Hastings, Overlord, 215
9. Fussell, The Boy's Crusade, 7

Chapter Five - Prelude

1. Mauldin, Up Front, 46
2. Bradley, A Soldier's Story, 296
3. McManus, The Americans at Normandy, 40
4. Sears, Eyewitness to World War Two, 50
5. Hastings, Overlord, 247
6. Grossman, On Killing, 122
7. Fussell, The Boy's Crusade, 164

Chapter Six - Capture of Gourbesville

1. McManus, The Americans at Normandy, 96
2. Fussell, The Boy's Crusade, 111
3. Neillands, The Battle of Normandy, 126

Chapter Seven - On To Cherbourg

1. Neillands, The Battle of Normandy, 227
2. Hastings, Overlord, 212
3. Ibid, 211

Chapter Eight - Crisis

1. McManus, The Americans at Normandy, 172
2. Hastings, Armageddon, 5
3. Eisenhower, Crusade in Europe, 269
4. Brown, Bodyguard of Lies, 731
5. Neillands, The Battle of Normandy, 203
6. Ibid 223
7. McManus, The Americans at Normandy, 175
8. Fussell, The Boy's Crusade, 45
9. Bradley, A Soldier's Story, 324
10. McManus, The Americans at Normandy, 199
11. Ibid, 216

Chapter Nine - Descent Into Hell

1. Hargreave, The Germans In Normandy. 122
2. Miller, The Story of World War Two, 310
3. Ambrose, Citizen Soldiers, 329
4. McManus, The Americans at Normandy, 202
5. Ibid, 201
6. Ibid, 211
7. Neillands, The Battle of Normandy, 224
8. Morning Report, 357th Infantry, July 8, 1944

Chapter Ten - Captivity

1. 90th Division History, 13
2. Hastings, Overlord, 249
3. McManus, The Americans at Normandy, 213
4. Johnson, One More Hill, 164

Chapter Eleven - Rescue

1. Johnson, One More Hill, 171
2. Time magazine, August 14, 1944
3. Eisenhower, Crusade in Europe, 256
4. Wette, 171
5. Ibid, 172

Chapter Twelve - On To London

1. Grossman, On Killing, xv
2. Ibid, 22
3. Ibid, 22
4. Ibid, 117
5. Ibid, 13
6. Ibid, 13
7. Fussell, The Boy's Crusade,
8. Stein, The Girl Watchers, 46
9. McManus, Deadly Brotherhood, 283
10. D'Este, Decision in Normandy, 506

Chapter Thirteen - London Under Fire

1. Brown, Bodyguard of Lies, 704
2. Ackroy, London - The Biography, 723
3. Ziegler, London at War, 11
4. Ibid, 305
5. Ibid, 273
6. Ibid, 132
7. Ibid, 147-152
8. Ibid, 298

Chapter Fourteen - London Under The Americans

1. Ziegler, London at War, 216
2. Hastings, Overlord, 49
3. Time Capsule, 1944, 73
4. Ibid, 70
5. Ibid, 145
6. Ibid, 73
7. Neillands, The Battle of Normandy 1944, 127
8. Hastings, Overlord, 167
9. Ambrose, Eisenhower, Soldier and President, 147
10. D'Este, Eisenhower, A Soldier's Life, 562
11. Hastings, Overlord, 247
12. Mauldin, The Brass Ring, 233

13. Bowen, Fighting With The Screaming Eagles, 76
14. Ziegler, London at War, 310
15. Ibid, 329

Chapter Fifteen - Hello Paris

1. Pyle, Brave Men, 484
2. Deever, Paris After The Liberation, 72
3. Jones, Paris - A Biography, xvi
4. Ibid, 90

Chapter Sixteen - An American in Paris

1. Deever and Cooper, Paris After The Liberation,
2. Ambrose, Citizen Soldiers, 336
3. Rooney, The Story of The Stars and Stripes, 174
4. Burkett, Stolen Valor, 165
5. Ibid, 165

Chapter Seventeen - Homecoming

1. Hastings, Overlord, 316
2. Mosier, Cross of Iron, 205

Mr. & Mrs. Carver McGriff

ABOUT THE AUTHOR

CARVER McGRIFF, A NATIVE OF INDIANAPOLIS, PASTORED ONE OF America's largest Protestant congregations, St. Luke's United Methodist Church, Indianapolis, Indiana, for 26 years. He briefly taught ethics at Butler University and, for eight years, was moderator of an award-winning current events weekly television show in Indianapolis during the Civil Rights and Vietnam War era. He was also a regular participant on Indianapolis religious television. He served in the Infantry in Normandy, receiving a Bronze Star medal and two Purple Hearts. He is the author of nine books and resides in Zionsville, Indiana, with his wife Marianne, and is the father of three daughters.